S0-BJB-851

Practiceopedia

THE
Big Book
OF
Practice
Help

Philip Johnston
www.insidemusicteaching.com

Published by
PracticeSpot Press
PO BOX 871
Mawson ACT 2607
AUSTRALIA
insidemusicteaching@gmail.com

Copyright © 2009 by Philip Johnston

All rights reserved. No part of this publication may be reproduced or distributed in any form or by any means, or stored in a database or retrieval system, without prior written permission of the publisher.

Also by Philip Johnston

- *Not Until You've Done Your Practice* (1989)
- *The Practice Revolution* (2002)
- *The PracticeSpot Guide to Promoting Your Teaching Studio* (2003)
- *Scales Bootcamp* (2009)

All previewable and available from **www.insidemusicteaching.com**

ISBN 0-9581905-3-4
Ver. 1.2 color

Exploring this book
Navigating the **world's largest guide** to practicing

O ver 370 pages. Hundreds of illustrations. Thousands of practice ideas and tips scattered through 61 chapters, and over *100,000 words* of information.

Ok, so that's plenty of help...but where on earth do you start?

You *could* read it from cover to cover, but who reads encylopedias like that? There are **smarter**—and much **faster**—ways to find what you need...

Start from **anywhere...**

This is not a book that you have to read from the start right through.

You **don't need** to read the early chapters to understand the later chapters. This has been carefully designed to be an **open-at-any-page-and-learn-something** resource that will help you for many years to come.

...or start with a **problem...**

This way, please, for:

The USHER ➲16 lists **common issues**, events and difficulties you might encounter—such as *"speeding up a piece"* or *"not wanting to practice"*.

It will then **direct you to** dozens of different solutions in the book for you to try. That way you can aways match your practice tools to the task at hand.

Create your own course...

Read a different chapter each week for your very own **year long course** in practice mastery—skills you can then apply for the rest of your life.

Preview any chapter...

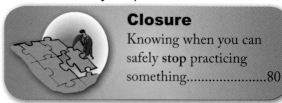

Closure
Knowing when you can safely **stop** practicing something 80

The CHAPTER GUIDE ➲10 provides **brief summaries** of every chapter in the book, so you can quickly **jump** to chapters that seem useful.

Skimread chapters and paragraphs

All chapters have been given subheadings for quick skimming, while the paragraph text is occasionally **bolded** to allow **easy scanning**. Blue boxes show **pullquotes** to give you an instant feel for the content. Orange boxes highlight **cautions** and **extra information**. There's a lot of information in this book, but it's packaged to be very easy to read.

Use **cross-references** for even more help...

ung your head together is a vital preparation task. Check VISUALIZING ➲364 for more

Each chapter in this book **links** to other **related chapters**, so there's always "more help" readily available, no matter what topic you're learning about.

That way, you can cover each topic in **as much** or as **little depth** as you need to. Look out for the RED TEXT—there are over 1,000 such cross-references(!)

Welcome to Practiceopedia

Developing the most important musical talent of all

ONE OF THE **most mischievous, misplaced, undervalued** and **overused** words in the world of music is "talented".

"Oh my" grandma will gush at the recital *"Well, I just have to say. Goodness gracious. Timmy plays so beautifully. He's so...talented"*.

Well, ok. Timmy might be talented, and good for him. But **what exactly** does Grandma *mean* when she uses that word? And why should musicians everywhere—not just Timmy—be suspicious that perhaps she's missed the point?

So what does she mean?

One common view of talent is as a measure of **how easily** particular skills come to a student. So if, for

example, you have a **good ear**, or find it easy to play from **memory**, or can quickly feel and play back **complex rhythms**, then you would be "talented". Congratulations.

It seems then to be something you are **born with**—which would mean that there's not too much you can do to acquire or rid yourself of such natural aptitudes.

But here's the thing. At my students' end of year concert, it's **not always** the "talented" students who shine. Often the best performances are given by students who DON'T have good ears, and who struggle to play from memory, and are frequently **befuddled** by rhythms.

These students shine because they have a **different talent** entirely—one that's not talked about nearly enough:

*Their talent is for **preparing**.* These are students who have a knack for practicing well. The way they work behind the scenes *works*, allowing them to turn brand new pieces into performances—with a minimum of fuss, and maximum effect.

And in the process, they **leave** many of my conventionally more "talented" students **in their wake**.

All of this got me thinking. Could it be that knowing how to practice well is not just an **overlooked** musical talent in it's own right…

…could it be that it's *the most important musical talent of all?*

In which case, music students everywhere should be **excited**. Because unlike perfect pitch, or the ideal embouchure, this particular talent can be *learned*.

Practice talent—a closer look

The most important musical talent is knowing how to practice well? That's a **big call**. Obviously practicing is useful to help you get ready for lessons and concerts, but would your life really be that different once you are a talented *practicer?*

You bet it would. Walk with me for a moment, as we take a **tour** of what's possible once you're a **master practicer**….because then the rest of this book is going to help you become exactly that.

The time discount

Improving your practice skills doesn't just mean that you'll

> # If you want to progress twice as rapidly, you don't have to figure out how to do twice as much practice. Instead, practice twice as *effectively*.

sound better. There's another **side effect** that you're going to love—especially if you're a **busy** student:

*If you have strong practice skills, you can get **more done** in much **less time**.*

Why? Because of two powerful changes that you will have made:

1) **Getting rid** of practice habits that don't work—so you stop *wasting* your time.

2) **Replacing** them with a brand new set of carefully chosen practice techniques that *do* work.

Because these new practice tools are **sharper**, and better suited to the task, they'll get the job done **faster**.

So while traditionally the practice battle has been about **more** practice, this book opens up the delicious possibility of *less* practice…as long as you are smart about **how** you work.

Practiceopedia is filled with ideas to help you make that transformation.

The accelerator effect

Being able to get more done in less time doesn't *have* to be used as a ticket to **less practice** overall though. It's also a ticket to being able to progress much faster than ever before on the **same amount** of practice that you've always done.

So if you have always been doing 25 minutes a day, six days a week, then you *could* **continue** to do that. It's just that with your new-found skills, you might cover as much in **one** week as you used to in **two**.

This means that if you want to progress **twice as rapidly**, you don't have to do twice as much practice. *Instead, work twice as effectively.* We'll take a look at hundreds of ways of doing exactly that in the chapters that follow.

Supercharging your lessons

The quality of your practice obviously has a huge impact on your playing and performances. But that's **nothing** beside the power it has over your **lessons**.

Your work in the six days *between* lessons **determines**—and **limits**—

everything that can happen in the lesson itself.

Remember, whenever you turn up to a lesson unprepared, it's not just that you failed to meet an obligation. You're actually **crippling your teacher** for the lesson that follows. Unable to move forwards into what logically *should* have been next, they're forced to drag you—as they would an **old, tired dog** that doesn't want to go for a walk—through the work you should have covered in the previous week.

By contrast, whenever you *do* turn up with everything done, a whole new world of possibilities opens up. *Your teacher is now free to focus on the things that you couldn't have done for yourself*—which is how they can help best.

So if you want to **pack your lessons** with feelings of "wow, I never realized that before" and "That's some great advice", then you have to **free your teacher** to be all they can be. Which means eliminating from their role the endless rehashes of what was supposed to be *last* week's work.

Discovering hidden abilities

Perhaps the **most exciting** benefit of all is that your smart practice can help you **develop** skills that you thought you'd never have.

So if you currently don't rate yourself as an effective sight-reader, you don't have to accept that you'll be that way forever. Changes in your practice can not only **eliminate** the weakness—you can actively turn it into a **strength**.

In this way, your talent for practice is a gateway to **brand new** abilities that you never knew you had.

The promise here? However good you *think* you might be as a musician, *you're actually much better*. The difference is going be in how you practice...which is good news, because by the time you've finished this book, you're going to be practicing very, very well.

More practice...by stealth

Practicing effectively may well be a ticket to less practice, but that's actually not what's likely to happen.

Once you start to experience what a huge **difference** effective practice can make, the process becomes oddly **addictive**. So while you have the *option* to do less, you'll probably find yourself doing more anyway...*without even noticing.* Time drags when practice is plodding along pointlessly—and it hurtles past when you're engaged and making a difference.

This twin combination of **efficient** practice, and **more of it** leads to an exciting outcome:

You'll discover the best you could have been.

This book is written especially for music students who want to find out just how good their best is.

So what exactly is "Practiceopedia"?

Let's **start** with what it's **not**. It's not a join-the-dots-how-to manual for individual practice sessions. It's not going to give you specific advice for your instrument. It won't tell you how to practice a particular trill, or how to make your playing more legato. It doesn't give out formulas like "always start with X" or "be sure to play Y five times every day".

In fact, it's not a set of practice instructions at all.

Instead, it's a set of **guiding principles** so that you can *create your own* practice instructions—no matter what the piece, or the situation.

It's a little like some books on chess. They don't necessarily recommend particular moves, but they do give guidelines for being able *to better select moves for yourself.*

After all, that's what you're doing in the practice room. It's always **your job** to select the next move. You constantly have to decide **what** you'll be practicing, **how** you'll be practicing, and when you'll be **moving on** to something else.

This book won't make those decisions for you, but it will arm you with powerful and effective ways to make your own choices.

It will also introduce you to practice techniques and ideas that you've never met before—brand new tools for your workshop—and then help you understand exactly what each tool is *for.*

If only I knew then...

Some of the principles in this book you may eventually have figured out by the time you have decades of practice behind you. Some of them might *never* have occurred to you. Either way, it's too long to wait, and you'll be wasting an unforgivable amount of practice time along the way.

In short, this book is saving you from the great lament:

"If only I knew then what I know now".

You *are* about to know it *now*—so you can apply it throughout all your musical training.

Welcome to Practiceopedia.

Day Zero

There's just one more thing.

As you're reading this, you will have your own practice track record...and maybe you're **not so proud** of what's happened so far.

Perhaps you're a student who **hasn't been doing much** practice. Perhaps you haven't been doing **any at all.**

It doesn't matter.

You should say it out loud.
It **doesn't matter.**

The practice you've done so far is **not** what determines your future. *It's the practice you do from now on.*

So when you turn this page, and start the Practiceopedia journey, it's also a *fresh* start. You get to make up your future as you go along, and you can make it **completely different** from what you've been used to.

Come on—let's take a look at what's possible...

Chapter Guide
Chapter summaries and locations

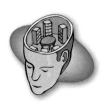

Randomizing

Restoration

Prototypes

Rogue cells

Recording yourself

Scouting

Recordings

Session Agenda

Reflecting

Shooting the movie

Speeding
The **hidden damage** caused by practicing **too fast**.....320

Triggers
Setting up **cues** that get you practicing in the first place.......................347

Stalling
What to do when a piece gets **stuck**.......................325

Turnaround time
Mastering **new pieces** in **weeks** instead of **months**......................352

Thematic Practice
A **powerful alternative** to practicing in sections.....330

Varying your diet
Freeing yourself from **dull**, repetitive practice.......... 360

Tightening
Making the leap from **good enough** to **excellent**.......337

Visualizing
The **most important** practice you'll ever do....364

Triage
When there's **too much to do**, and **not enough time** to do it..............................342

Your practice suite
Setting up the ultimate practice space.................231

Practiceopedia Usher

Directing you to the **help** you need for the **problem** you have

Your practiceopedia is a **big book.** The information you need is almost certainly in here...somewhere...but **where?**

If your problem fits roughly into any of the **common issues** below, the Practiceopedia Usher can show you **straight to** the chapters that can help.

This way, please, for:

Can't see your issue here? Try the CHAPTER GUIDE *➲10 instead.*

Directing you to the **help** you need for the **problem** you have

Not wanting to practice

It's not quite the disaster it seems—when students don't want to practice, there's **always a reason**. If the *don't-want-to* bug strikes you, the solution is to **change** whatever it is **you don't** like about practicing. (Yes, you're allowed to).

So what can you change? Just about everything...read on to find out how to **reinvigorate** your practice by **reinventing** it...

Essential Help

- NOT WANTING TO PRACTICE ➲200
  Understanding **why** you don't want to, and learning **how to fix it.**
- EXCUSES AND RUSES ➲128
  The **classic excuses** for not practicing exposed. You'll see yours here.
- TRIGGERS ➲347
  Ensuring that your lack of practice is not just because you **forget** to.

Removing the negatives

- VARYING YOUR DIET ➲360
  Stopping practice from being the **same old** drills all the time
- CLOCKWATCHERS ➲76
  Removing the **tyranny of time quotas** from your practice room
- STALLING ➲325
  When **slow-to-no progress** is what's killing your motivation
- TURNAROUND TIME ➲352
  Minimizing the time spent slogging through notes in **new pieces**.
- SCOUTING ➲299
  Pre-practicing your pieces so practice itself will feel friendlier
- DESIGNER SCALES ➲106
  Making your **scales** and technical practice feel **relevant**

Removing the negatives (cont.)

- TRIAGE ➲342
  When there's always **too much** to do, and not enough time
- ONE WAY DOORS ➲208
  Removing the need for **constant revision**
- ISOLATING ➲164
  When you're being driven mad by problems **colliding**
- CLEARING OBSTACLES ➲72
  Strategies to **win the battle** with passages that are frustrating you
- SHOOTING THE MOVIE ➲315
  Freeing yourself from having to learn your pieces **in order**
- RANDOMIZING ➲262
  When your practice feels like the same **predictable** tasks every day
- PRACTICE SUITE ➲231
  Ensuring that the problem is not due to **inadequate resources**
- CLOSURE ➲80
  So you know when you can safely **stop** practicing something
- PRACTICE TRAPS ➲236
  Common **practice disasters** that can rob you of motivation

Directing you to the **help** you need for the **problem** you have

The power of targets

- CAMPAIGNS➲58
  Finding out how **today's** practice helps the **big picture**
- LEVEL SYSTEM➲182
  Rapid-fire short term goals to keep you moving forwards
- MARATHON WEEK➲191
  Restarting the fire by **tackling the impossible**...and succeeding

Methods of motivation

- BREAKTHROUGHS DIARY➲46
  A growing list of **evidence** that your practice **actually works**
- PRACTICE BUDDIES➲226
  Someone to be **accountable** to... and in **competition** with
- LESSON PREFLIGHT CHECK➲174
  Your midweek **wake-up call** if practice has been a little...sparse
- COUNTDOWN CHARTS➲99
  Curing you of the **"I've got plenty of time"** attacks of sloth
- RECORDINGS➲277
  Reminding yourself just why this piece was so good in the first place

Making it fresh again

- RECORDING YOURSELF➲270
  Introduce a powerful and versatile **new tool** to your practice room
- THEMATIC PRACTICE➲330
  Switching to **issues based** rather than **segment based** practice
- FRESH PHOTOCOPIES➲151
  Using **multiple scores** to bring new focus to your practicing
- EXPERIMENTING➲135
  Creative and unpredictable practice for fine-tuning interpretation
- VISUALIZING➲364
  Powerful practice that doesn't even require your instrument
- COLOR CODING ➲84
  An intuitive new way to **keep track** of corrections and suggestions
- HORIZONTAL VS VERTICAL ➲158
  Changing the **alignment** of your practice to better suit you
- EXAGGERATING ➲124
  Reinforcing key ideas by **parodying** what you need to remember
- FITNESS TRAINING ➲146
  A sideways shift to **basic skills building,** rather than repertoire

Not wanting to practice (cont.)

Directing you to the **help** you need for the **problem** you have

Getting your piece up to tempo

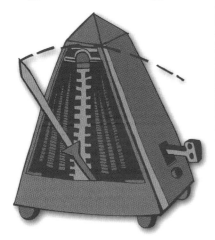

Y OUR PIECE IS ASKING for 180bpm, but you can only manage 92—and even that **feels like a stretch**. Don't panic though. Every brilliant fast performance you hear was **slow and struggling** once. But the *way* you work is going to be critical—brilliant fast performances don't just happen **by accident**...

Is it *ready* to speed up?

- PROTOTYPES➲257
  Don't even **think** about speeding it up until you've **built this**
- DETAIL TRAWL➲110
  Making sure you're speeding up what's **actually there**
- CAMPAIGNS➲58
  When you should be starting your push for full tempo

Getting you there

- METRONOME METHOD➲195
  Sneaking up on full tempo so gradually, you won't notice it.
- CHAINING➲69
  When you're **impatient** to hear results straight away.
- LESSON AGENDA➲171
  Working **with** your teacher to reach the target
- VISUALIZING➲364
  Ensuring you're not **undermining** yourself with negative thinking
- HORIZONTAL VS VERTICAL➲158
  Competing orientations for getting your piece to tempo

If it resists

- ISOLATING➲164
  Targeting possible problem **causes**, one issue at a time
- BUGSPOTTING➲53
  Pinpointing the exact **locations** of what's holding you up.
- CORAL REEF MISTAKES➲89
  Making sure you can detect **harder-to-find** underlying problems
- CLEARING OBSTACLES➲72
  Eliminating **easy-to-fix causes** of your problem
- REFLECTING➲283
  Because you won't overcome resistance just by **playing**
- EXPERIMENTING➲135
  ...but not with dynamics—with **technical solutions** to playing fast
- EXAGGERATING➲124
  So you **won't forget** the key elements of your solution
- BOOT CAMP➲43
  Shock therapy for the won't-cooperate passages
- STALLING➲325
  When the resistance is **long term**, and full tempo seems impossible

Directing you to the **help** you need for the **problem** you have

Tracking your progress

- FRESH PHOTOCOPIES⊃151
  You'll want to **reserve one** just for your speeding up campaign
- BREAKTHROUGHS DIARY⊃46
  Daily record of your progress to full speed.
- COLOR CODING⊃84
  So you can see **at a glance** how far each passage has to go
- PRACTICE BUDDIES⊃226
  It's more fun when you can **tell someone** about your new PB
- COUNTDOWN CHARTS⊃99
  Recording your results and setting yourself **date-based targets**

Permanent speed boost

- FITNESS TRAINING⊃146
  Behind the scenes work that will help you play *all* pieces faster.
- DESIGNER SCALES⊃106
  Mastering the **raw material** that makes up your fast passages

If you can't get there...

- COSMETICS⊃94
  When the concert is **too soon** to get the piece up to speed

If you can't get there (cont.)

- EXPERIMENTING⊃135
  Discovering compelling **slower interpretations**

Other relevant chapters

- SPEEDING⊃320
  When speeding up goes overboard—a **cautionary tale**
- VARYING YOUR DIET⊃356
  Speeding up pieces shouldn't be the **only thing** you're doing
- DRESS REHEARSAL⊃115
  The **ultimate test** of whether you can cope with the tempo

Getting your piece up to tempo (cont.)

How much time you have between eighth notes...			
Grave	0.75 seconds	**Allegretto**	0.30 seconds
Largo	0.65 seconds	**Allegro**	0.26 seconds
Adagio	0.58 seconds	**Vivace**	0.24 seconds
Andante	0.50 seconds	**Presto**	0.21 seconds
Moderato	0.37 seconds	**Prestissimo**	0.16 seconds

Directing you to the **help** you need for the **problem** you have

Preparing for Performance

THIS IS THE END GAME—a completely **different** type of practice that kicks in as your concert looms. You've done the **hard work** to learn your piece in the first place...now it's time to **showcase** it in public. So what can you do in the **practice room** to ensure you sound great on the big day?...

Performance security

- DRESS REHEARSAL ➲115
  Testing your piece under performance conditions
- FIRE DRILLS ➲139
  Damage control simulations so you don't need to fear mistakes
- CORAL REEF MISTAKES ➲89
  Ensuring **hidden** errors don't ambush you on concert day
- BUG SPOTTING ➲53
  Surveying for any last minute trouble spots
- PRESSURE TESTING ➲249
  Ensuring your piece can deliver **every time**, and under pressure
- PRACTICE BUDDIES ➲226
  A great source of **support** and **advice** as your deadline approaches
- SPEEDING ➲320
  Ensuring your **choice of tempo** is not wrecking your preparation
- VISUALIZING ➲364
  Essential **mental preparation** for any major event
- RANDOMIZING ➲262
  So you're ready for the **unexpected**, and tough to distract

Final polishing

- OPENINGS AND ENDINGS ➲215
  Nailing the **two most important passages** in your performance
- PAINTING THE SCENE ➲222
  Using **imagery** to intensify your performance
- RECORDING YOURSELF ➲270
  Find out exactly what your **audience will hear** when you play
- EXPERIMENTING ➲135
  Testing any **last minute** interpretation changes
- THEMATIC PRACTICE ➲330
  Polishing your performance, **one issue at a time**
- TIGHTENING ➲337
  Making the jump from "Good Enough" to "Excellent"
- EXAGGERATING ➲124
  Highlighting **key moments** and issues to remember in your performance
- BRIDGING ➲50
  Ensuring your performance works as a **seamless whole**

Directing you to the **help** you need for the **problem** you have

Final polishing (cont.)

Problem Passages

Project Management

Other relevant chapters

Preparing for performance (cont.)

Directing you to the **help** you need for the **problem** you have

Managing Deadlines

A s a music student, you're always going to be juggling deadlines—from having to prepare a dozen works in time for a **major competition** next year, to simply being ready for **next lesson**.

Even if you don't rate yourself as organized or efficient, there's good news:

These skills can be *learned*...check out these Practiceopedia chapters.

Project Management

- CAMPAIGNS➲58
  Shaping the **big picture**, from first reading to first performance
- COUNTDOWN CHARTS➲99
  So you always know what's **coming up**, and **how far away** it is
- SESSION AGENDA➲305
  Creating the **to-do list** for the work you're about to do **today**
- TRIAGE➲342
  Managing **multiple deadlines**, too much to do, and **not enough time**

Fanatical Efficiency

- ENGAGING AUTOPILOT➲120
  One of the greatest **enemies** of getting anything done
- BLINKERS➲38
  Shutting out everything except what you're **supposed** to be doing
- ONE WAY DOORS➲208
  Ensuring **pointless revision** is not holding you up
- LEVEL SYSTEM➲182
  Microsteps approach to **quickly learning** new pieces
- SHOOTING THE MOVIE➲315
  Being smarter about choosing the **order** you learn new pieces in

Fanatical Efficiency (cont.)

- PROTOTYPES➲257
  Insuring yourself against having to **un-practice** anything later
- ROGUE CELLS➲293
  Tiny moments of practice that can **undermine** your whole campaign
- SCOUTING➲299
  Pre-practicing new pieces to learn them faster.
- CLOSURE➲80
  The art of knowing when you can safely **stop** practicing something
- CEMENTING➲64
  A time **saver**—and a time **waster**. It all depends on *when* you use it
- LESSON REVIEW➲178
  So that your teacher never needs to make the **same correction twice**
- CLOCKWATCHERS➲76
  Save time by **ending your obsession** with time
- BEGINNERS➲33
  Another huge **timewaster** to guard against
- LESSON AGENDA➲171
  Ensuring you always get the **follow-up help** you need
- BREAKTHROUGHS DIARY➲46
  Staying accountable by ensuring there's always something to record

Directing you to the **help** you need for the **problem** you have

Managing Deadlines (cont.)

Directing you to the **help** you need for the **problem** you have

Learning new pieces

For many students, it's the slowest, most frustrating part of practice. Polishing existing pieces isn't so bad—but learning brand new ones...ugh

Problem is that until you get this out of the way, there is nothing to polish. **Worse still** , there's nothing for your teacher to work on either.

So how can you get new pieces **up and running** without all the **pain?**

Essential Help

Ways of working

Ways of working (cont.)

Obstacles to progress

Directing you to the **help** you need for the **problem** you have

Obstacles to progress (cont.)

- CLOCKWATCHERS➲76
  Why **obsession with time** just makes everything **take longer**
- ROGUE CELLS➲293
  When **practice cells** are out of control, **nothing** is getting learned
- BEGINNERS➲33
  Because the beginning is **not always** a good place to start

Making it accurate

- PROTOTYPES➲257
  Everything you want the **final version** to be—minus the speed
- DETAILS TRAWL➲110
  Making sure you don't **overlook anything** in the score
- PRESSURE TESTING➲249
  Proving that you know **exactly** what the notes and rhythms are

Learning pieces faster

- MARATHON WEEK➲191
  Redefining assumptions about how long learning new pieces takes
- FITNESS TRAINING➲146
  Long term **upgrades** of your ability to learn pieces **fast**

Other relevant chapters

- FRESH PHOTOCOPIES➲151
  Create **custom scores** and markings just for learning your piece
- EXAGGERATING➲124
  A **slightly weird** way to get your new piece to stick in your mind
- BLINKERS➲38
  Narrowing your focus in otherwise enormous pieces
- VARYING YOUR DIET➲360
  If you're **going insane** from spending all your time learning notes
- STALLING➲325
  When it feels like you'll **never** get there

Learning new pieces (cont.)

Directing you to the **help** you need for the **problem** you have

Staying Focused

Just because you're practicing **doesn't** mean you're automatically **making progress**. Like any other activity, it's possible to make yourself furiously busy without actually getting anything done.

So how can you save yourself from this? Could it be that by **thinking differently** you could get the same work done in a fraction of the time?...

Essential Help

- ENGAGING AUTOPILOT➲120
  What happens when **plug in** your autopilot...and **unplug** your brain
- BLINKERS➲38
  Making sure you can't even *see* passages that you **shouldn't practice**
- ROGUE CELLS➲293
  How unsupervised **moments** of practice can **wreck** your pieces
- TURNAROUND TIME➲352
  The **ultimate reward** for focusing—more done with less practice

Dangers of drifting

- BEGINNERS➲33
  Avoiding problems of **mindless loops** from the 1st measure
- CORAL REEF MISTAKES➲89
  Errors in your piece that **remain invisible** if you're daydreaming
- CEMENTING➲64
  A vital technique, but also a practice **trap** if you're **not thinking**
- SPEEDING➲320
  A **disaster** that awaits when your brain **drifts** and your notes **fly**

Making it interesting

- VARYING YOUR DIET➲360
  Regularly **changing the ingredients** of your practice sessions
- PRACTICE BUDDIES➲226
  Because it's always more engaging when you **don't work alone**
- FRESH PHOTOCOPIES➲151
  Multiple copies of your score, each with a different focus
- RANDOMIZING➲362
  Ensuring **no two** practice sessions are ever the **same**
- EXPERIMENTING➲135
  Discovering magic in your pieces that you never knew was there
- BOOT CAMP➲43
  The **only way** to survive this technique is to be **thoroughly engaged**
- SHOOTING THE MOVIE➲315
  Permission to switch to **new sections** when the old one gets tired
- HORIZONTAL VS VERTICAL➲158
  Switching between **wide** and **deep** to keep your practice fresh
- RECORDING YOURSELF➲270
  The **wake-up call** when you hear what you really sound like

Directing you to the **help** you need for the **problem** you have

Using targets

- SESSION AGENDA➲305
  Turning your **daily to-do list** into a focal point for your practice
- LEVEL SYSTEM➲182
  To create a series of **rapid turnover** short-term targets
- LESSON PREFLIGHT CHECK➲174
  Creating a **progress checkpoint** in the middle of your week
- COUNTDOWN CHARTS➲99
  Ensuring your practice session is focused on **upcoming deadlines**
- BREAKTHROUGHS DIARY➲46
  Because if you work aimlessly, you'll have **nothing to record**
- MARATHON WEEK➲191
  Sharpening your focus with an **insanely tight deadline**
- ONE WAY DOORS➲208
  The **ban on revisiting pieces** later forces you to get them right now

Concentration barriers

- PRACTICE SUITE➲231
  Changing your workspace to make focusing easier

Concentration barriers (cont.)

- CLOCKWATCHERS➲76
  So you're not constantly distracted by the **time**

Other relevant chapters

- BUG SPOTTING➲53
  Working out **what** you should be focusing on in the first place
- REFLECTING➲283
  Ensuring that you're taking the time to **think** while you work
- ISOLATING➲164
  Creating distraction-free focus on **single musical elements**
- CLOSURE➲80
  Preventing pointless practice by clearly marking tasks as **done**
- LESSON REVIEW➲178
  Ensuring you're concentrating on the **same things** as your teacher
- PROTOTYPES➲257
  Focusing to create the **ultimate** slow motion version of your piece
- TIGHTENING➲337
  Because tightening is **impossible** unless you're fully focused

Staying focused (cont.)

Directing you to the **help** you need for the **problem** you have

Saving Time

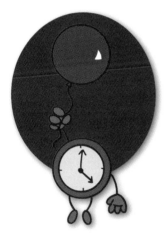

If you're like most students, music lessons won't be the **only** activity competing for your time and attention. And since you're only going to keep **getting busier**, learning how to work fast is **more important** than ever before.

So if you're serious about getting maximum results in minimum time, what **changes** can you make?...

Essential Help

- PRACTICE TRAPS ➲236
  Classic practice inefficiencies that **burn** through your time
- RECORDINGS ➲277
  One of the best piece-learning **accelerators** ever invented
- SCOUTING ➲299
  Ensuring you have a huge **head start** when beginning a new piece
- TURNAROUND TIME ➲352
  Essential tips for getting your pieces concert-ready **sooner**
- PRACTICE SUITE ➲231
  Ensuring everything you need is always **to hand**

Cutting non-vital work

- CLOSURE ➲80
  So you're not wasting time practicing issues that are **already fixed**
- THEMATIC PRACTICE ➲330
  Saving time by working on **similar issues** piecewide
- SESSION AGENDA ➲305
  Ensuring **100%** of your practice spent on your **todo list** tasks
- TRIAGE ➲342
  Bumping non-vital work to the bottom of your list

Cutting non-vital work (cont.)

- BEGINNERS ➲33
  Eliminating **commuting**—one of practicing's biggest time-wasters
- DETAILS TRAWL ➲110
  To ensure you're not practicing things that **aren't really there**
- LESSON REVIEW ➲178
  So your practice time is actually spent on your **teacher's requests**
- PROTOTYPES ➲257
  Matching **all** your practice to the performance model you create

Eliminating *un*practice

- CEMENTING ➲64
  Saving you from **unpractice** by being careful *when* you cement
- EXAGGERATING ➲124
  Making sure changes **stick**—so they don't need further work
- SPEEDING ➲320
  Avoiding the **extra work** that practicing too fast creates

Training to work faster

- DESIGNER SCALES ➲106
  Saving time by **pre-practicing** elements in future pieces

Directing you to the **help** you need for the **problem** you have

Training to work faster (cont.)

- MARATHON WEEK➲191
  Redefining what's really possible
  with limited time
- FITNESS TRAINING➲146
  Training to make **everything**
  happen faster, and more easily

Other relevant chapters

- COLOR CODING➲84
  So you don't have to waste time
  hunting for reminders
- STALLING➲325
  Getting things **moving again** when
  progress has stopped
- SHOOTING THE MOVIE➲315
  Getting the job done faster by
  working **out of order**
- VISUALIZING➲364
  Using the power of **projection** to
  accelerate mastery
- BLINKERS➲38
  Eliminating all but the practice
  you really need to do
- CLOCKWATCHERS➲76
  Ensuring your obsession with time
  is not **costing** you time
- LEVEL SYSTEM➲182
  Using **micro-steps** to accelerate
  the learning of a new piece

Other relevant chapters (cont.)

- FRESH PHOTOCOPIES➲151
  So your **score** focuses on what
  you're trying to focus on
- ISOLATING➲164
  Solving problems faster by tackling
  them **one at a time**
- REFLECTING➲283
  Ensure that you're not wasting
  time by heading the **wrong way**
- ROGUE CELLS➲293
  Ensuring your **smallest units** of
  practice run efficiently
- ONE WAY DOORS➲208
  Practice it once, practice it well...
  then **never** practice it **again**

Saving Time (cont.)

Directing you to the **help** you need for the **problem** you have

Dealing with problem passages

Sooner or later you'll encounter passages that are a mess, **refuse to improve**, and seem destined remain that way forever.

That doesn't mean **game over** though—it just means that the way you've worked *so far* hasn't worked.

Fortunately, there are plenty of other options to try...

Essential Help

- STALLING➲325
  Tactics to get your stuck passages **moving again**
- BOOT CAMP➲43
  The **no-mercy** approach for passages that give you a hard time
- VISUALIZING➲364
  Because if you can't **picture it**, you won't be able to **play** it either
- CLEARING OBSTACLES➲72
  Discovering what is really **causing** the tricky bit to be tricky
- PRACTICE TRAPS➲236
  Ensuring that the way you practice is not **contributing** to the problem

Targeting the problem

- BUG SPOTTING➲53
  Narrowing down exactly where the problem is really located
- ISOLATING➲164
  Ensuring you're only targeting **one problem** at a time
- BLINKERS➲38
  Ensuring your focus stays **exactly** on these trouble-makers
- COLOR CODING➲84
  Making sure problem passages are always **easy to locate** in the score

Targeting the problem (cont.)

- FRESH PHOTOCOPIES➲151
  Dedicating a special copy of the score just to solving the problem
- DESIGNER SCALES➲106
  Creating your own technical exercises to target the problem

Fixing the problem

- EXPERIMENTING➲135
  Testing out different possible solutions to the problem
- HORIZONTAL VS VERTICAL➲158
  Seeing if a change of orientation helps **soften the ground**
- PRACTICE BUDDIES➲226
  Because **two heads** is better than one when you're solving problems
- PROTOTYPES➲257
  Ensuring you will **recognize** the "fixed" passage when you hear it
- LEVEL SYSTEM➲182
  Sneaking up on the fix, one **tiny step** at a time
- DETAILS TRAWL➲110
  Checking that the problem is not caused by a simple **misreading**
- LESSON AGENDA➲171
  Ensuring you get any additional **help** you need next lesson

Directing you to the **help** you need for the **problem** you have

Fixing the problem (cont.)

- LESSON REVIEW➲178
  So you don't overlook solutions that have **already** been recommended

If full tempo is the issue

- CHAINING➲69
  If full speed in bits is an option, but the **whole passage** fast is not
- METRONOME METHOD➲195
  Microsteps approach to getting to full speed

See also GETTING YOUR PIECE UP TO TEMPO➲19 in this Usher

Making the fix stick

- CEMENTING➲64
  Locking in whatever solution you eventually come up with
- EXAGGERATING➲124
  Reinforcing the key elements of the solution
- PRESSURE TESTING➲249
  Making sure you can deliver the solution **reliably**

If a concert's looming...

- COSMETICS➲94
  If all else fails—creating a musical makeover to **disguise** the problem
- FIRE DRILLS➲139
  Rehearsing **damage control** for any possible problems.
- DRESS REHEARSALS➲115
  To ensure the **rest** of the performance is still in good shape

Other relevant chapters

- BREAKTHROUGHS DIARY➲46
  Recording the evidence that you're making headway
- CHAINING➲69
  If the stubborn section refuses to go at **full speed**
- CAMPAIGNS➲58
  Reminding yourself that you don't have to be victorious immediately
- FITNESS TRAINING➲146
  Immunization against another outbreak of the problem in the future

Dealing with problem passages (cont.)

Beginners

Curing your addiction to the start of your piece

T he **start** of Hailey's new piece is sounding fantastic. In fact, the start of Hailey's pieces *always* sounds fantastic.

But the *end* of her pieces are a **different story**. No matter which piece she plays, the closer she gets to the **last measure**, the worse her playing becomes...until everything **collapses** in a tangle on the last page.

What's going on? Why do her pieces sound **great** at the start, get **sick** in the middle and **die** at the end?

THERE'S A SONG in *The Sound of Music* that says something about the beginning being "a very good place to start". That might be true if you're **reading a novel** or competing in the **100 metres final** at the Olympics, but it's *not* always great advice when you're practicing.

For a lot of students though, the beginning of their piece isn't just a very good place to start...

...it's the *only* place to start.

No matter **what the task** in front of them, they always handle it in exactly the **same way**:

Task: To memorize the **development section** of the new sonata

Solution: Play from the **start** of the piece

The *start?* That's **nowhere near** the development section...

...but that's how the Beginners Trap works. No matter where your target *actually* is, you start from the first square on the board.

Here's the same student handling a completely different task:

Task: To work on the tricky cross-rhythms in **measures 327-351**

Solution: Play from the *first* measure   (?!)

And if the student suffers from this disease **badly enough**—if the start of their piece is the only section they *can* start from—then even the following insanity is possible:

Task: To work out an effective fingering for the **final** 6 measures of my *Theme and 41 Variations.*

Solution: Give me a second, I just need to play from the start...

Of course, the result of building **bias** like this into your practice is that the **opening** of your piece just keeps getting better and better, while the **end** sounds as though it's hardly been practiced at all...

...which is largely because *it's hardly been practiced at all.*

What's really interesting here—and what all "beginners" should understand—is *why* that's the case though. Always starting from the top puts in motion a whole series of **unintended consequences**...

Unnecessary commuting

"Beginners" don't actively discriminate against the end of their piece. They're just **not factoring in** the reality that regions most distant from the start can take serious practice time *just to get to.*

To take an **extreme example**, let's imagine that you had a piece that was **25 minutes long**, and your task was to **tidy up the ending**. If you're starting from the beginning, *it will take you 24 minutes of playing just to get to your target...*

...which in a half hour practice session leaves **6 minutes** to actually work on the problem.

You might as well have started from where you needed to, and then only done 6 minutes of practice.

So the first **price you pay** for being a "beginner" is extra practice, to cover the **commuting** you need to do each day—from the start of your piece all the way to the passage you really needed to fix.

But this **wasted travel time** is only part of the problem.

Stopping to pick weeds

The 24 minute commute might sound **bad enough** by itself, but that assumes that you're playing **straight through**.

The reality is that if you always start from the beginning, you'll notice things that need work **while you're traveling.**

And so, like a hiker with a pebble in their shoe, you'll *stop*. After all, you've **noticed a problem**, and you'll want to **fix** it. Hard to argue with that.

> # The first price you pay for being a "Beginner" is extra practice... to cover the commuting you need to do each day...

But since you've stopped, *none of the problems that come after the one you're working on will be visible to you yet.* They'll only be covered once your journey resumes, and **if there's time.**

Worse still, for hard-core beginners, **the journey might** *not* **resume.** Having dealt with the problem they spotted, they dust their hands off, roll up their sleeves...*and start again from the beginning...*

Stuck in a stationary line

All of this creates an imbalance:

• **Problems near the beginning** are guaranteed to get noticed, because the journey to them is **short**, fitting neatly into even the briefest practice session.

• **Problems near the end** though *are waiting in line*—and it's a line that items from the beginning can **push in** whenever they feel like it. If the practice session **ends** before you get to them, then that's tough—they'll have to wait until **next time...**

...except that, if you're a beginner, next time you'll start at the beginning again too...*so there is no "next time".* The problem at the end of

the piece is **always at the back of the line**, and the line never seems to progress. You're stuck on hold for eternity, and the only muzak on offer is the opening measures of your piece...

The result? Large slices towards the end of your piece remain not only *under*practiced but sometimes *un*practiced entirely—no matter how hard you may have been working.

And if things go wrong on concert day...

...there's only **one thing** you'll know how to do. You won't be able to just **pick up** from near wherever you got lost, because that's something you've **never done**. (See FIRE DRILLS ➲139)

Instead, "Beginners" handle that problem the **same way** they handle every problem in their practice sessions: *They start again from the beginning...*

The groans from the audience will be almost loud enough to cover the sound of your teacher sobbing.

Signs you might be a "Beginner"
• If you find it difficult to **pick up** from the places your teacher asks for
• If your pieces **sound great** at the start, and **get worse** the further you get into them
• If, despite that, most of the issues you notice and work on seem to be in the **first half** of your piece

Creating new home bases

If you're a Beginner, then it's not all bad news—with all the attention it's received, the **beginning** of your piece will be in **great shape**. (See OPENINGS AND ENDINGS ➲215) You can then use similar **bias** in your practice to ensure the **rest of the piece** is in great shape too.

Remember, you didn't end up being that good at the beginning because the beginning was *easy*. Or because you *liked* it more. It happened simply because that was always the place you **started from**.

If you had a **new** place that you always started from, then the same thing would happen. Because of the **commuting** factor, passages near that new start point would receive

more attention than the rest of the piece...*which is great news if they need more attention than the rest of the piece.*

This is exactly how you can turn the Beginners Trap—always starting from the same place—into a **powerful practice weapon**. The idea is to continue to work with a "home", but to ensure that the home is located **near** wherever most of your **assigned tasks** are.

So if most of your jobs this week are in the **development section** of your piece, then your "home" for the week *should be the start of the development section.*

If that means dedicating some initial practice time just to being able to pick up from there, then that's **time well spent**—it's like the

time spent establishing a base camp for a climbing expedition.

You are now welcome to start from there **every time** you practice if you wish—it's acting as your **new beginning.** It just happens to be much better located than the old one.

Because your practice tasks will change, you need to **review** the **location** of your "home" every few days, to make sure that it's **still** near the work you need to do.

So in our example above, if you've taken care of most issues in the development section already, then it's time to pitch your tent near a **different problem.**

Evolve to nomadic practice

Being smart about the location of your "home" for the week is a **great start** to correcting some of the imbalances that Beginner practice causes.

But in the end, you want your practice to evolve so that there's no "home" at all—that instead, you're able to zoom in and **start** directly from **whatever** the problem you're

> # The groans from the audience will be almost loud enough to cover the sound of your teacher sobbing.

trying to fix. That way, **every note** you play is geared towards troubleshooting, and improving your piece.

You'll be stunned by the amount of practice time you can save when you work in this **commute-free** way—and by how much more even the quality of your piece will be.

Using positive discrimination

If your piece has **already** been affected by the "Beginners" practice trap, then you don't need to panic. It's just time to even the score a little. Starting immediately, you would work **exclusively** on the **last page** of the piece—if you need to, use BLINKERS➲38 to ensure that you can't even *see* the rest of the piece.

This bias in favor of the end would continue until it's the **same standard** as the beginning. Given that the beginning has had a tremendous

head start, this might take a while.

And then, when everything is square once more, you'd focus on the **second last page** of the piece— again, until it's caught up.

Because it's that much closer to the beginning though, it will probably have had a little more **attention** than the very end originally had, and so shouldn't need to **pedal as hard** for as long to catch up. Ditto for the page before *that*—so this process gets easier and easier as you gradually get closer to the start.

Your next new piece...

Consider using SHOOTING THE MOVIE➲315 to **mix up** the order you learn your piece in the first place. It's very hard to suffer from "Beginners" syndrome when the beginning was actually the 14th section in the piece that you tackled...

Blinkers

Shutting out the things you shouldn't be working on

Logan does plenty of practice, but only a **small part** of that is focussed on what he's *supposed* to be working on. The rest is spent on **old** pieces, or **favorite passages** in his current pieces.

His teacher is getting **frustrated** because Logan is regularly turning up to lessons unprepared. Logan protests that he *is* working.

But how can he **focus** that work on **what's needed?**...

YOUR PIECES WILL BE a **mix** of passages that **need work**, and those that you can **safely leave**. The idea is of course that you should focus your practice on those sections that really **need the help**, together with those that your teacher wants to **hear next lesson**.

Unfortunately, that's **not** always how things work out:

- Some students always seem to practice from the **start** of their piece—whether it needs it or not (see BEGINNERS➲33)

- Others only practice the bits they can **already play well** (See "Polishing Shiny Objects in PRACTICE TRAPS➲236)

- Others always end up playing the **whole piece** whenever they practice, so that their practice is always a DRESS REHEARSAL➲115

- There are also students who **lose track** of what they're supposed to be practicing, and just *play...* (see ENGAGING AUTOPILOT➲120)

The result is the same. These

students end up **wasting plenty of time** playing over sections that don't need work, while **ignoring** the passages that do.

There's a way around this though, as any horse-riding traffic cop will tell you...

When horses get distracted

To keep horses **focussed** on what's in **front** of them—rather than, say, the traffic that's *around* them—they are sometimes fitted with special eye-shields called "blinkers".

These eye-shields don't **magically** remove all distractions, but they do the **next best thing**. They ensure that the horse can't *see* the distractions in the first place.

So just by **limiting its vision**, you get a horse that is focussed on where it's **supposed to be going**—without the need for carrots or sticks.

Your very own blinkers

Practice blinkers work in much the same way. They'll make it impossible for you to see certain things—in this case, *passages that you shouldn't be working on*.

Since you're **not a horse,** we're going to make a slight modification though. Instead of fitting the blinkers to your **head**, you're going to fit them to the **music itself**.

What you'll need:

- Scissors
- A sheet of paper that is the same size as a page of music in your book
- Your music
- A list of *exactly* what you need to work on this week.

How to make them

If you were to take that piece of paper and simply **place it over** a

Blinkers in action:

On this page of music, there's only 8 measures the student needed to work on. So the cutout is created, and placed over the music...

...and only those 8 measures are visible.

For students who rely heavily on the score, this makes it very hard to practice anything other than what they're supposed to.

page of your music, you obviously wouldn't be able to *see* any of that page. That would be like **blindfolding** the horse.

The idea behind blinkers is to allow you to see *some* of the page, but to be able to control exactly *which* bits. To achieve this, you're going to **cut "windows"** out of a sheet of paper, so that when you place it over the music, *you can only see the passage(s) that you're supposed to be targeting.*

These relevant passages appear in the windows. Everything else is **hidden**. The rule then is, if you can't **see** it, don't **practice** it.

For students who **rely on the music** when they practice, it's a very effective way of **guaranteeing** that they only ever work on what they're supposed to.

Matching your blinkers to your todo list

Because your blinkers are going to **narrow** your focus, you have to **be careful** that they're helping you focus on the **right things**:

• The very first windows you create should reveal the passages your **teacher** asked you to focus on this week.

• The next set of windows would then focus on any other passages that genuinely **need your attention**.

Any passage that does not fit into at least one of those descriptions should be covered up. It might still be an **important** passage to the piece as a whole, but it's **not a priority** right now. (See Triage⊃342)

See no evil, practice no evil

Once you try blinkers for the first time, you'll quickly realize how closely what you *practice* **matches** what you can *see*. This is why if you're able to **look** at the wrong passages, you'll be very tempted to **practice** them too.

But whenever your blinkers **cover up** an irrelevant passage, you have just guaranteed that it will get **less practice** than it would have otherwise.

In fact, it usually won't get any at all.

Immunity for memorizers

There's a **caution** for memorizers though. If you're doing most of your practice without the music anyway, then blinkers are not going to make any difference to you.

Yet another reason that you should be using the music at least **some** of the **time** when you work. (See "Ignoring the Map" in Practice Traps⊃243)

But even if your preference for memorizing means that you don't end up actually using the blinkers, simply **working out** where they would have gone is a huge step towards **switching your focus to** where it needs to be.

Themed window sets

Sometimes your focus shouldn't be so much on specific **passages**, as it should be on specific **musical elements**. (See THEMATIC PRACTICE ➲330)

So for example, last lesson, your teacher might have spent time talking through a new approach to **playing staccato**.

To help you focus on—and quickly find—passages relevant to this, you'd create a **special** "staccato" window sheet, behind which all the staccato passages would be visible.

But when the time comes to work on **intonation** instead, you may well need to be working with completely **different** passages. That's no problem—you'd create a separate window sheet called "intonation" which makes visible those passages

> # Relevant passages appear in the windows. Everything else is hidden. The rule then is, *if you can't see it, don't practice it...*

in which intonation has been an issue.

So if there were 12 different issues you were going to cover, you would have **12 different sheets**, each revealing a different set of passages in your piece. Just pull out the window sheet you need, lay it on top of the music, and all your attention will be focused on the passages you need for this issue. (See also COLOR CODING ➲84 as another way to handle **multiple practice themes** like this.)

Blinkers as memorization aids

If you're having trouble memorizing your piece, window sheets can be a great way to *gradually* remove the **trainer wheels** that is your score.

The idea is that you'd create a **graded** series of windowed sheets, each **covering up more** of the score than the last.

So the very first windowed sheet would reveal **all but the easiest** couple of passages on the page. As soon as you can cope with that, use the next window sheet in the series instead—it would cover the passages you already had, *plus a couple of new ones...*

In this way, just by **gradually decreasing** the size and number of cutouts, you can sneak up on memorizing the entire piece...while having the score in front of you the whole time.

Boot Camp

Where you send passages that won't behave

Ian has a passage that **trips** him up every time he plays it.

There's a part of him that thinks perhaps the section is too hard...

...but another part that knows he's never really **got serious** with it yet.

So what would "getting serious" with it really mean? What can you do if you **really** want to **get tough** with a problem passage?...

ALMOST EVERY PIECE has trouble spots. Moments of trickiness that cry "gotcha!" when you play them, and then **lie still** and **coiled**, waiting to **strike again** next time you pass.

It might be a jump you always miss. Or an accidental you always misread. Or a complicated run that always ends in a tangle.

But **whatever** it is, if it's been giving you a hard time regularly, the question is this:

What are you going to do about it?

You can run from the fight...

You'd think when a mistake bites like this, that the student would always **react** to it somehow.

That, like a school teacher who had been hit by a paper plane, they'd **stop everything** and say "Right! Who was that?", and then teach that section to never—*ever*—mess with you like that again.

But in the practice room, it **doesn't work this way**. All too often, when students are tripped up by misbehaving sections they simply think "Rats. I *always* mess that up"

And that's it. They **admit** they were tripped. They admit it's happened before. *And they move on, without doing anything about it.*

If that's what happens when you practice, then you *deserve* to be tripped up—and you're guaranteeing that it will happen over and over again.

This is exactly why some sections never seem to get better...

...because apart from **complaining**, you've never really done anything about them.

...or cry "Enough!"

If you're really serious about turning trouble sections around, instead of **meekly continuing on** when you're tripped, it's time to assert yourself. So next time one of these passages ambushes you, stop and turn around slowly...

..."You" you'll say "Yeah, *you. Come here.*"

Which means just **one thing** for this misbehaving passage.

Boot Camp.

It's a place missing from most students' practice, but it can make a **spectacular difference**.

Boot Camp: The Basics

Boot Camp is where you'll take passages that have been giving you a hard time, and go and give *them* a hard time.

It means **stopping** all other practice temporarily, while you **focus** all your energies on this one problem. You'll be throwing at it every practice technique you know. And then you'll be scouring this book and asking your teacher for techniques you *don't* know.

Just when it thinks that you're done, and it can **finally exhale**...

...you come back for **more**. Always more. With the metronome. Without the metronome. At half speed. At full speed. Five times in a row, no mistakes. With the music. Without the music. With your eyes closed. A *hundred* times in a row. With your little sister scrutinizing—any mistakes and you tidy *her* room for a week. Recording it. Writing it out. Analyzing it. With the dynamics as marked. With reverse dynamics. With accents on every second note.

Every time the trouble spot emerges, red faced, panting and dizzy, you send it off for **another challenge**.

> *"Is that all you got, private? Give me another 20! My great-grandmother can do better metronome playthroughs than that. Push it, push it, push it!"*

Your aim? That this section will be telling its *grandchildren* about how tough Boot Camp was.

And that with all this attention, it's going to be almost impossible for the trouble section *not* to improve.

> **Boot camp is where you'll take passages that have been giving you a hard time...and give *them* a hard time.**

After Boot Camp

Once the section is behaving itself better, you can **reintroduce** it to the rest of the piece, and resume your regular practice.

If it trips you up then, at least you'll know it's **not because** you'd been ignoring it—instead, it's a sign that there actually are more serious problems. But more often than not, it will have learned its lesson.

If Boot Camp didn't work...

Sometimes the **brute force** that is Boot Camp doesn't produce the results you were hoping for. If that's the case, then you need to switch to some more precision instruments to cure what ails you—boot camp is designed to rectify **lack of attention**, rather than fixing any deeper flaws.

First of all, **add** this section to your LESSON AGENDA➲171, so you can talk about it with your teacher. Anything that remains unimproved by boot camp is going to need **all the help** you can get.

But probably most useful is also a special section in the Practiceopedia Usher dedicated to DEALING WITH PROBLEM PASSAGES➲31. It will **recommend** the chapters in this book that can give further help.

Breakthroughs Diary

Keeping track of your progress

K aitlyn is feeling **discouraged**. "I'm practicing a lot" she thinks "but I really **don't** feel like I'm **achieving very much...**"

She's right. She *is* practicing a lot—Kaitlyn has a **chart** where she records **how** much practice she does, and it's full of **big numbers**.

But that's **not** helping her **feel better**.

"Your problem is that you're working with the **wrong chart**" her teacher says. "Don't record *minutes*. Keep track of **this** instead..."

What did her teacher **have in mind**?

WHEN YOU'VE **FINISHED** practicing for the day, before you fold up your music stand and congratulate yourself on a **job well done**, there's a **question** you need to ask.

And it's not "**how much** practice did I do?".

It's "**What did I** *achieve?*"

That question is so important that it's worth actually **recording** the answer...

...which is one of the reasons every music student should **create** and **write in** their own Breakthroughs Diary.

What? But that's just going to take *more* time!

Not at all. It's an example of **spending time** to **save time**. As we'll see, this daily ritual of recording *outcomes* actually changes the way you practice in the first place.

We'll take a look in a moment at what a "breakthrough" might be, but know this:

> **August 3rd**
> Can play page 1 from memory
> Worked out fingering for measures 34-55
> Dress Rehearsal performance of Etude
> Passed 3 in a row test with Eb Major scale
> Can now play development section with metronome
> Completed detail trawl of Sonatina
> Filled in page one of my theory assignment

If you're practicing well, you'll have plenty of such breakthroughs every day.

Taking the time to acknowledge each one by jotting a note sounds like an insignificant thing, but it's actually **hugely motivating**—it means you end every practice session with evidence of the **difference** your practice has made.

Those breakthroughs listed were *only* possible because you practiced today...which is great encouragement to practice again tomorrow.

Breakthroughs...such as?

A breakthrough is anything that you could do by the **end** of a practice session that you couldn't do when the session **began**.

It might be:
- **a new section** that you can play through from **memory**

- a passage that is now **faster** than it used to be

- a tricky section that you finally worked out a **fingering** for

- a tough **reliability test** that you were able to pass for the **first time** (see PRESSURE TESTING⮌249)

- Being able to play a passage with the **metronome** for the very first time

- A DETAILS TRAWL⮌110 that you completed

- A BUGSPOTTING⮌53 test that come up **clean**

Whatever your breakthroughs for the day happen to be, they're worth being proud of—and proof that you're moving yet another step closer to being ready for next lesson.

The best time to make any note is **immediately after** the breakthrough has happened—when your triumph is still glowing red. That's when the breakthrough will be **freshest** in your mind, and you'll be feeling most proud of it.

And over the course of a few months, you'll be amazed how much the book will **fill up**.

Making, not just recording history

Your breakthroughs diary isn't just a recording device though. It actually **influences** the very thing it supposed to be capturing.

Just knowing that you have to record *something* at the end of each practice session will **completely change** how you work during that practice session. Your practice will have to be geared towards getting jobs done, *otherwise you'll have nothing to report.*

Not being able to write something is a **terrible feeling**—it's almost admitting that your practice session has been a waste of time.

Keeping it brief...

Your notes don't need to be beautifully constructed English. **Bullet points** are fine:

> • Rondo: Measures 24-35 now up to 120bpm
>
> • Etude: page 1, 3 in a row, no mistakes
>
> • Scales: Added Ab major to my "familiar" list

The idea is to ensure that the note only **takes seconds** to write, while still telling you everything you need to know.

So even better might be using some shorthand—you'd create a **quick-to-draw symbol** for each of the

common breakthrough types that you record.

So for example, instead of writing *"listened to the recording, and followed the score for the first movement"*, you might simply put:

 1st mvt

Similarly, if you needed to record "successfully played through the coda, three times in a row, no mistakes, metronome at 120 bpm", you could use symbols to record:

Coda, 120bpm ③

That way you can record comprehensive information about each breakthrough, **without interrupting** your practice.

When breakthroughs stop

Don't be alarmed if breakthroughs come **less frequently** for pieces you already know. Breakthroughs tend to come thick and fast when a piece is new, but then can slow down as the piece gets closer to being ready. It doesn't always mean that you're not practicing well. (see Tightening ➲337 and Stalling ➲325)

Showing your teacher

A list of what you achieved each day this week is **very** useful to help your teacher plan *next* week. So bring your Breakthrough Diary to the lesson for a little show-and-tell, and a review of the week that was.

Your teacher can then **recommend** additional breakthroughs for you to pursue when you next practice.

Matching it to what was needed

A central aim in practicing is to be ready for each lesson—it's no good filling your breakthrough diary with achievements that don't help you complete what your teacher needed.

Ideally, your breakthrough diary entry should **match** or **exceed** your agenda for the day. (see SESSION AGENDA➲305). Do that, and something magic happens...

...you'll always be ready for your next lesson.

A growing history

Your diary is useful for motivating you from day to day, but it eventually will show **complete journeys**— from the first time you tentatively sightread a piece, through to the time you first perform it.

A running history like that is a great way to understand how you actually work, so you can work better in the future. Often, it will inspire you to aim for **different breakthroughs** for your next piece, so you can improve your TURNAROUND TIMES➲352.

Learning what works

As you keep these records, you'll quickly discover that there are **certain types** of practice and concentration levels that lead to regular breakthroughs, and others that are just paddling around, **using up time**.

So for example, it's one thing to *read* in this book that **practicing too fast** is counter-productive (see SPEEDING➲320), but you'll truly understand it once you're keeping the breakthroughs diary...

...because on the days where your practice is all too fast, *you'll have nothing new to record.* It's all just been sound, fury and sixteenth notes, signifying nothing.

And so you'll file "playing too fast" as a breakthroughs diary "blank page!" technique. Keen to avoid more blank pages, you'll be less likely to play too fast next time.

Experience is a great teacher—but it's an even better teacher when you take the time to note what it was trying to say.

Bridging

Smoothing the bumps *between* sections

Thomas has been working on a *Theme and Variations*. Thanks to some solid practice, he can play **each variation** easily and well.

But when he tries to play the **whole piece**, it's a **different story**. He keeps stumbling at the instant where he has to **switch** from one variation to the next.

Extra practice on the variations **hasn't helped**. What can he do?...

YOU WON'T NEED THIS book to know that practicing in **sections** is usually a good idea. Most pieces are simply **too big** to tackle as a whole.

But if you *always* practice in segments, and those segments are *always* the same, then there's a nasty side-effect waiting for you:

Ugly things can start to grow in the joins between sections. (see "**Bad Bricklayers**" in PRACTICE TRAPS ➲246)

How does it work? You've done section A. You've done section B. But you've never **combined** them. So the join was always going to be **rough**, simply because it's **under-rehearsed**.

It's the reason that triathletes don't just practice swimming, riding and running. They practice getting **out** of the water, and **onto** their bike. And then they practice getting **off** their bike, and **into** their running gear. Otherwise, they can lose precious time with clunky changeovers.

Bridging is about practicing those connections, removing the bumps, and ensuring your piece can **flow** from beginning to end.

Scouting for bridge locations

If your piece is divided up into 5 segments (A,B,C,D and E), you'll need four bridges:

- From A into B
- From B into C
- From C into D
- From D into E

If you think about it for a moment, you'll realize that in a piece with no repeats, this **always holds true**—there will always be one fewer bridges than there are segments.

So for a piece with plenty of segments, that also means **plenty of bridges**. (In fact, if your piece goes all the way up to "Z", you can expect 25 of them)

Don't forget repeats

Finding bridge locations is not always as straightforward as **saying the alphabet** though. Courtesy of repeats, codas or first/second time

bars, you might have to rehearse a link between the end of D and the beginning of B. Or the end of T and the very *start* of the piece.

Take a moment to factor in these joins too. (In fact, they're often among the most badly in need of a bridge).

Building the bridge

Once you know **what** the bridges are supposed to be joining, you can set the **boundaries** of the bridge itself. Remember, *the bridges are really just a set of new sections that happen to span the boundaries of the old ones.*

Normally a bridge would run from

a few measures **before** the end of a section, to a few measures **into** the next section. Like a **gangnail** across two pieces of timber.

As a result, bridges are usually **much shorter** than the original sections, because the only thing they have to take care of is the join.

Changing geography

It's not unusual for bridges to connect quite **different** types of **playing**—after all, those differences are probably what defined the sections for you in the first place.

Part of bridging is being able to **shift instantly** to a new tempo, or tone color, or rhythmic figuration, or range—**without** needing to have a few beats to **warm up** into it.

So if the first half of your bridge needs duplets, while the second half suddenly requires triplets, you're going to have to be very good at **switching** from duplets to triplets... which sets up a **practice task** in its own right (see ISOLATING➲164)

Don't throw out your sections

The point of Bridging is to allow you to **keep working** in sections, not to have you **feeling guilty** about using sections in the first place. Make no mistake, sections are still a great way of making **large** pieces feel **small**—now that you're using Bridging too, your section-based

approach won't have any **unpleasant side-effects**.

The ultimate test...

...is to be able to play the piece to somebody else *without them being able to tell where the sections originally were*.

Like **quality carpentry**, you've paid attention to the joins, and made sure they're a seamless part of the whole.

Bridging in action

Let's imagine for a moment that you needed to rehearse the song "Twinkle Twinkle Little Star".
You might have divided it into **three sections** to do most of your practice.

A: *"Twinkle, twinkle little star. How I wonder what you are"*
B: *"Up above the world so high. Like a diamond in the sky"*
C: *"Twinkle, twinkle little star. How I wonder what you are"*

But then to ensure that you can **connect** these sections, your bridges will be A-B: *"...what you are. Up above the..."*, and B-C *"...in the sky, Twinkle twinkle little..."*. It's really that easy, but bridges like this are often overlooked.

Bug Spotting

Because you can't fix what you don't know about

Penny keeps **being surprised** at lessons by mistakes that she never knew were there.

What frustrates her though is that they feel like mistakes she could **easily correct** herself...if only she were able to spot them at home.

"It's **not** that they're **hard to find**" says her teacher "It's just that you have to **remember** to look for them."

Look for **bugs** in your pieces? How do you do *that*?

Practicing is largely about **solving problems.** It's about figuring out **how** to get this piece up to full tempo, or **which fingering** will make that passage work. It's about discovering **why** that section on page three sounds so...flat...and how to stop the coda from **getting faster.**

The more you practice, **the better you'll get** at solving problems like these—this book is filled with ideas to give you a **head start.**

But there's a danger that you need to be aware of:

You can't solve problems that you don't know are there.

You might be *perfectly capable* of tidying up some incorrect rhythms in your new piece...if **only you had known** they were wrong in the first place...

So **why does it matter** if you miss things like this? Surely your teacher will find them anyway?

1) It wastes lesson time
Your teacher has lots of roles, but pointing out things you could have **found for yourself** really

shouldn't be one of them. (See Details trawl➲110)

If you come to the lesson **having already found** and dealt with these issues, then your lesson time has to be spent on other more useful things.

2) It delays the start of repairs
Instead of starting work on the problem when the evidence first appears, you'll have to **wait** until your lesson comes around—cutting down the amount of time you then have to actually *fix* the problem.

2) It embeds the error
With no evidence of an error, you may well decide it's time to Cement➲64 this passage, playing it over and over to lock it in. With every pass, the missed issue becomes **harder to resolve**—and, because you're getting used to how it sounds, even **harder to spot.**

Spotting bugs for yourself
Sometimes you'll be lucky enough to spot bugs just as part of playing the piece—a clumsy passage might just **leap out** at you.

But most bugs won't just turn themselves in like that. If you want to be **sure** of finding them all, you have to stop your regular practice, and actually **look** for them.

How? There are a few options...

Bugspotting 1: "Spot" Method
Like most of these techniques, the "Spot" Method is not so much a practice tactic as a **survey.** It's job is not to fix things—it's simply to **identify** what needs fixing.

Of all the Bugspotting techniques, the "Spot" Method is the best at identifying *where* issues are:

1. Start by playing from the **beginning of the section** that you want to survey.

2. You would then keep playing until the very first thing happens that you **wouldn't** be happy to have happen **in a recital**.

It might be a wrong note, or a badly ended phrase. It could be sloppy rhythm delivery, or a fingering disaster.

3. Your job then is to **stop playing**, and put a **tiny spot** above the exact location of the problem in the music.

4. Pick up from where you were up to, and **continue the process**. So you'd keep playing until the very *next* thing happens that you wouldn't be happy to have happen in a recital. Stop, mark the spot, pick up again...and so on.

5. When you get to the end of the section, simply **loop back** to the start and **continue**. If a mistake appears in the same measure on the second pass, then it will get another spot.

After you've looped half a dozen times, you'll notice that some measures are clear, some have one or two spots...and others look like they have the **measles**.

When you next practice this passage, you'd start with the measures that are spottiest.

Using color to help with "what"

While the spot method is very good at helping you identify *where* issues are, it provides **little information** about *what*

the concern was in the first place.

Rather than cluttering up your score with written notes every time you stop, consider using COLOR CODING ➲84 to help you remember what each spot was for.

So, for example, a red spot might mean "misread note". Light green might mean "Rhythm needs tightening". Blue might be "not legato enough".

In that way, you can leave yourself reminders—and keep your score relatively clear.

Bugspotting 2: **Record & Review**

Sometimes it's easier to hear issues if you're not actually **busy playing** at the same time (see RECORDING YOURSELF➲270 and YOUR PRACTICE SUITE➲231)

This time, instead of stopping every time you notice a mistake, record a **complete playthrough**.

Then you'd listen to that recording, while carefully following the score. As you **notice** areas of concern, mark them in.

Again, you're not trying to fix anything...all you're doing is **flagging** areas as being high priority for future work.

Multiple passes

A sample of one can be a **little misleading** sometimes—to ensure that you're making recommendations based on typical playing, it's a good idea to record **several takes** consecutively.

Make separate notes for each take... and then, like the spot method, give highest priority to those issues that keep reappearing.

Bugspotting 3: Stress Testing

When engineers want to ensure that a bridge is going to be safe, they will usually test it with loads that **far exceed** the demands it would normally face. So if they know that it has to be able to cope with 4 tonne trucks, then they will subject it to testing that is the equivalent of a 7 tonne truck.

One way to identify possible trouble spots in your piece is to set up similar stress tests. **Demand more** than you need, and see if any **cracks** appear.

So, for example, if the passage is designed to be played at 120bpm, you might test it at 150bpm...just to see what's still **fine**, what **wobbles**, and what **collapses completely**.

Of course, you don't *need* to be able to play at 150, but the sections that give way first are usually those that are **most likely** to be trouble at 120 too.

And of course if you can handle 150, then you have the **added bonus** on concert day of knowing that you're performing 20% slower than you know you can manage.

Bugspotting 4: Thematic listening

Instead of focusing on the **location** of errors, thematic listening has you concentrating on **types of issues**— wherever they may be in the piece.

So you might play right through, listening just for **precise delivery of rhythm**. Make a note at the end about the extent to which that's a problem in the passage.

Then you'd switch issues—perhaps this time focusing on **articulation**. Again, jot down a quick impression

of the health of this issue in your passage.

Next might be **matching dynamics** to the score. Or elegant **fingering**. Or maintaining a **steady tempo**.

By the time you've been through a dozen issues, some will have put their hands up as being major concerns. Others you might get an all-clear for.

Either way, you'll be much better equipped to answer the question "what should I work on next?"

How to exterminate your bugs

It's very unusual to be able to squish a bug with just one practice technique—normally you'll need to use a mix of complementary techniques.

Some things to try:

CLEARING OBSTACLES⤸72—so that you can discover what is causing the bug in the first place

ISOLATING⤸164—so that you can work on the bug without cross-infection from other simultaneous issues.

BOOT CAMP⤸43—when you're ready to get tough with a bug that's been tough on you.

EXPERIMENTING⤸135—to trial possible solutions to the problem

CEMENTING⤸64—once you've settled on the best technical approach to kill your bug.

EXAGGERATING⤸124—to embed and make yourself highly aware of the behavior that kills the bug.

PRACTICE BUDDIES⤸226—you never know, they just might have dealt with bugs like this before, and have a suggestion or two.

If they're **still resisting** after all of that, then your teacher will need to help—but you'll find that most bugs are easily squishable once found.

When you can't find the bugs

If you've got the awful feeling that something is wrong in your piece, but that it's **hiding** from you, then check out the chapter on CORAL REEF MISTAKES⤸89

In short, they can hide, but they **can't run**...

Keeping a bugs journal

If a bug is important enough to make a **note** of, it's important enough to **keep track** of. As well as marking bug locations, you might want to try keeping a separate Bugs **Journal**. The aim of the journal is for you to **track** the **progress** of the bug—from the day it was first identified, until the day you declare it Exterminated. Each page in the journal would be dedicated to a particular bug. You'd record underneath that:

- **When** and with **which** practice techniques you have been targeting the bug
- Any **suggestions** your teacher may have given you
- Any **questions** you have about the bug that you want to raise at your lesson
- **Results** from any PRESSURE TESTING⤸249 that you may have run

That way you can see what **you've** been doing about the problem, what your **teacher** thinks you should do, while the tests allow you to **measure** your progress.

Campaigns
Connecting your daily practice to the big picture

Carrie has just been given a **brand new piece**, and has been told that she will be getting it ready for a performance...

... in **eight months' time.**

"Eight months!" she says "That's *forever!* I'll be so **sick of** practicing it by then..."

"Not true" says her teacher. "Each of those months of practice will be **completely different** to all the others."

Carrie pulls an I-don't-believe-you face. It's the **same piece.** She'll **know how to play it** in *one* month. What are the other seven **for?**...

CAMPAIGNS ARE the **largest unit** of measurement in the practice world.

They *have* to be large—a campaign covers everything you do from the very **first time** you meet a piece, through to a point in the future when the piece **needs no further practice**.

Depending on the piece and your own TURNAROUND TIME➲352 skills, that can take weeks, months... or even years. Campaigns are definitely about **Big Picture**, and are nothing short of a journey.

Zooming in...

If you look at a campaign closely though, you'll see that it's **not** just a **single entity**. Campaigns are made up of hundreds of practice sessions, and if you zoom in on *those*, you'll see that they're made up of **cells**—practice segments so **short** that they sometimes last only a few seconds. (See ROGUE CELLS➲293 for more information on these atom-sized practice segments)

The idea is that *cells* should work towards **session** goals, while each of those *sessions* should then work towards goals for the **campaign**.

Sound confusing? It's not really.

It's similar to an athlete **preparing for the Olympics:**
- The entire preparation over the course of several years is the **campaign**.
- When they turn up at the track at 10am to train on a particular day with their coach for two hours, that's a **session**.
- And if, during that session, they're doing 50 abdominal crunches, then that's a **cell**.

Of course, that set of abdominal crunches won't be the **only cell** in that session. Another cell might be spending a few minutes **analyzing** a video of the last time they competed. Or rehearsing **faster starts**. Or building endurance by **running uphill** on sand.

In fact, in the two hour session, there might be a **dozen** or more individual cells—each covering a different skill, but all helping the athlete and coach complete their **goals** for that session.

And then, as part of a three year campaign for the Olympics, there will be **many, many hundreds** of sessions.

An example

Ok, so you might not be preparing for the Olympics, but let's imagine that you have just been given a brand new sonata by your teacher.

As soon as they tell you about your new piece, the **campaign has already started**—and it will continue up until you've performed the work successfully several times.

On **each day** of that campaign, you will schedule one or more **practice sessions**. These sessions will have targets designed to move your campaign forwards.

For example, you might have a passage in the development section of your Sonata that is desperately in need of a **better fingering**. Just before your next practice session starts, you would **set yourself the target** of figuring out and embedding an improved fingering for the passage.

Now that your session has that goal, you then might run the following practice cells so you can meet that goal:

- **Trialling** alternative fingerings
- **Writing in** the best of those fingerings
- **Highlighting** crucial fingering transitions
- **Rehearsing** the new fingering slowly
- **Memorizing** the new fingering
- Using Metronome Method ⮌195 to **speed up** the new fingering
- **Testing** yourself by writing in the fingering on a Fresh Photocopy⮌151
- Cementing⮌64 the new fingering

At the end of which, your target for the session will have been met. (Can you even *imagine* how good your fingering is going to be after all those cells?) And long term, you've just **solved a problem** for the entire campaign.

Because the fingering is now fixed, you would set a **new goal** for the next practice session, and there would be a **brand new set of cells** to support that goal. There *has* to be a brand new set of cells—*yesterday's cells were designed for yesterday's problem.* They won't help at all with today's.

How campaigns unfold

The **type of work** your piece needs will **change** as the campaign progresses. That's really not too surprising—obviously your practice immediately before your first performance will be very different

from the practice you did when you **first met** the piece.

So how might your practice change through a campaign?

Campaign start

Because you've never worked on this piece before, your early sessions will normally involve Scouting⮌299 . That way, you'll form strong and accurate impressions of the piece—even before you've played a single note.

A lot of students skip this step... and then have to do hours of additional **unnecessary practice**.

Early campaign

Here's where you actually **learn the notes**—the aim of this phase being to end up being able to play the piece from beginning to end.

For many students, this is their least favorite part of the campaign. You usually don't sound so good, there's lots of reading, you'll be playing slowly and in small segments.

As a result, a lot of campaigns get bogged right here—although if you used something like LEVEL SYSTEM➲182 , you can unstick yourself very quickly.

Middle campaign

By now you can play the piece from beginning to end, and the focus switches to issues like getting it up to speed (see METRONOME METHOD➲195 , CHAINING➲69), making it reliable (see PRESSURE TESTING➲249) and adding your own interpretation stamp (See EXPERIMENTING➲135 and PAINTING THE SCENE➲222)

Late campaign

Your piece will be in good shape by now, but this phase is about **not accepting** that as being good enough. You'll be focussed on making the jump from "very good" to "excellent", which will involve plenty of TIGHTENING ➲337, and some of the most careful listening you've done so far.

End game

This is about getting ready for the concert, and is more about preparing **you** than preparing the **piece**. Depending on the progress of the piece, you'll use techniques

> # Depending on the piece and your own Turnaround Time skills, a campaign can take weeks, months...or even years. Campaigns are definitely about Big Picture.

such as VISUALIZING➲364, FIRE DRILLS➲139 , DRESS REHEARSALS➲115, and (hopefully not) COSMETICS➲94 .

Of course, sometimes the best End Game practice is **no practice at all**...if leaving well enough alone is genuinely what you need with two days to go, then so be it.

Overlapping campaigns

Unless you're in the unusual position of only having one piece to work on, you'll find you have **several campaigns** running at the same time.

These campaigns will be **different lengths**—simply because some

pieces require more extensive preparation than others.

They also will have **started at different times,** so at any one time you're likely to have a campaign that's **brand new**, a couple that are **well established**, and perhaps another that is **winding down**.

So a typical scenario might be that you have been working on a huge piece that you've been practicing for a year already...while learning the notes of a brand new **snack-sized** encore...and speeding up **a month-old** etude.

That's three **very different** stages of three very different campaigns.

The fact that they overlap is **good news** though—it means you can **vary** the type of practice you're doing. So if you're completely sick of practice tasks that are based around **scouting** (which is where your Campaign-Start encore piece will be up to), then instead of your only alternative being no practice at all, you have **other types** of practice you can switch to:

• Switch to performance-based challenges, (your End-Game year-old big piece).

OR

• Switch to tempo-boosting and reliability challenges (your Middle-Campaign etude).

In that way, you can keep a healthy mix, and still keep all your campaigns moving forwards. (See VARYING YOUR DIET ➲360)

Campaigns and your schedule

Another way to structure and vary your sessions is to build your practice schedule around **rotating** through each of your campaigns.

So if you have 4 campaigns running at the same time:

1) **Major Sonata** (Late campaign)
2) **Encore piece** (Campaign start)
3) **Etude** (Middle Campaign)
4) **Romanian Dance** (Early Campaign)

you might schedule things like this:

Monday

Session 1: Encore Piece (*start*)
Scouting - listening & following score

Session 2: Major Sonata (*late*)
Tightening - eliminating Tempo Creep

Tuesday

Session 1: Romanian Dance (*early*)
Level System - 12 new Levels

Session 2: Encore piece (*start*)
Scouting - break the piece up into segments

Session 3: Etude (*middle*)
Experimenting - randomizing dynamics on page 2

Wednesday

Session 1: Major Sonata (*late*)
Tightening - double checking articulation marks

Session 2: Etude (*middle*)
Metronome Method - Page 3, 92 bpm - 160 bpm.

...and so on.

You'll notice that it's not just the

campaign that varies each day—it's also the **type of practice** that you're doing. It's hard for things to become stale with variety like that.

Putting campaigns on pause

It's not all forward motion though. Sometimes you'll need to **suspend** campaigns temporarily:

• If you've reached a point where a campaign is **stalling**, and no further improvement is occurring. (although there are alternatives to suspending the campaign - see STALLING ➲325 for some suggestions)

• If a change in your deadlines or circumstances mean that other campaigns now need to **demand all of your time**.

So, for example, if you find that you've a **school concert on short notice,** you might have to temporarily suspend all campaigns apart from the one that prepares you for that concert.

If you do ever need to suspend a campaign (and you will), it's not necessarily a bad sign. If you've been practicing well in the first place then you **won't slip backwards** too far (in fact, often you won't slip back at all—see ONE WAY DOORS ➲208)

Conducting campaign *reviews*

Every few weeks, it's worth **downing tools** for a moment or two and reviewing your progress on the current campaign:

Is it moving forwards? How quickly? Is there a **deadline** the campaign is working towards? If so, does it seem that you'll be **ready in time**?

Which **phase** of the campaign are you currently up to? What **still** **needs to be done** before you can move onto the next phase?

How well are you **juggling** this campaign with the others? Are they all getting the **attention** they need? Is it worth **suspending** one of the more developed campaigns briefly, while you **catch up** on the others?

Is there a campaign that you're working on that is perhaps **no longer needed**?

Or another that's **almost finished**? And if so, how will you be able to tell when it's **time** to put it behind you? (See CLOSURE ➲80)

Remember, your practice cells only exist to serve your practice sessions, and the sessions only exist to serve the campaign—so if you **get things wrong** at the campaign level, it will **undermine** everything else you do.

Counting balls in the air

How many campaigns should you have **running at once**? There is no ideal number for everybody—but there almost certainly is an **ideal number for you**.

Some students work best when they can narrow their focus to **just one or two** campaigns at a time. Instead of enjoying the variety that half a dozen campaigns can provide, they actually find it **distracting**.

Others get twitchy and irritable **unless** they're working on a dozen at once.

You need to discover what's best for you—*and it might be different from what your teacher has been automatically setting for you so far.* (If you've never tried **fewer** or **more** balls in the air, how will you know?)

It doesn't mean more or less practice. It just means **distributing** your practice differently.

Cementing

Locking in the version you want to keep

Ella has worked **very hard** this week, but at her lesson, her piece is a **complete mess**.

"I **don't understand**" she complains to her teacher. "I played this **over and over and over** at home."

Her teacher smiles. "Ella" he says "That's exactly *why* your piece is a mess."

What did he **mean**? Surely **repetition** is *vital* when you practice?...

CEMENTING INVOLVES **using repetition** to deeply embed a particular way of playing something.

The idea is that if you deliver a rhythm the same way a **thousand times,** then you'll almost certainly deliver the rhythm that way on **concert day** too.

It's a concept most students are thoroughly **familiar** with.

But here's the **problem**, and it's a **big one**:

A lot of students confuse cementing with practicing.

And so they use the technique **all the time,** usually because it's the only technique they know.

As we'll see in a second, cementing is a *final stage practice technique only.* Using it too early is not just ineffective—it's actually a sure way to make your piece **worse.**

So how does cementing work? And why should you normally **postpone** it?

The backyard path

Let's imagine for a moment that I want to make a **path** in our back-yard—something my kids can **ride around** on their bike.

I could make this path out of dirt, but I want something that's going to be **permanent** and **solid**. So I make the whole path out of **cement**.

A day in the sun and the cement has dried. As intended, the path is both permanent and solid. And so I pace along it, admiring how strong it is.

It's only then that I **realize something awful.**

The path is really *not* well placed. It's too close to the fence on once side, and runs right through a space we had originally set aside as being a vegetable garden on the other.

Worse still, at one point it's within half a metre of the pool—a pool which, under council regulations, we will be required to fence in before we fill it.

In other words, in **summer** when my kids are riding their bikes, when they get to that section of the path they'll have to **get off** the bike, open the pool fence gate, wheel their bike through, close the gate, **ride for two metres** inside the fence, then open another gate, wheel the bike out, close that gate...

...you get the idea, but it's not exactly wind-in-your-hair free-wheeling fun.

Looking at it now, I can see an alternative route the path could have taken—one that would have solved all these problems.

Unfortunately though, this cement is **permanent** and **solid**. It's going to be a heck of a job to make changes now.

In fact, I'm not even sure it's going to be **possible**.

Permanent changes

What you have to understand is that cementing is a *very* powerful technique to ensure that a passage is **always** played the **same way.**

The repetition at the heart of cementing is designed to **lock in** behavior, and it's an essential part of the practice process. You *need* your performance locked at some stage. Otherwise concert day is just a roll of the dice.

But cementing **does not look closely** at *what* is being made permanent like this. It **does not distinguish** between correct notes and incorrect notes. It **doesn't care** about missed accidentals, bad fingerings or unworkable bowings.

It simply takes whatever you're **already doing,** and makes sure you *always* do that.

If what you're already doing is carefully checked and well thought out, then this is **great news.** Cementing is your **best friend.**

But if there are errors in there, then all you're doing is turning them into **fossils.**

> # Cementing is a *final stage* practice technique only. Using it too early is not just ineffective—it's actually a sure way to make your piece *worse*.

In the backyard scenario on the previous page, the **cement was not the problem.** At some stage this path *had* to be cement. The problem was that the cement was introduced before I was 100% certain of *what* I was about to make permanent.

A little checking—and preparation—would have made a lot of difference.

Pre-cement preparation

If you've reached the stage where you feel ready to lock in a passage, there are a couple of **last minute checks** that you should run first—just to make sure that you're not about to embed errors.

Note and detail trawl

A wrong note is one kind of problem, but a *cemented* wrong note...you'll need a crowbar to remove it. Similarly, you don't want to embed an accent or staccato that isn't really there. See DETAILS TRAWL➲110 for more information.

Rhythm check

Are you *sure* that your understanding and delivery of the rhythms in this passage are correct? Wrong rhythms are particularly hard to shift once they've been embedded. Run some last minute counting or check the RECORDING➲277 just to make sure.

Fingering/bowing/tonguing

Again, you're about to lock in the way you're already doing this. Are you *sure* this is what you want to keep? Forever?

Announcing your prototype

All this preparation is really helping you create a **prototype** of the passage (See PROTOTYPES ➲257)—a model you'll be able to point to and confidently say.

"*This* is how I want this passage to go. These are the **notes** I want, those are the **dynamics**, and these are the **articulations** I need. The **rhythm** is supposed to sound like this, and the passage needs the following **fingering**".

It's an exciting picture. It's what you want the passage to eventually be.

But at this stage, it's just an idea. Now it's time to ensure that the passage is delivered that way **every time.**

Which is where cementing comes into its own.

The cementing begins

Having **triple checked** that you're about to cement the right things, and created a clear picture of the prototype for this passage, it's now all about **repetition**.

You're going to be playing this passage **over and over** again, until you *simply couldn't imagine it being any other way.*

All those carefully worked out fingerings, notes and articulations go from being just **good ideas** to something you can **reproduce** anywhere, anytime.

Even more exciting is that with every pass, the cement grows stronger— but this time, because you've **checked everything in advance**, that's a cause for celebration, not concern.

In fact, without the cement, your

prototype would **remain** just as an **idea.** You could certainly explain it to somebody, but there's no guarantee you could actually *play* it that way.

Checking that the cement is strong enough

If cementing is about repetition, the next question is "how many times?". You **can't** answer that with a **number** (see CLOSURE ➲80), but instead you need to PRESSURE TEST ➲249 the passage. The tougher the test, the better.

If you pass the test, that's enough repetition. If not, then you're not done just yet.

When the cement won't set

If after plenty of repetition, the passage is still not reliable, then the cause is usually one of three things:

*1) You were **not sufficiently clear** about what the final cemented version **should contain.***

If you are at all muddled about what notes you should be playing, or which fingering you should be using, then the cement will **never** set.

Why? Because in such a case *you're not really using repetition.* Your uncertainty will mean that each playthrough will be **slightly different.** This time it's an F. Next time it's an F#. And the time after that you leave it out entirely.

That's like trying to **learn a spelling word** by writing it out over and over again...but **varying** the spelling in those writeouts. Sometimes you use two "p"s. Sometimes one. Sometimes none at all.

Which spelling is the real one? You **won't know**...which means that you won't know in your **spelling test** either.

The same is true when you're practicing. If each of your playthroughs are **slightly different,** you have no way of knowing which one is the "real" one. In which case, **get ready for a surprise** on concert day—you could produce any of these versions. (Very bad for your teacher's blood pressure)

If this is happening to you, stop the cementing (it's not doing anything for you), and go back to your **prototype.** Double check the things you're not sure of, and then try cementing again.

2) *You **are clear** about what the final version should be, but **sloppy** about ensuring each playthrough **matches that** vision.*

Again, the cement won't set because you're not really repeating anything.

You have to concentrate hard when you're cementing, ensuring that every playthrough contains **exactly** the elements you want the final version to contain.

3) *You **are clear** about what the final version should be, you're **concentrating hard,** but the passage is just proving **too hard to play.***

This is a different problem entirely, but again, you can't cement under these conditions. Try slowing the passage down, perhaps working directly from your Prototype➲257.

Alternatively, you might need to spend a little time working out why the passage is hard to deliver. (See Clearing Obstacles➲72),

or check out the Usher entry on Dealing with Problem Passages ➲31.

Consistency vs Quantity

Because of the fact that cement **only sets** when you're playing exactly the **same** thing over and over, consistency has to be your **first priority.**

Unfortunately though, when students are in cementing mode, the focus usually becomes **how many times** they can play the passage. If 50 is good then 100 seems better. Twice as good, in fact. *But that doesn't count for anything if you've been "cementing" slight variations.*

So before you get too carried away with **numbers,** remember this—your cementing will have been much more effective of you spent **5 minutes** getting a score of :

10 correct attempts
0 incorrect attempts

than if you had spent a **whole week** on:

6500 correct attempts
4275 incorrect attempts

In other words, if you're casual about this, you're just **throwing away** practice time.

Chaining
Getting to full speed, one segment at a time

Caleb has a piece that he can't play at **full speed**—yet. He's been trying to speed it up with METRONOME METHOD➲195, together with plenty of slow practice, but is frustrated by the rate of progress.

"Is there some way I can speed my piece up **without** having to practice **slowly** all the time?" wonders Caleb.

You bet, Caleb. Although this is not *instead of* slow practice, this is *as well as*, and it turns everything **upside down**. Here's how it works...

Most of the practice techniques designed to **speed pieces up** are based around **slow practice** initially.

So, for example, Metronome method➲195 works by starting with a **slow and comfortable tempo**, and then steadily **increasing the speed** after each successful play-through.

Some students find this bottom-up approach frustrating though.

Chaining **works from the top down.** You actually start by playing at **full speed** straight away.

As ever though, there's a twist.

The Chaining Compromise

Instead of compromising **tempo** (which is how metronome method works), chaining compromises the **length** of the passage.

You start by playing a **fragment** at full speed—just the first two notes of the passage—and then gradually **increasing** the number of notes in the chain.

So once you've got a full speed chain that's four notes long, you'd be looking to extend it to five.

When do you add to the chain?

The **rule** is that you **don't** ever extend the chain until you're **coping** at **full speed** with the chain you've already got.

And "coping" doesn't just mean somehow **tripping** through the notes. It means being able to **control** how you're playing them. If you can't keep it **even**, or produce the **dynamics** you want, or stick to the **bowing** you worked out, then your chain shouldn't be growing just yet.

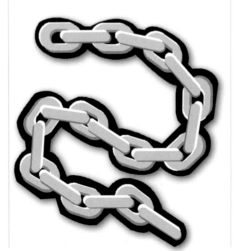

When the chain won't grow

After a while, you'll find that your initial chain will **stop growing—** that if you try any more notes at full tempo, you start to **lose control.**

That's **no problem**—in fact, it's part of the process. Simply **start another chain** somewhere else in the passage. Grow the new chain as much as you can.

When **it too** becomes as long as you can cope with, **start another one...** and so on.

You'll end up with **lots of chains** scattered throughout the passage, some **overlapping,** some **not.**

Fragments of full speed

These **scattered chains** now mean that while you may not be able to deliver the **entire passage** at full tempo yet, you will have **plenty of fragments** in the passage that will go that fast now.

The rest of your chaining work will involve continuing to **lengthen these fragments,** and then **joining fragments together**—with the aim that eventually **every measure** in the passage will become part of the same big chain.

In the meantime, enjoy the fact that the **percentage** of the passage **now covered** by these full-speed chains is **always growing**, even if individual chains aren't.

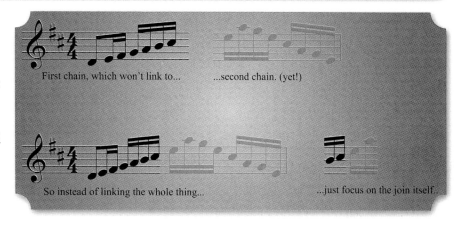

First chain, which won't link to...   ...second chain. (yet!)

So instead of linking the whole thing...   ...just focus on the join itself.

Getting beyond "I can't"

As soon as your very first chain is in place—even if it's short—it's much harder to undermine yourself with thoughts such as "**I can't** play this passage at full speed. I'll **never** be able to play this passage at full speed".

Instead, you're able to say "There are **44 notes** in this passage. I can already handle **3 of them** at full tempo. **By this afternoon** it will be 6. **By tomorrow** it will be 14."

As the **number of notes** that form part of a chain **grows**, so will your **confidence**. Playing fast is not some far-off-maybe-one-day thing. You just *did* play fast.

When chains won't link

Every so often, you'll come across

chains that simply **refuse to link**. They work fine by themselves, by when you try to turn them into a single extended chain, everything falls apart.

This is not a sign that these sections will always be unlinkable, but there are two things you need to try if you want to make further progress:

1) Instead of trying to link ALL of the first chain to ALL of the second chain, try just working on the **join** itself. (See illustration above)

Similar to BRIDGING➲50, you might start just by joining the **last note** of one chain to the **first note** of the other. Then the last two notes of one chain to the first two notes of the other...and so on.

2) Instead of leaving it at "I can't link these", try to find out *why* by CLEARING OBSTACLES ➲72. There will be a reason—perhaps a bad fingering, or a jump that you need to handle in a different way. Find the reason, and you can fix the link.

It's part of a team

Chaining is just **one of many** practice techniques designed to help you speed your piece up, and they work best if they all have a part to play. So if your chain doesn't quite end up covering the whole piece, **don't panic**—check out what the Practiceopedia Usher has to say about on GETTING YOUR PIECE UP TO TEMPO ➲19.

Clearing Obstacles
Finding what causes tricky bits to be tricky

Ella is not having a very **happy day**. She's been trying to fix a tricky run in her piece, but it's just not getting any better.

"This bit's stupid!" she yells as she flings her book off the music stand. "I'll **never** get it! I've played it a **hundred times** already and I've had **enough** and music lessons are **stupid too** and I never, never, never, **ever** want to play the stupid violin again and...and....*boo hoo hoo*."

Poor Ella. The thing is though, she could probably have saved herself this misery. Not by working **harder**.

By working *differently*...

W E'RE ALL taught that if you want to **master tough passages**, you have to play them over and over and over. That if a section is **still not behaving itself** after you've played it 100 times, it's just a sure sign that you really needed to **play it *200* times instead**.

Let's take a closer look at this, because I'm **not convinced** it's such a great idea.

The play-it-a-lot-to-fix-it model can be **described** in three steps:

> **STEP 1:** Play the passage
>
> **STEP 2:** Did you play it well?
> *(Yes/No)*
>
> **STEP 3:** If **no**, go back to Step 1

Ouch. Written out like that, it doesn't look like **such a *smart* idea after all**.

Let's take a look at why it doesn't work, with an illustration straight out of your **kitchen...**

...The Bad Toaster

Let's imagine you have a kitchen appliance that is **driving you crazy**—a toaster that's always **burning** your toast. Every time you have breakfast, your bread pops up looking like a **relic from Pompeii**.

Using our just-repeat-it model, you'd fix the problem like this:

> **STEP 1:** Put a slice of bread in the toaster, and wait till it pops up
>
> **STEP 2:** When it popped up, was the toast burnt? *(Yes/No)*
>
> **STEP 3:** If Yes, get another slice of bread, go back to Step 1 and repeat.

So the method for dealing with the problem is to **keep putting slices of bread in**, hoping each time that THIS time, it will cook properly.

If you've already put 100 slices in, and you're still getting nothing but burnt toast, you would **keep going**—*you obviously just haven't repeated the process enough yet.*

It's what **some musicians call "dedication"**. I think that's a very nice word for something that is a **colossal waste of time**.

Instead of simply looping something that's not working, you have to **interrupt the process**, and try to figure out *why* the toast is getting burnt in the first place. Ah, there we are. The toaster had been turned up too high! Silly me! Turn it down, and problem is fixed—without having to waste any more bread.

Sometimes persistence **is not the answer**—*analysis* is. Figuring out why your sections are misbehaving in the first place.

If at first you don't succeed, *stop and think*

It's been said the definition of insanity is **doing the same thing** and expecting a different result.

If you've already thrown plenty of practice at a passage, and it's not responding, **simply doing more** practice is **not** going to **get the job done**. In fact you're probably just reinforcing whatever was causing the passage not to respond in the first place.

So your **very first step** has to be to STOP what you're already doing. Catch your breath…and then find out **what's really going on**.

Analyze, test and *then* practice

Once you've stopped the practice that *wasn't* working, clearing obstacles is a three step process:

STEP 1: Analyze the passage to identify what the obstacle actually is.

STEP 2: Brainstorm and test possible solutions.

STEP 3: CEMENT➲64 the solution

> **If you've already thrown plenty of practice at a passage, and it's not responding, simply doing *more* practice is not going to get the job done.**

that delivered the greatest improvement.

Let's take these one at a time:

1. *Analyze* the passage:

It's **not enough** just to say "this bit is hard". What **exactly** is it that makes it hard? Is it a tricky **jump**? An awkward **register change**? A **rhythm** you can't feel? A chord you can't reach?

Naming the problem is nine-tenths of fixing it—and while the problem remains unidentified, **no amount of practice** will improve things for you.

2. *Test possible solutions:*

Once you've named the problem, it's time to **brainstorm possible solutions**. If it's a rhythm that you can't feel, perhaps counting while you play will help. Perhaps ignoring the notes and tapping it is the

way to go. (See ISOLATING ➲164) Perhaps listening to the recording might create an "aha!" moment (see RECORDINGS ➲277). Or maybe it's worth doubling every note value to make the rhythm friendlier to the eye and ear.

Armed with a **list of possible fixes**, try them out. See what works, what doesn't, and then…

3. *Cement the solution(s) that delivered the greatest improvement*

If one of your possible solutions actually helped, it's worth **building into** your playing.

So if you had a theory that perhaps relaxing your hand and dropping your shoulder would make a fatiguing passage easier to deliver, and you were **proved right**, then you need to practice doing exactly that.

So no matter what you may have been told about posture, if leaning forward makes the passage easier to play, *then it makes it easier to play.* Lean forward, **save yourself** the unnecessary practice you would need to do to cope with leaning back.

Start with the usual suspects

In your hunt for obstacles, there are three that between them, account for the **vast majority** of passages that don't seem to improve with practice. Before you start looking for more complicated causes, take a moment just to **rule these out:**

• **Being unclear as to what notes or rhythms actually are.** It sounds obvious, but it's amazing how often students will start repeat-playing sections that are filled with basic notereading errors—and then wonder why it keeps sounding wrong despite all their "practice"

• **Unworkable fingerings or bowings.** Your choice—you can either spend 5 minutes working out a better fingering, or 5 weeks struggling to master the old bad one. (In fact, there are some fingerings that are so bad you will NEVER master them)

• **Insane tempo.** Often the simplest explanation of all—you can't play this bit, because you're trying to play *too fast*. You dope. See SPEEDING ➲320.

The zero practice result

Removing an obstacle doesn't just cut back the amount of practice the passage needs—sometimes it can actually mean that you *don't need to practice the passage at all.* After all, if the cause for a passage being difficult has been removed, the passage should no longer be difficult.

If it *is* still difficult, then there may be **more than one** obstacle. Go back, take a closer look.

When you can't find the obstacle (or the solution)

Sometimes you can run a microscope over a passage and still can't discover why it's so hard. And sometimes you will have isolated exactly what's so difficult, but haven't a clue what to do about it.

Record the location of the problem passage in your LESSON AGENDA ➲171, together with what you've done about the problem so far.

Your **teacher** can take it from there. (They've had a lot more experience than you at identifying and clearing obstacles, and can work even better if you flag areas for "please help!")

Clockwatchers

Curing the unhealthy obsession with *time*

Everyone who knows Benjamin talks about how hard he works. In fact, he does **forty minutes** of practice every single day. Even on his *birthday*.

Mind you, it's always **exactly** forty minutes. Never forty-one, or thirty-nine. And lately, he's just **not ready** for lessons.

It's hard to see what he's doing wrong though. Or is it?...

CLOCKWATCHERS HAVE an obsession with **how long** they've been practicing. The **more minutes** they use up, the **better** they think the practice session is.

So while other students are **checking** fingerings or **listening** to phrasing, the clockwatcher's attention is **on the time**, and their mind is filled with thoughts like this:

"Great! Only a quarter of an hour to go!"

or

"I can't believe all those scales only used up three minutes..."

No concern for the health of the pieces, or their task for the week. Their job is to pass the time, and they keep willing the minute hand to go **faster**, as if they were a frustrated motorist stuck behind a slow truck.

Clockwatcher logic smashed
Clockwatchers are **right** about one thing. Doing a good job can take a **long time**.

However, it **doesn't necessarily follow** that if you've taken a long time, then you must have done a good job.

Think about it for a second:

Let's imagine you were told to **tidy your room**. You could spend 12 hours moving your bed **back and forth** from the left wall to the right wall.

At the end of that time, your back would be sore, you'd be worn out... and your room would **still be a mess**.

What clockwatchers don't understand is that it's not **how long** you take. It's **what you get done**.

Their practice might *seem* ok...
To outside observers, clockwatchers can seem **hard working enough**. Because they watch the clock, they'll rarely do less than they're supposed to.

If their teacher had **asked** for **half an hour** of practice every day, then the clockwatcher will have done exactly that.

And I mean *exactly* that. There's no way a clockwatcher is going to do **21 minutes** if they're asked for **20**. They'll **abandon** their practice mid-phrase as soon as the countdown timer **hits zero**.

It's all part of a spirit of work which is **not interested** in what's actually happening, as long as it takes the **set number of seconds**. We should all be hoping that **surgeons** don't work this way too. ('I've now spent 2 hours transplanting this liver, that's long enough')

...but they're often not ready
Because they're so focused on the clock, Clockwatchers **fall victim** to any number of PRACTICE TRAPS ↪236, usually without realizing

it. At the very least, the fact that they're **not paying attention** to what they're doing means that they are almost certainly ENGAGING AUTOPILOT➲120.

As a result, when a clockwatcher turns up to their lesson, it might well be after **lots** of practice—but they often still **won't have completed** the tasks their teacher needed.

They could do *less* practice...

Here's the irony. If clockwatchers focused **less** on the clock, and **more** on what they need to get done, they could actually be ready each week with **less practice overall**. (see SESSION AGENDA➲305)

It's not about **minutes spent**. It's about what you **get done** with those minutes.

So if you're clock watching because you want to do as **little practice** as possible, the **best thing** you can do is become an **expert** on practicing—*that way you can get everything done in less time.*

> **"If your schoolteacher asks you how your homework went this week, he or she wants to know if it's *done*—not how long you spent on it."**

Use the Captain Hook solution

The fastest way to **cure yourself** of clockwatching is to make sure that you have **no way** of telling the **time**. Ban all clocks and watches from the practice room. It's not going to **keep crocodiles away**, but it will stop you from checking the time every 90 seconds—so you can concentrate on your **music** instead.

Figuring out when to stop

Because the Captain Hook solution now means that you can't tell the time any more, you'll suddenly find that you now **don't know** when you're supposed to **stop** practicing. You're going to have to find some other trigger for CLOSURE➲80, so that you're not just stopping whenever you **feel like it**. (You might feel like it very quickly...)

Recording what you achieve

Clock Watchers always know **exactly** how much practice they did in a session, and will often proudly record the results on a chart. Instead, they should know exactly **what they accomplished** in that time.

The question to ask is "how did all that work **help** me be **ready** for my next lesson?"

If the answer is "I don't know" or "It didn't really help me with my next lesson", then it **doesn't matter** how much time you threw at your practice—your lesson is still going to be **painful** for you and your teacher.

To help you **match** what you're *actually* doing to what you're *supposed* to be doing, consider using a BREAKTHROUGHS DIARY➲46 to record your achievements—so you can **see for yourself** what your hard work is really **producing**.

Explaining this to parents

If the **rule** in **your house** is half-an-hour-of-daily-practice, you can't just **announce** that you're switching to a new model that doesn't need clocks. It's going to sound like you have plans **not** to practice **at all.**

Show your parents this *Practiceopedia* entry, so they understand what you're trying to do. You should also show them your Breakthroughs Diary, so they can see for themselves just how much you're actually getting done.

That way, they'll realize that you're not simply trying to dodge work—it's just that you'll be working **smarter** from now on.

"So, how was this week?"

You don't need to answer your teacher's question any more with **meaningless numbers** such as "I did 30 minutes every day".

Remember, if your school teacher asks you how your homework went this week, he or she wants to know **if it's done**, not **how long** you've spent on it.

Similarly, knowing that you've spent 30 minutes every day really **doesn't tell** your music teacher **much** about how your practice has gone this week—except that there was obviously **210 minutes** spent doing **something**.

So when your teacher asks you the question, show them your Break-throughs Diary instead.

Or better still, **play the piece** and **demonstrate** that everything they asked for has been done. If you've been careful each day to set your session agenda, and then complete everything on the agenda, that demonstration is going to be just fine.

Not *watching* time is different from not *spending* time

Don't misunderstand this chapter—abandoning clockwatching **doesn't mean** that you're entering a wonderful **fairyland** where you can spend no time practicing and still sound great. If you're going to get through all your tasks each day, it's going to take time. It's just that the point is the **tasks**, not the **time itself.**

This builds into your practice a **reward** for practicing efficiently and concentrating hard—*you'll get through your work sooner, which means less practice.* But it also builds in a **penalty** that has not existed before:

If you're goofing around in there, you could be practicing all day. Remember, you get to stop your practice for the day **as soon as** you've completed everything on your agenda...

...but **not until**.

Closure

Knowing when you can safely *stop* practicing something

Allan has been practicing the **same section** for 10 minutes now, and feels like he's made good progress.

He's got **plenty of other work** to get on with, and is **tempted to move on** and practice something else…

…but should he?

How can he *really* tell when he's **finished** with something?…

C LOSURE IS THE art of knowing when to **stop** practicing something, and it's an essential skill that hardly ever gets talked about.

It's essential because when you're practicing, until you stop what you're currently doing, you can't **move** on to **what's next**.

Which means "what's next" isn't getting done—it's **waiting in line**. Along with all the other tasks on your list that are waiting in line behind *that*.

So if you're really finished with a task, but keep working on it anyway, don't fool yourself. You're not being dedicated or thorough. You're just **stealing time** from other tasks.

More than just *overpracticing*

The reverse is true too. If you move on from your current practice task **too soon**, then you're going to fall victim to the *Skimming* practice trap (See PRACTICE TRAPS➲239)

Moving on before the job is done just means that you have to **revisit** the job again—or risk turning up on lesson day with the job not finished.

Looks like you're in a **pickle** here. If you stop too late, you're wasting time. Stop too early and you do a half-job on your current task.

So how do you judge it correctly? Before we have a look at how to tell when it really is time to move on, let's look at how *not* to tell.

Examples of *bad* closure

Students have all sorts of reasons for moving on to what's next. You might recognize some of these:

1) I'm **sick of** this bit now

That's not a reason for moving on. Your job is to complete the practice tasks, not wait until you're "in the mood". Get on with it.

2) **That'll do**

Maybe...but how do you know? Did you PRESSURE TEST➲249 it? Would your *teacher* think it's ready enough when he or she hears it?

3) I've spent (insert your favorite upper time limit here) **on that** already now

If you get nothing else out of this book, please understand that how long you've spent on something tells you nothing about how ready it is. It just tells you how much **older** you are then when the practice session started.

4) Ok, that time, it was **finally right**

Yes, but that doesn't count for much if you screwed it up 25 times first. *Once-right* doesn't mean *lesson-ready*. It usually just means *lucky-shot*.

Which means you're going to have to get lucky on lesson day too, otherwise you're going to have to resort to "...but it didn't sound like this at home" (yes it did, 24 out of 25 times).

Again, make sure you've read the chapter on PRESSURE TESTING➲249

5) *I'll finish that off* **some other time**

Well, you're going to *have* to now that you've abandoned it. Wasn't the whole point of starting with this task today to get it done though?

Using this particular reason for moving on is a great way to ensure that you have dozens of half-completed tasks at your next lesson.

Unfortunately, these are not just bad reasons for moving on. They're the reasons students *usually* use. (How many of those have you used?)

Better reasons for closure

Ok, so if those are bad reasons for moving on, what are *good* reasons?

1) *I've* **Pressure Tested** *this task now, and it's* **lesson ready**

This is the single best way to be sure that you can safely stop what you're currently doing.

Because you tested it, there was no chance of a fluke. You've *proved* you're ready to move on—you can do so with a clear conscience.

> # Closure becomes an issue whenever you *think* you've finished with something, but aren't really sure if you should stop just yet...

2) *This has* **stopped improving**

At the very least, the fact that it's stopped improving is a sign that you're wasting your time practicing exactly as you are.

You either need to practice the same section in a new way, or move on to something else entirely. See STALLING⊃325

3) *I have* **time constraints** *on my practice that mean I cannot afford to* **ignore** *the rest of my task list* **any longer.**

Remember, while you're bogged down with this section, nothing else is getting done—including items that you really could have dealt with quickly and easily.

Move on, win some battles with other practice tasks, and then

come back recharged. But do come back. (Otherwise this can easily become a variation of "I'll finish that off some other time")

What else needs closure?

Closure becomes an issue *whenever you think you've finished with something, but aren't really sure if you should stop just yet.* So it applies to a **lot more** than simply deciding whether or not to move on to the next practice task:

• *I've done* **lots of practice** *already this afternoon. Can I stop the* **entire session** *yet?*

Just like closure for tasks, "Lots of practice" might sound a sign you're done, but it is **not** a reason for closure. In fact, the *amount* of practice you've done is really not relevant to anything.

Having completed and tested all your tasks for the day is a reason for closure though. (See SESSION AGENDA➲305)

• *My **concert is tomorrow,** my piece seems **fine** whenever I try it… should I play it through **just one more time** to be safe? Or should I just leave it?*

Especially before a concert, you want to leave well enough alone. If your piece seems fine, then let's make sure you walk onstage still feeling that way about it.

Going over and over a piece that is otherwise behaving itself will eventually uncover new things for you to worry about during your performance.

• *Should I schedule **more practice tomorrow** for the passage I was just working on, or is that now **ready** for next lesson?*

Check out the chapter on ONE WAY DOORS➲208 for help with this. The answer is often "don't".

These seem like a **mix** of closure questions, but they're all really asking the **same thing:**

What do I have to do to be able to mark this as "completed?"…and to therefore move on to the next task (or a break!) with a clear mind and conscience?

There's a way to answer that every time…

…all you have to do is set some **triggers.**

Setting closure triggers

Instead of asking yourself "can I move on yet?" *while* you're practicing, figure out in *advance* what your trigger for moving on will be.

That way, you'll know when the time is right, because you'll **recognize the trigger**—no guessing needed.

You'll normally phrase your trigger in the following way:

"As soon as I can [insert details here], *then I can move on.*

Some examples:

• *As soon as I can play this entire passage **from memory**…*

• *As soon as I have written in a **workable fingering** for this passage…*

• *As soon as I can play this passage with the **metronome** set at 140 bpm…*

• *As soon as I have* COLOR CODED ➲84 *all the dynamic markings in this piece…*

• *As soon as I have cleanly made this jump five times in a row…*

Once you have defined your trigger, keep an eye out for it while you practice. And as soon as it appears, **move on**—without guilt, and without delay.

Color Coding

A whole new dimension to marking your score

Nathan's music teacher has just given him a **present**—and it's not even his **birthday**.

"Open it" she says "I'm giving one to every student in the studio. It's a new **practice tool** that's going to transform how you work."

Nathan is very curious...but then quickly **disappointed** when he sees what's inside.

A pack of color markers? How could *this* possibly be a **practice tool?** Has his teacher gone **mad?**...

Y ou've probably been told that you should only ever use **pencil** if you're going to write on your music. That way, you can always erase it so you can have a clean copy (see Fresh Photocopies ➲151)

There's a **problem** though. Add enough markings, and they all start to **look the same**. Pretty soon they just become as everyday and easy to ignore as the details they were supposed to be highlighting.

Worse still, a measure can have a circle around it, but you'll have **no idea why**—and so you start to feel **guilty** about everything in that measure: *Urk! A circle. Is there a wrong note? Am I playing too loudly? Was I forgetting to observe the rest? Was something maybe an octave too high? I know I had to remember SOMETHING here…"*

It's as useless as if your teacher had pointed to that passage at a lesson and said "**Don't forget** what you're supposed to do with this bit".

If you could remember *that*, then there would be no need for a reminder in the first place…

The circle-it trap

Students sometimes wonder how pencil marks can **breed so quickly** on their music—it's because as a one-size-fits-all reminder, if you need a lot of **reminders**, you're going to need a lot of **circles**.

Here's how it usually works:

> *Need to remember a **tempo change**?*
> ❖ *Circle it.*
>
> *Forgot to **observe the rest**?*
> ❖ *Circle that too.*
>
> *Didn't spot the C#?*
> ❖ *Circle that accidental.*
>
> *Need to apply **rubato** here?*
> ❖ *Circle it, so you remember.*
>
> *Playing the turn incorrectly?*
> ❖ *Yep, you'd **circle** that too…*

…and so it continues. Before long, your piece is **covered with circles**, an insanely one-sided tic-tac-toe game, failing to remind you of anything, because each individual pencil mark *looks exactly like all the others*, and conveys no more information than "watch out for this".

For this reason, some teachers will **supplement** these markings with shapes and symbols as well…but even then it can still be hard to see at a glance what all these boxes and squiggles actually *mean*. And whether it's circles, squiggles, boxes or polyhedrons that are covering your score, it all adds up to one thing:

Clutter.

There's a much better system—one that is compact enough to **eliminate the clutter**, while saving you loads of time when you practice.

The power of color

If you've ever tried to **put a computer together**, you'll know that it can be difficult to tell **which lead** is supposed to plug into what.

One manufacturer had the bright idea that they would make their leads **different colors,** each matching the port they were supposed to plug into. Red lead goes into red port. Green lead goes into green port.

Suddenly, putting the computer together is something **any bright four-year-old** could do.

It's time to leave behind the world of **Grey Reminders** in your **music** too. Because as you'll see in a second, colorful markings are more than just decoration.

Setting up color categories

So how is color going to help? Surely it's just replacing one type of clutter with another?

Color is obviously going to stand out, making it more likely that you'll notice reminders in the first place.

But even more important is that you'll be able to tell—at a glance—**what** *sort* **of reminder** it is.

Was a reminder needed because you were running a DETAILS TRAWL ↪110 and had noticed a staccato you had previously missed? That's no problem. **Overlooked score details** might all be marked in **red,** which is how you'll mark this one too.

Was it perhaps instead a passage that **wasn't quite in time?** Again, you'd have a color for that too. Whenever that particular problem occurs, you might mark it in **yellow.**

Passages that are **uneven** might be **green,** sections that you're playing **too fast** might be **orange,** while runs that still **need to be faster** might be **blue.**

Your **teacher** can help you **set up** the categories you need, and let you know about any colors that they already use.

Highlights, not circles

The other great advantage of color is that you don't have to draw an entire shape to communicate meaning. *As soon as the color is visible, you can tell what it represents*—which allows for some very **small markings.**

Color overload

If you try to work with too many colors, you'll end up confusing yourself and your teacher. So if your initial list looks like the one below:

RED: **Misread** note

MAROON: Overlooked **score marking**

TURQUOISE: Need to **rework fingering**

VIOLET: Needs to go **faster**

AQUA: Needs to go **slower**

BEIGE: Rhythm is **uneven**

GOLD: Watch your **intonation**

INDIGO: All in **one breath/bow**

LIME: **Pedal change** needed

MAGENTA: Keep the tempo **steady**

CYAN: **More projection** needed

ORANGE: Be careful with **balance**

TAN: **Phrase off** here

...it's time to trim things back. Aim for **4-6 colors,** to cover the **most common** reminders you need. There's no point in permanently setting aside "Azure" to mean "watch out for the **hemiola**", but you **will** want to have a color for misreadings.

You can always **add** more colors later, once your initial half dozen are automatic for you.

So instead of drawing colored circles, use a **highlighter** directly on the relevant notes or markings. This means that if you're using red for misread notes, *you can actually highlight the note itself.*

This allows for highly compact and highly targeted markings, because you don't have to draw around the note...you can draw *on* it:

OLD: Yet another pencil circle. What exactly were you supposed to remember here? No accent? Not too loud? Wrong note? Check your fingering? Watch your intonation?

NEW: Highlighter, red to indicate a misreading. Compact, eye-catching, and targetting exactly *what was overlooked.*

You'll be able to pinpoint the **exact moment** in the passage that needs the reminder. So the reminder in the example above could have been **even more compact** by *just highlighting the natural*—if that's what was being overlooked.

Color for practice instructions

Once you and your teacher have **agreed** on colors for categories, your teacher can give a practice instruction as simply as **highlighting a passage** with the appropriate color. So if purple means "Rework the fingering", then all your teacher would have to do is highlight the relevant run in purple—you'd know **exactly** what to do.

The next lesson, your teacher could go right through the score, **one color at a time**, and ensure that everything was completed.

They would then give you a Fresh Photocopy⊃151, and make **new** color markings for the **upcoming week**.

In this way, and using **less space** than regular circles, color not only tells you *where* to work—it tells you exactly *why* you'd be working on that bit in the first place.

Themed practice sessions

Color coding like this makes life very easy if your practice session is based around Thematic Practice ⊃330.

If your theme was "passages that aren't quite in time", you won't have to go **hunting** for them any more. *They're the yellow markings in your score, and should jump right out at you—no matter where they are.*

Smart color coding means you spend less time trying to **find** relevant passages, and more time **actually practicing**.

Up-to-date with photocopies

Even if you're using color, your score will quickly become **impossibly cluttered** if you keep every single marking you've ever made.

A reminder to play an F# might be useful when you're **first learning** the piece, but you **don't** need your music to keep **yelling** that at you once the F# is safely part of every performance you give.

It's another reason to make extensive use of photocopies when you practice. Your original would never have markings on it, but every few weeks you would create a new **up-to-date marked score**. It would only contain those color code reminders that you still actually **need**.

So your color coded photocopy from your very first week with a piece will look **very different** from a copy from the week before the performance.

But your latest color coded photocopy will still **tell you everything** you need to bear in mind as you work at home—without muddling you with things you needed to bear in mind three months ago...

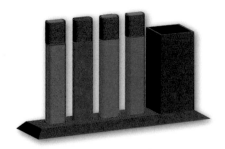

Alternative uses for color

Color coding doesn't just have to be limited to flagging issues. There are a range of other reasons you might want to keep the markers handy...although you shouldn't use **more than one** color system at once. So choose one use for colors, and then stick to it.

Using color to *label structure*

If you're learning a fugue or other contrapuntal work, colors can help you see at a glance where subject entries are.

You can then use different colors to indicate retrograde entry, or strettos, or episodes...using your palette to **lay bare the architecture** of the piece itself.

If the structure of your piece is complex, it's worth dedicated a photocopy of the score just to this purpose, so that you understand exactly how every measure fits into the bigger picture.

Using color to *prioritize*

It will be a rare week that you only have one thing to work on at once. For that reason, you're always going to be facing **tough decisions** about what gets practiced, and when.

The chapter on TRIAGE ➲342 outlines some techniques for determining what your work order will be...you can then use color coding to record the results.

So highly urgent passages might be marked in red, while passages you can safely ignore might be green. Orange would be "if you have time"

Again, it provides a whole lot of useful **at-a-glance** information that is much tougher to display meaningfully in plain pencil.

Using color to *track*

If you decide run a battery of PRESSURE TESTS ➲249 for every section in your piece, you can track your completed tests by **assigning colors** to each test type.

So as section A is delivered flawlessly three times in a row (with the metronome, and from memory), instead of having to record...

Section A, delivered flawlessly three times in a row (with the metronome and from memory)

...or **inventing a graphic** to communicate all that, simply decide that blue means exactly that, and then put a small blue spot above Section A.

In this way, with tiny colored dots, you can mark off each of the pressure tests as you complete them—and by looking out for missing colors, see which pressure tests still need to be administered to which bits.

Coral Reef Mistakes

Detecting invisible trouble spots

Mackenzie has an **uneasy** feeling. She's been playing over her piece, and everything seems fine...

... but that's just the trouble. Everything's going too well. It's almost as if it's one of those movie scenes where it's quiet...*too* quiet...

She's now worried that there might be problems in the piece, but that they're **hiding** somehow.

What can she do to have them **show themselves**? And how can she make sure that this happens in the practice room, and not at her lesson... or worse still, her *recital*...

THE CHAPTER on BUG SPOTTING ➲53 highlighted two different types of mistakes:

① Mistakes that are **immediately obvious**—clanging wrong notes or passages that fall apart.

② Mistakes that you'll only detect *when you look a little closer*, normally through some **bug-spotting checks**, such as Spot Method.

There's actually a **third type** though.

These are mistakes that *want* to remain hidden, and which even Bug Spotting **might not reveal**. Mistakes like this do everything they can to remain invisible, hoping that you'll just practice **straight past** them.

It's a little bit like cute coral reef fish trying to **blend in** with the background when a shark comes. As long as they're not spotted, they're safe.

Well **guess what**. These coral reef mistakes in your piece might be hiding, hoping not to be detected, but otherwise you **shouldn't mistake them** for cute coral reef fish. There's

nothing cute about them.

They're actually **monsters** waiting patiently for their moment of glory. A moment when they can **reveal themselves** without you being able to do anything about it...

Concert day.

You *have* to get them in the practice room, before they get you in public.

But to do that, you need to understand how their **camouflage** works—otherwise you'll never spot them in the first place.

Refusing to play their game

Coral Reef Mistakes might sound terrifying (impossible-to-detect disasters waiting to ambush you on concert day can't be all good) but

they actually have a **critical weakness.**

When they hide, they're counting on certain behavior from you to remain hidden.

In other words, they can only remain camouflaged **with your help.** If you refuse to behave in the way they expect, the game's up, they'll reveal themselves, and your concert is safe.

So what are these behaviors they're counting on?

Practicing too fast

If you're practicing a passage at full speed, it's *very* easy for a Coral Reef Mistake to go unnoticed. It will be just one of the masses of notes that are **flying past** at 180 bpm.

It's why **three-card-hustlers** move the cards so fast. If they worked in slow-motion, they wouldn't fool anybody.

So every time you practice fast, remember *that's just how the coral reef mistakes like it.*

(See SPEEDING ➲320)

Not practicing in segments

This is a great way of providing **safety-in-numbers** for the coral reef mistake. If you're silly enough to play through the **entire piece** every time you practice, they'll have hundreds—*maybe thousands*—of notes to blend in with.

It's like a **purse-snatcher** disappearing into a rush hour crowd. They don't even have to *run* any more.

> These are monsters waiting patiently for their moment of glory...
>
> ...you have to get them in the practice room before they get you in public.

By contrast, coral reef mistakes get **very nervous** if you are just focusing on a single phrase at a time. That's like our same purse snatcher trying to hide in an **elevator**—and then having every elevator in the building **searched** by police, *one elevator at a time.*

Your coral reef mistake will be trying to hide in a **phrase**—if you're serious about catching it, you'll be searching these phrases one phrase at a time. With confines like that, and your attention focused *on* that confine, the mistake has no chance of escape.

(See *"Gluttons"* in PRACTICE TRAPS ➲242)

Practicing with your brain off

Sometimes you'll look **right at** the mistake, but because you weren't looking *for* a mistake, you just won't see it.

If you're not **actively listening** when you practice, coral reef mistakes might not even need to hide—they just need to hold their breath and wait for you to pass.

In fact, if you're really daydreaming badly enough, they could even *wave* at you.

But they'll be doing that with an **evil smile**. As they watch you disappear into the distance again, they know their hour of triumph is drawing ever closer.

(See ENGAGING AUTOPILOT ➲120)

Ignoring the score

If you always practice without the music, then there will be plenty of mistakes that can hide by **pretending** to be **authentic notes.**

Remember, not all wrong notes *sound* wrong. Some of those passages that sound fine to you might be filled with **attractive mistakes** ...you won't know unless you check the music once in a while.

As a result, coral reef mistakes love it if you always play from memory, and break into a sweat whenever you start checking the score.

(See *"Ignoring the Map"* in Practice Traps ⟳243)

Focusing on sections that you've already thoroughly polished

You might be **sounding good** when you practice like this, but don't congratulate yourself. You're **playing right into** the Coral Reef Mistake's hands.

It's the same as if the police from the **bag-snatching scenario** were spending all their time searching an elevator that they have previously checked, *and know is empty.*

If you're spending all your time on passages that are **nowhere near** your coral reef mistakes, then as far as the those mistakes are concerned, *you can practice as much as you like.* They're completely safe.

(See *"Shiny Object Polishers"* in Practice Traps ⟳237)

Not checking all elements

You might have checked a passage thoroughly for accidentals, key signature, rhythm, dynamic mark-ings, articulation and phrasing...

...but if your coral reef mistake is a **bad fingering**, *and fingering wasn't on your list*, then you still won't find it.

Remember, your **mistake detection** will only be as comprehensive as the list of elements you check for.

(See Thematic Practice ⟳330)

Not spending enough time checking a passage

If you quickly shine your flash-light on a passage **once**, and then **move on**, there's every chance that any coral reef mistakes will have gone undetected.

However, if you were to dedicate **an entire practice session** to checking that same passage, you would be much more likely to find what you need.

Checking passages carefully for all musical elements is **time consum-ing**—it takes time to actually play the passage, and then even **more time** to play it enough so that you can methodically work your way through your elements list.

No matter what it is you might be trying to locate—misplaced carkeys, a pencil sharpener, a phone number—a "quick look" usually means you won't find it.

Coral Reef mistakes know this. And so when you visit their part of the piece, they hope you won't be staying long.

(See *"Skimming"* in Practice Traps ⟳239)

Not being aware of what you're really playing

Sometimes actually **playing** a passage can take so much of your concentration that there's little left over for anything else—such as **listening** carefully for evidence of any possible coral reef mistakes.

So if you're **barely coping** with delivering an extended run of accidental-filled sixteenth notes, then **don't be surprised** if you miss a coral reef mistake relating to articulation.

If this is happening to you, then it's time to temporarily divide playing and assessing into **two separate stages**—check out the chapter on RECORDING YOURSELF➲270.

Not checking the passage under pressure

Some coral reef mistakes only **come out to play** when the pressure is on. So unless you want that playtime to be your **concert**, then you need to subject the passages to pressure tests in the practice room first.

Make those tests **tough enough**, and anything that's hiding in the piece will be forced into the open.

(See PRESSURE TESTING➲249)

Spotting coral reef mistakes

Once you've stopped the practice behaviors coral reef mistakes rely on to hide, *you usually won't have to "spot them"*. With their optimum hiding conditions **stripped away**, most coral reef mistakes will be just as easy to find as any other error.

But if you really want to be sure, once you've double checked that the **practice conditions** you have set are making it impossible for *anything* to hide, run the **following checks:**

• DETAIL TRAWL➲110 will help you find any **score indications** that you had overlooked.

• RECORDING YOURSELF➲270 will allow you to **compare that score** to what you're *actually* playing.

• Spot Method (see BUG SPOTTING➲53) will reveal the errors that happen **regularly**.

• PRESSURE TESTING➲249 will reveal those that only come out **occasionally**, and when the **stakes are high**…

…Remember though…

…**spotting** mistakes is different from **eliminating** them. Once you've located your coral reef mistakes, you'll still need to do the work to get rid of them.

Check out the chapters on CLEARING OBSTACLES➲72 or TIGHTENING➲337

Cosmetics

Minimizing the impact of weak passages on concert day

Taylor has a **concert** in **three days**. Everything's ready... except for **one small passage** near the end. It's really hard, and it's a **mess**.

With another month or so of practice, she could probably turn it around. Problem is, she's **out of time**. 72 hours to go, and then she's onstage.

Can anything be done? Is there some way of **rescuing** this?...

Every so often, you will have a **performance looming**, but you'll have a passage that has **resisted** the **best efforts** of you and your teacher. Maybe another couple of **months** of practice might fix it, but you've only got a **couple of days.**

When that happens, you've got **three choices:**

- *Elect not to play the piece at all.*

  Just because *one passage* is not ready? That's like **cancelling** an entire **Olympic Games**, just because the ten-metre diving towers aren't complete.

- *Get ready for a crash*

  This simultaneously **accepts** that you'll never deal with the problem—while **actively planning** to *have* the problem in the first place. If that's me, I'm going to be walking very, very slowly to the stage on concert day.

- *Mask the problem*

  Making **small but critical changes** to what the score asks for, so that any negative fallout from the passage is **minimized.** Cosmetics is about applying this third option.

An example: the swordfight

It's not just musical performances where cosmetics can work their performance-saving magic. Let's imagine that you were **directing a play** that asks for a **swordfight.**

If, despite your best efforts, your leading actor still **can't swordfight** convincingly **the week before** the performance, you can either **abandon** the idea of a fight scene entirely—or you can apply **cosmetics** to it:

- Make it a **fistfight** instead.

- Use a **stunt double** for the swordfight scene.

- Run the swordfight scene behind a veil, so the audience can only see the **shadow**.

- Choreograph the fight so that the **better** of the two swordfighters does **all the work**.

- Change the fight so that the leading actor's character has his sword **knocked from his hand** at the start—he can then spend most of the fight dodging and running, instead of swordfighting.

- Use **strobe lighting** so the audience only sees freeze frame versions of the fight.

- Deliberately have the fight—and all onlooker reactions—in **slow motion**, giving your actor time to get things right.

- Or, if they're absolutely hopeless, run most of the scene **off-stage**, and handle the whole thing with **sound effects**.

It's not a surrender
These options are **not merely a lesser evil** than forging ahead with

a lame-looking swordfight. They're **compelling and legitimate options** in their own right—*which should always be your aim when using cosmetics in your own pieces.*

Your cosmetic choice and application shouldn't just **mask** the original problem. It should **enhance** the performance in some way.

> # The very thought of "cosmetics" is going to upset some musicians. But remember, it's an extraordinary solution for extraordinary circumstances.

Some musical examples

• Let's assume you have a passage that contains a **turn,** but that despite plenty of attention, it always seems to mess up the notes that follow.

One cosmetic solution is to **rework** the passage so that it doesn't include the turn in the first place.

Another is to include **rubato** throughout the turn—to take the time you need to be able to deliver it with control.

Neither option is in the score, but both are better than a clunky-but-as-written delivery on concert day. Practice them both, see which works best.

• A pianist might face a passage in **double thirds** that's meant to be brilliant and quicksilver... but instead sounds like it's being dragged through wet cement by a team of **elderly oxen**.

Rather than playing every painful third on concert day, they're better off **reworking the passage** so

that it's just **single notes** in each hand—that way it can still be brilliant and quicksilver. Much better the criticism be "*that was weird...my edition has double 3rds...*" than "*ouch...that passage was ploddy and painful*"

To be used, but not lightly

Before you even **think** about using cosmetics, you need to ensure that you've already mounted a **sustained** and **focused campaign** to deliver the passage **as written.**

Cosmetics are an important **last resort**—it's always better than **performing the muddle**—but they are exactly that. A last resort. They're **not** intended to be a **cheap** and **easy** cover-up for a passage that careful work would have fixed anyway.

They're also **not** designed to be your **automatic solution** to troublesome sections. Use them only when all else has failed, and you can see the whites of your deadline's eyes.

Some cosmetic techniques

So what can you do to help **minimize damage** from a problem passage?

Your choice of cosmetic technique will depend on the passage itself, and there are many more options than the list below highlights:

- Introduce rubato or a rit to **credibly slow** the passage down to a manageable speed

- "Thin" the passage by **omitting notes**, turning sixteenth notes into eighth notes, and only playing every second note. Truly. Still guaranteed to harmonize with any other ensemble parts—and as long as the tempo does not change at all, it's astounding how often people don't notice.

These are the same people who *would* have noticed your badly delivered sixteenth notes if you had stuck to the original.

- Rewrite notes in the passage to take it out of an **uncomfortable range**—usually just an octave transposition.

- **Shorten** unwieldy or overly elaborate ornamentation—especially if your delivery is so awkward that the ornament draws attention to itself, and away from the melody.

- **Simplify** a rhythm that you can't feel—and therefore always play out of time—into one that you *can* deliver with precision. If that means those quintuplets marked "with Hungarian Swing" become straight duplets, then so be it.

- **Omit the passage entirely**. Extreme, but it your entire development section is genuinely an underprepared and irredeemable catastrophe, then you're better off leaving it out altogether than playing it badly.

Simply work out how to move gracefully from the end of the passage **before** to the beginning of the passage **after**. You might need to add a couple of joining notes to smooth the transition if the keys are completely unrelated.

Then rehearse this join using Bridging ➲50 so that it's completely seamless, and then reveal the Director's Cut of your piece on concert day.

Again, it's astonishing...and more than a little frightening...*how many people won't notice*. All of them would have noticed your pox-ridden development section though, so it's just as well they didn't get to hear it.

Sir! You can't be serious!

Don't look so shocked. **Of** *course* all of this is cheating and a quick fix.

This is cosmetic practice—it *has* to be cheating and quick, otherwise you won't **meet** your performance **deadline**.

If there **isn't a deadline** that's imminent, you **shouldn't** be using cosmetics in the first place. You should be trying to **fix it properly**. Check out *Dealing with Problem Passages* in the Practiceopedia Usher ➲31.

Ensuring you don't *need* cosmetics next time

It may have been necessary **this time** to treat your problem passage with cosmetic practice—but you don't want to have to handle things that way **every time** you meet a similar passage.

There are two steps you can take to ensure your next performance is cosmetic free:

1) Better campaign management

If you had to resort to cosmetics because your deadline hit too fast, it's no good blaming the deadline —or the passage.

The problem here was your own **project management**, and specifically how you planned the **campaign** for this piece. (See Campaigns ➲58)

When you're setting yourself performance deadlines, make sure you set yourself a **checkpoint deadline** of "concert-ready" that is at least a month before the big day. That way, if you discover problems, you still have plenty of time to correct them. (See Countdown Charts ➲99)

2) Technique upgrade

If instead the cosmetics were necessary because the passage was **genuinely beyond you** technically, then you don't have to accept that this will *always* be the case. Sure, concede defeat **this time**, but as soon as the concert is over, that passage goes on a long term development list.

Your job then is to work to **improve your technique** so that next time, you can play passages like this one *as is*. It beat you up once, but that doesn't mean you have to be **easy pickings** second time around.

For the purists who are about to email me...

The thought of "cosmetics" is going to upset some musicians. But remember, it's an extraordinary practice solution for an extraordinary occasion. You would **only** use it where your sole alternative is an **on-stage calamity** that would require therapy for you and the audience.

Remember, your job as a performer is **not** to make the piece perfect. It's to give the **best performance** you possibly can. Playing **98% of what's there**, but playing it **100% well** almost always produces a more satisfying performance than the reverse. As a result, cosmetics practice sessions are about:
- **Choosing** the "98% of what's there" change that adds stage-ready flow to a passage that would be clunky or broken if you played it exactly as written.
- **Practicing** that change so the delivery is natural and effective, and the piece feels like it is supposed to sound like that anyway.

And then, when the concert is over:
- **Working** to ensure that next time, you can handle passages just like this—*without make-up...*

I'm at **insidemusicteaching@gmail. com** though if you're still cross :)

Countdown Charts
Factoring your deadlines into your practice

Ethan has just realized with a **shock** that there's now only a month to go until his major recital.

"I don't understand" he says "I thought this concert was **six months away**."

"It *was* six months away," says his teacher "when you first found out about it **five months ago**. Looks like it's been sneaking up on you in the meantime. Welcome to October."

Ethan feels like he's been **ambushed**. But how could he have managed this better?...

I**T'S THIS SIMPLE.** If you don't always have your deadlines right where you can **see them**, you'll get **ambushed** by one of them eventually. Like a lion tamer, you always need to maintain eye contact and never, ever **turn your back**.

This chapter is all about managing your dates, deadlines and commitments—because as a music student, you're going to get plenty of them:

- The **piece** that needs to be ready for **next lesson**
- The **concert** in **six months**...and the other one in **six weeks**. And yet another towards the **end of the year**.
- The **rehearsal** with the accompanist in three **weeks**
- The **competitions** in May and September
- Your **grandparents** staying with you in the holidays (they always expect to hear you play...and you can't play them half a piece)
- Your **theory assignment** due on the first Wednesday next month

And that's not even taking into account a **similar list** that you'll have for **school**.

Where's the 7th Lion?

Most students don't worry too much about **keeping tabs** on lists like these—after all, it's only a dozen items or so. They're sure to remember most of it.

And they're right. They *are* sure to remember *most* of it. But that's like being in the lion's cage and positively knowing where 6 out of 7 of them are.

It's that 7th lion you need to be afraid of.

When deadlines pounce

Deadline ambushes don't work **quite** the way you might **think**. It's not as if you'll be lying in a

hammock, reading a book, when suddenly you smack your hand to your head, thinking "Arggggh! May 13th! Don't I have a concert today???".

Deadline ambushes are not nearly so **unsubtle**. They don't usually ambush you by simply making you **miss** important dates.

They aim to cause much more pain than that.

They ambush you by reminding you about the date...*once there's no longer enough time to prepare.* You know they've pounced when you **suddenly notice** that it's November, and the "concert at the end of the year" is **not in the distance** any more. It's now two weeks away...and you can still only play the first page...

So the first pain you experience is that your life is turned upside-down while you try to **panic practice** your way to **safety**.

And then, while you're still exhausted from the practicing frenzy, the **killer blow** is struck. Because you tried to compress what should have been six months work into two weeks, the piece will be badly underdone on concert day. Not rare. *Raw.* Just how lions like it.

Like the warning says, *Objects in This Mirror may be Closer than they Appear.* Your concert might be six months away **at the moment.** But every day that distance shrinks. At some point, it will be tomorrow...

Countdown charts is all about giving yourself **early warnings** that tomorrow is coming.

Building a Countdown Chart

Each countdown chart is designed to keep track of **one deadline**, which means that you'll normally have a small stack of countdown charts in your practice room.

The stack would be sorted by how far away each deadline is—the countdown charts for your **nearest deadlines** will be on top of the pile.

So if you have a piece to prepare for next lesson, that will be the **top chart.** A concert at a festival in the middle of next year will probably be at the **bottom.**

Once the deadline has **passed**, you **won't need** that countdown chart any more, so you discard it. This means that there will then be a **new** countdown chart on top of the pile—whichever upcoming date is due soonest.

What you'll need
Building these charts is quick and easy, but you do need to get yourself a few essentials:

- A big sheet of cardboard.
- Some colored markers (you should have some of these in your practice room anyway—see Color Coding➲84)
- A ruler

Put the name of the deadline as a big heading at the top of your sheet. So if the deadline is "School Talent

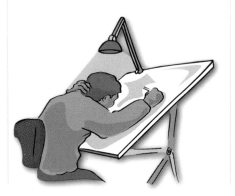

Night", then that's your heading. Then you need to work out exactly **how many days** there are to go until the Big Occasion. Not just the date—the actual number of days is critical. Don't round it up or down. If it's 99, then it's 99, not 100.

Your sheet of cardboard is going to become a **custom designed calendar**...but instead of having 30 squares (as you might expect to have on a regular calendar), it will have *one square for each day between now and the performance date.*

So there might be 25 squares, there might be 160—it all depends **how far away** the event is.

Using the ruler, create a grid so that you end up with enough squares. If you group them in multiples of **seven,** you'll also be able to use your chart for instant how-many-weeks-to-go snapshots.

Once you've done that, it's time to start **labeling** the squares. But don't write anything in yet. You're going to **color code** this to make the whole thing more dynamic—and intuitive.

Color coding your chart

The idea behind the color coding is to make sure you're **constantly being reminded** of the fact that your deadline is drawing nearer, and to add **fresh bursts of urgency** to your campaign.

How? As the deadline draws nearer, *the color you use to label the number of days to go will change.*

Pretending for a moment that the deadline is **86 days away,** the colors you use to write the "days to go" label might be as follows:

86-75 days to go: Light Green

75-50 days to go: Dark Green

49-35 days to go: Light Blue

34-25 days to go: Dark Blue

24-15 days to go: Purple

14-8 days to go: Orange

7-1 days to go: Red

Concert day: Black, with yellow highlighter over the top.

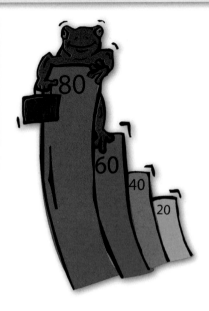

Once you have worked out your color plan, **write in** each of the numbers using the colors you decided on. Don't make the numbers too big—you are going to want to leave room in each square for some other things.

As you cross the squares off the chart each day, you'll notice any color changes as **landmarks.** So once you hit the 75 days to go mark, and everything is suddenly dark green, it will feel as though the campaign has entered a **new phase**—it's a natural reaction then for this to trigger a fresh burst of practice.

Adding stepping stones

With your chart as it is now, you'll always be able to see how close your deadlines are, and have an easy way to see the urgency ramping up as each deadline draws nearer. That's **half the battle won**—now it's going to be very hard for dates to sneak up and ambush you.

The **other half** is project managing all of this—to take this huge deadline, and break it down into a series of **smaller milestones.** Let's refer to these mini deadlines as "Stepping Stones" and look at how to build them into the countdown chart, because they really do make your preparation much easier.

Let's imagine that you have a performance exam in 100 days, at which you have to play **four different pieces**—a Gigue, an Etude, a Sonatina and a Blues Waltz—and some set **scales.**

To make sure that you **stay on track** throughout the preparation campaign, you might create the following **Stepping Stones:**

93 days to go: *Be able to slowly play right through the Gigue.*

That's only a week from now, but remember, you've only got 100 days to get all four pieces learned, polished and up to speed. So it's not merely a week—it's actually 7% of your time used up.

86 days to go: *Must be able to slowly play right through the Etude, and the Gigue at three-quarter tempo.*

67 days to go: *Be able to play through **all four** pieces from beginning to end.*

55 days to go: *All pieces learned, fingered, dynamics and phrasing worked out and polished.*

40 days to go: *All pieces to be memorized*

30 days to go: *Monster scales test* (every scale listed in the syllabus for the exam, done in every imaginable way!)

20 days to go: *Mock exam with your own teacher.* Which means everything in the program ready to go—pieces AND scales.

12 days to go: *Mock exam with another teacher.* Again, it's a run through of the whole program,

but this time you'll be a little more nervous because it's not with the person you usually see each week..

So with 12 days to go, **you're in great shape**—your stepping stones were demanding, but have prepared you very well for the deadline itself.

Which is the whole point of stepping stones. As long as you meet the deadline for **each Stepping Stone**, you shouldn't ever find the major **deadline itself** a problem.

Being accountable to yourself

The deadlines you use **probably won't match** the examples above exactly, but whatever your list contains, you will know EARLY in the campaign if you are starting to **slip behind**.

So in the example above, if in 7 days from now, you can't play through the Gigue, it's time to **get moving**.

This **early warning** about any lagging is a huge advantage for both you and your teacher. It allows both of you to **react** to getting behind schedule while there is **still time** to do something about it.

Recording other breakthroughs

Your countdown chart will now have the **major deadline** at the final square, and then **stepping stones** scattered throughout. This leaves plenty of otherwise empty squares...

...which can then double nicely as a Breakthroughs Diary↪46. So every time you're able to do something new—the first time you play a particular passage from memory, for example—you'd make a note on that day's square.

In that way, your countdown chart is not just a reminder of your deadlines—it's a great way to **keep track** of your progress.

Managing multiple deadlines

So far the focus has been on getting your **first countdown chart** up and running. But remember, the plan was to have several charts—one for each major deadline.

Before you start a practice session on a piece, you'd check out any **countdown charts** that have deadlines for that piece.

So if you had an Etude which was

scheduled for a performance at a school concert, **and also** forms part of your program for of an end-of-year exam, you'd pull out your **"School Concert"** and **"End of Year Exam"** countdown charts.

Then you would just look for the **nearest Stepping Stones** on each countdown chart—this would give you a clear picture of where the etude needs to be up to in the short term.

So instead of **wondering** whether you need to memorize the piece, or whether it's time to start learning at the final page yet, the countdown charts **tell you** exactly **what** needs to be done, and by **when**.

You can then use that to **plan** what needs to happen in **today's practice** session with this piece.

Two targets with one shot

If you have a **lot** of performance deadlines that all involve the **same piece**, you might find that different charts give you wildly conflicting Stepping Stones.

For example, if your etude is featuring in *three* concerts—one in **three weeks**, one in **six months**, and another a **year from now,** then those countdown charts will have very different Stepping Stones.

The "Year from now" Countdown Chart will have **widely spaced** and gentle stepping stones, because the event is **so far away**. For a distant deadline like this, the Stepping Stone requiring full tempo playing might not be scheduled for another **10 months**...

...of course, that would come 9 **months too late** to help you with the performance you're supposed to give in only three weeks. The "full tempo" Stepping Stone for *that* concert is actually only 8 days from now.

Because you're only ever looking for **nearby** Stepping Stones, you **won't even notice** the 10 month version yet—you don't need to. However, you **will** see the 8 day version, because it's coming soon, so you have to practice for it now.

In 8 days time, when you tick that Stepping Stone, there's then a bonus. *You can also tick the 10 month stepping stone too*, because it has the same requirements. (And you've just met them!)

So sometimes you can complete one Stepping Stone, and then cross off several **other instances** of exactly the same Stone. It's almost like you get them for free ☺.

The Master Chart alternative

Some students don't like having separate charts for all their deadlines—instead they want a **constant bird's-eye view** of *everything* that's coming up.

If that's the case, then you're going to need a slightly **different chart**. In fact, your best bet is a BIG regular calendar.

Creating your Master Chart

You'd start by putting in all your deadlines—the concerts themselves. Then you'd **work backwards** and create Stepping Stones that will get you ready for each of those concerts.

A different use for color coding

Instead of using color coding to indicate how the **countdown is progressing** (you can't, because this chart has several countdowns running simultaneously), use it so that you can tell at a glance **which stepping stone** belongs to **which deadline.**

So you might label your School Talent Night in **red**. Any stepping stones designed to prepare you for that deadline would then also be labelled in red.

All the **green** stepping stones might be for your exam, while the **blue** ones refer to the winter studio recital.

Working with the Master Chart

As you work each week, no matter what the color, you look for the **nearest stepping stones.** You then plan your practice sessions each day to **prepare** you for those stepping stones.

Again, if **all you do** is ensure that you're prepared for every stepping stone as it falls due, you'll be **ready** for the concerts too.

The Master Chart doesn't have the same **countdown urgency** of the traditional Countdown Charts—you miss out on the impact of watching the numbers tumble down. But it does give you a better "what's going on" picture for everything you're doing.

You don't have to fly solo

No matter which type of Countdown Chart you use, you don't have to work on them **all by yourself.** Your teacher is almost certainly going to want to have some input into **what** your Stepping Stones should be, and **when** they fall due.

So work out a **rough draft**, but then show your teacher what you're thinking. They'll be able to steer you away from any traps you might have set for yourself.

Designer Scales

Choosing technical work that supports your pieces

Daniel has a **core** of scales that his teacher has given him to work on, but beyond that, his scales work is **up to him.**

Because he knows scales can make a huge difference to his playing, he's happy to include **additional scales** work in his practice—but apart from the teacher-set scales, he's confused as to **which ones** to focus on.

Where should he start? Or doesn't it matter?...

MUSIC STUDENTS

MUSIC STUDENTS all over the world are told that it's **important** that they practice their scales.

It's good advice. Scales *are* important—they can make a **huge difference** not just to the pieces you're playing now, but to pieces you haven't even met yet.

However, the problem is that "scales" is such a **vast universe**. Like stars, however many you might *think* there are, there are many, many more...

...which means that try as you might, *you'll never cover them all.*

This leaves any music student with a problem—and some tough choices. We'll look at how to choose your scales in a moment, but first, let's take a look at just how out-of-control the options are.

The vast scales universe

"You'll never cover them all?"... Sounds like an extravagant claim— let's start though with the scales you can see with the naked eye, and then start reaching further out

into scales space, and see what's out there...

As you would be expecting, there are the **majors** and **minors**...which for many students is as big as the scales universe seems to get. But remember, minors come in **three main flavours**—harmonic, melodic and natural. So barely out of earth's atmosphere, and there are 5 scale families already.

But it's in deep space that things start getting weird...and the deeper, the weirder.

You've got all the modes, pentatonic scales, chromatic scales, whole tone scales, octotonic scales, blues scales, while **meteor fragments** from the edges of the Solar System contain traces of Hungarian minors, Enigmatic scales, Lydian Augmenteds, Double harmonics...and **that's not even including** the stuff from distant

galaxies, such as Super Locrian, Neapolitan Minor or Japanese In Sen scales...

...and even then, the list is **far from comprehensive** (ask any jazz professional...or Jean Luc Picard)

You then take all of that, and **multiply it by 15,** to get all the possible keys and their enharmonic equivalents as starting notes...

Type all this into a calculator and **see for yourself.** We're already talking some big numbers here.

But that's just the beginning. You're going to have to throw away your calculator for what's next, because the numbers just aren't going to fit.

Permutations and combinations

Here's the really scary thing:

*It's not like all those scales can only be delivered in **one way**.*

As a pianist, for example, you can play any given scale separate hands or together, in parallel octaves, 3rds, 6ths or 10ths.

There are double thirds and double octave scales—and of course then the **range** of the scale can vary, along with the speed, direction, articulation, dynamics...heck, sometimes there are even **alternative fingerings**...

...and we haven't allowed yet for broken chords, or arpeggios, or contrary motion...

With all of this, there's a **horrible reality** that you have to accept:

No matter how much you practice, you won't be able to master every possible scale in every possible format.

In fact, if you were to practice for 12 hours a day for the rest of your life, you wouldn't even *meet* every possible scale in every possible format.

So when you're practicing scales, **it's about choosing.** Which scales to include. Which to leave till later. Which to ignore completely. And then how to play the scales you do choose.

You might as well choose **carefully**.

Choosing scales that help most

There's **no point** in spending hours mastering **Mixolydian b6** scale if the music you normally play is never going to feature that. (In fact, if just reading the phrase "Mixolydian b6" makes you go "huh?", then it's a pretty good sign that you can leave the scale alone for the time being)

However, if two of your current pieces are in E Major, then that's **definitely** a scale you want to be concentrating on...*even if it's not on your current "official" scales list.*

So before you decide which scales to work on, ask yourself a simple question:

*Which keys **feature heavily** in the pieces I'm currently working on?*

They're the scales you need. You won't have to wait years to **enjoy the benefits** of the work you do— you'll see improvements straight away in your pieces.

Not only that, the scales practice you do will feel relevant and helpful, rather than a compulsory but **entirely useless add-on**, like long division or naming state capitals.

So if your pieces are in g minor and A Major respectively, with liberal dollops of D Major thrown in as a modulation key, then your scales practice should focus on g minor, A Major and D Major.

That's **not** to say other keys are a **waste of time.** Your teacher might have good reasons for some other scales that aren't on this focused list.

But you can be certain that these three particular scales will come in handy, and come in handy soon.

Figurations too, not just keys

Once you've **narrowed down** candidate keys, you still need to choose exactly *how* these scales should be played. Again, make sure it mirrors your pieces.

So if your piece is an **adagio** with a slowly moving legato melody line, then slow legato scales are going to be closest to what's required. While you're practicing your scale, you can be working on **exactly the same** tone production and articulation that you need in your piece anyway.

If another piece features a fast **two octave arpeggio** as a part of a recurring melody, then fast two octave arpeggios are on your menu.

It's part of ensuring that your scales—your Designer Scales, if you like—are actively **preparing** you for your existing repertoire.

So it might be a small part of the scales universe...but it's a part that is **most likely** to help the pieces you're playing.

Two for the price of one

Because your Designer Scales are based directly on the **key** and **type of writing** in your current pieces, *time spent on them doubles as time spent on the pieces themselves.*

As these scales **improve**, you'll find there are passages in your pieces that seem to improve "all by themselves". No extra practice needed.

They're not really improving by themselves. Your targeted scales work has loosened the jar lid.

Preparing for the future

If your teacher has particular pieces planned for later in the year, it's worth **finding out** as much as you can about those pieces now.

That way you can start working on scales that are based on those pieces, so you can hit the ground running when the time comes.

Making scales permanent

Practicing your scales might be hard work, but there's **good news:**

Once you've learned them, you'll never forget them.

In this way, scales are like your times tables, or the alphabet. The scales you master now will stay with you **forever**...and **every piece** in the world that is built around the scales you know will be just a little easier for you to learn.

If you're a **pianist** and you're serious about making your scales permanent, I've put together a **special practice book** that does exactly that. Complete all the challenges for any scale in the book, you'll know that scale **for life**...

...whether you practice it ever again or not (!)

You can take a detailed tour of *Scales Bootcamp* at:
www.insidemusicteaching.com

Details Trawl
Ensuring you know what's *really* in the score

Anthony's problem is that he keeps **missing details**. A sharp here. A flat there. A pianissimo on page three. An entire passage that should be staccato on page four.

His teacher gets **frustrated,** because she has to waste lesson time pointing out things Anthony could easily **find for himself**—*if only he'd look...*

What can Anthony do? Is there a **foolproof** way he can pick up these details in the practice room?...

S OME STUDENTS have the funny idea that sheet music is split into **three types** of information:

1) *Essential* **information**...

....by this, they usually mean noteheads and rhythms. Most students are careful to check these, or at least are clear that they're *supposed* to.

2) *Probably important* **information**...

...these are items that you can leave out and still usually recognise the tune, so heck, maybe you can live without them. Which means living without things like rests, ties and accidentals.

3) **Trivia**...

...fingerings, dynamics, tempo changes, articulation marks, phrasing, pedalling, bowing....

Hmmm. Problem is, your teacher (correctly) is **not** going to see these items as trivia at all, leading to...

...massive waste of lesson time

Because these details actually **do** make an enormous difference to

how your piece sounds, your teacher *has* to point them out whenever you miss them.

Unfortunately though, during that time, your teacher is not helping you become a better player, or showing you **new tricks**. There's not much room for them to be fun or interesting. (Just how fun can you make "um...there's no flat in front of that B"?) They're just covering ground you could cover yourself —you don't even need a lesson.

But **somebody** has to, and you didn't.

So what you've done is taken your teacher—someone who might have **decades of training** in music—and reduced their job to point-out-the-details-my-dopey-student-missed.

It would be like paying an expert for **creative writing lessons**, and then have that expert spend their time fixing sloppy spelling mistakes. Sure, they *can* do that, but every second they spend doing that is a second you're **missing out** on the good stuff.

So every time your teacher uses lesson time pointing out a detail you could have picked up for yourself, you should **ask yourself** this:

"What cool new thing could my teacher be showing me right now instead, if only I had checked this myself?"

What indeed. Let's look at some ways to make sure your lessons are never wasted like this again.

Setting up a details trawl

The aim behind a details trawl is not just to spot a **few more** score details than you might otherwise.

It's to scan **every last surface** of every page for anything that even looks detailish. Like a **forensic officer** at a crime scene, you will be bagging even the most insignificant marking.

Nothing will escape. Nothing will go unnoticed. Not the smallest staccato dot, or the most harmless looking sforzando mark. There's nowhere for details to run or hide when your trawl starts—you'll capture everything.

By the time you've finished, the aim is for you to be nothing short of the **single biggest expert** on the **planet** on what is actually in that score. (You might even know more about the score than the *composer* does.)

Which means that from now on, if you don't play that crescendo on page 3, it's not because you **didn't know** it was there. (And if you *know*

it's there, why wouldn't you play it?)

So how are you going to become an expert like that? As you'll see below, there are actually **two different types** of details trawl—try them both, see which works better for you.

Driftnet detail trawl

Driftnet trawling is just like its ocean counterpart—*nothing* escapes. A single trawl only takes a couple of minutes, and by the time you're done, you'll end up with a comprehensive picture of **all score markings** in your chosen segment. It won't help you **remember** these

markings (there's a separate technique for that which we'll look at in a moment), but it will ensure that you have *collected* all the markings in the first place.

To ensure nothing gets through though, Driftnet Trawling is **slow** and **methodical**. It's not how you'd want to spend a Sunday afternoon, but the good news is, you only have to do it **once** for each piece.

Setting up

Setup couldn't be easier. You'll need:
- a **copy of your score**
- a **ruler**
- a **pencil**
- a sheet of **paper**

You'll also need somewhere to work where you won't be disturbed... driftnet trawls only work if you can give them your **full attention**.

Now place the ruler **vertically** at the start of the very **first measure** of the piece.

You'll now steadily and slowly **move the ruler to the right**, advancing along the first line of music. Any time the ruler touches a *detail*, **write down** the detail itself on the sheet of paper.

So what's a "detail"? *Anything in the music that isn't a notehead, a stem, a barline or the stave.* So that will include (but not limited to) all dynamics, fingerings, accidentals, ottava markings, articulation marks, key signature and tempo changes.

For this trawl, you don't need to record *where* each detail is, you just need to record *what* it is.

Once you you've trawled to the **end of the line**, go back and **repeat** —just to make sure nothing escaped (although it's VERY hard for details to escape even **one** pass of the slowly advancing driftnet-ruler-of-doom).

> # Nothing will escape. Nothing will go unnoticed. Not the smallest staccato dot, or the most harmless looking sforzando mark...you'll capture *everything*.

What you'll end up with is a page of assorted markings **floating** in space—but no notes to attach them to.

That's fine. Because now to **test yourself,** you'll be working with the very reverse.

Pin the notes on the donkey
Your job now is to write each of those score markings in their correct location on a **stripped photocopy** of that opening line. (There's more details on how to create these in FRESH PHOTOCOPIES ⊃151—in short though, a stripped photocopy is a copy of the score that has had all details apart from notes **removed**.)

If this leaves you flummoxed, then use a stripped photocopy that has **boxes** *wherever details should appear*—you can then test yourself by writing the **correct detail** in the **correct box.**

But eventually, you should be able to correctly mark in all the details **without** having location prompts.

Once you're able to do this...
...actually **play through** that line a couple of times, and EXAGGERATE ⊃124 the listed details wherever possible. That way you're not just noting the score detail as an abstract idea—you're actually turning it into a **musical reality**.

Once you're done, go back and start a driftnet trawl through the **next line**. Test it when the trawl is complete...and then move on to the line after that.

Eventually, when you've trawled and tested **every line** on the page, play "pin the notes on the donkey" again, but with a stripped photocopy of the **whole page**. Your quest is almost complete.

And your graduation task?

Pin the details on a stripped photocopy of the **whole piece**.

By then, the "driftnet and test" process will ensure you know **what** is in the score, exactly **where** it is, and that you will have **played** it too—all of which will transform your knowledge of the score's contents.

It won't **guarantee** that you never, ever need to be reminded about a score detail again, but it will **dramatically slash** how often that happens.

In the meantime, all that **reclaimed lesson time** will have been used for more productive things, so you'll probably be playing better too.

Category Detail Trawl

This trawl is just as meticulous, but instead of being **line-by-line**, it's **issue-by-issue**. (See THEMATIC PRACTICE ➲330)

So you might start by doing a trawl through the score for all **staccato marks**. Note how many there are.

Then get yourself a **stripped photocopy** (see FRESH PHOTOCOPIES ➲151) If you noted that there were 12 instances of staccato in the original score, now comes the big question:

Where?

And so now you'll try to place them on the stripped score. Get your

pencil out and start putting in dots. Then compare with the original. Repeat the process until you can accurately place them. (Which is why it's always worth having plenty of stripped scores on hand).

Again, it sounds worse than it actually is. Before long, you'll know **exactly** where all the staccatos are. Choose a new category at that point (eg. "rests" or "two note phrases" or "diminuendos"), and repeat.

Sometimes you'll get it all right. Sometimes you won't. But one thing is for sure—work this way **just once**, and you'll be stunned by how many of your past scores you've obviously have no idea about...but **played in front of people anyway**...

Beware edition variation!

One slightly unfair element in all of this is that details can actually **differ** from edition to edition—sometimes significantly.

You don't want to do all this work only to have your teacher correct you anyway, because they were working from a different version.

Wherever possible, the score you work with at home should be **exactly the same** as the copy your teacher will use in the lesson. If that's **not possible**, then you need to sit down with your teacher and make any necessary alterations to your score BEFORE you start any sort of Details Trawl.

Dress Rehearsals

Setting up your own concert simulator

Angela's concert is **next week**. Everything seems ok—her pieces are in good shape, and last lesson her teacher couldn't have been happier.

But she's **worried**. Sure, everything sounds fine in the practice room and at her lesson...but **on stage**?

How can she **prepare herself** for performing under **concert conditions**?...

YOU BETTER BE **ready** when you try this. This special practice session is actually a performance of your entire program—under the most **realistic concert conditions** you can arrange. Beginning to end, no stops, and with all the flair and energy you want the concert itself to showcase.

All designed to make you more relaxed about the concert itself, by giving you **practice** at coping with the unique pressure that comes from having to get things right **in front of somebody**.

Put away your wrench

We'll look at how to put your dress rehearsal together in a moment, but key word you have to remember throughout is *performance*.

You're **not** trying to improve weak sections, or fix problems. Instead, you're **testing** the piece, to find out what actually happens when you play it under concert conditions. (You've got to find out sometime—better now than at the concert itself)

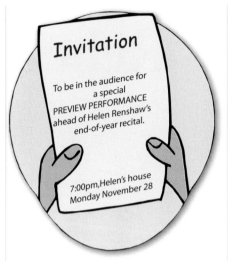

> **Invitation**
>
> To be in the audience for a special PREVIEW PERFORMANCE ahead of Helen Renshaw's end-of-year recital.
>
> 7:00pm, Helen's house Monday November 28

Pre-season reality checks

Musicians are not the only people who have test runs like this—sporting teams usually arrange **pre-season trial games** for the same reason.

They use what happens in the trial game to plan future training sessions, and to fine tune plans for the season proper. Your Dress Rehearsal session is fulfilling exactly the **same role**, and at a similarly critical time.

Trial games also allow for **experimentation**—trying different combinations of players, trialling tactics—all in an environment where the **final decisions** don't have to be taken just yet.

Dress Rehearsal experiments

You'll learn plenty the first time you run the Dress Rehearsal, but you'll learn even more the **second** time—because you now have something to **compare** it with.

So when the second performance has finished, ask yourself some questions:

• Were **problems** from the first performance resolved?

• Were there **new issues** in the more recent performance?

• Were there areas of excellence **common to both**?

• Which performance was **better**? And most critically: *why?*

The answer to *that* question will help you optimize delivery of the concert itself. So instead of **wondering** about various performance decisions, you can construct an "ideal" performance that contains the **best** of each of your Dress Rehearsals so far.

So, if the **brisker tempo** of the 2nd Dress Rehearsal meant that the performance flowed better, then perhaps a brisker tempo is a good idea on concert day too.

You might then combine that tempo with the **warm dynamic approach** of the 4th Dress Rehearsal, and the **dramatic ending** you tried during the 1st.

The special hybrid version that you then put together for concert day will **carefully avoid** the bad elements from each Dress Rehearsal, and instead be a **highlights package** of your best playing and ideas.

Making it real

If you want your Dress Rehearsal to **work** it has to **feel real**, which means there's a little setting up you need to do first.

- No performance is complete without an **audience**. Talk to family, friends, neighbors—anyone who can fill a chair and clap hard.

If you're scheduling multiple Dress Rehearsals (and you should be), try to organize a **different audience** for each time...

> ## This special practice session is actually a performance of your entire program—under the most realistic concert conditions you can arrange.

...even if it's just an audience of one. There's nothing quite like playing to people who **haven't heard** the program yet.

- Make an **actual time and date** for each dress rehearsal. And then give **tickets** to your invited audience, so you're committed to going through with it...and so they're committed to turning up.

- Before you start your performance, **do the whole "onstage" thing.** Bow. Tune your instrument. Have the houselights dimmed. Do **whatever** you would do in a proper concert. You want these rituals to feel comfortable and familiar, not like a trip to the dentist's chair on the day.

- Remember, it's a *performance*. So once you start, there's **no stops.** No "Whoops!, I'll try that again!". Why? *Because you can't in the concert itself.*

No matter what happens, keep going—it's advice you've heard before, but "just keep going" is not as easy as it sounds... ...which is **precisely why** you need to practice it.

Don't try this too early...

There's no point in running a Dress Rehearsal with a piece you don't know yet (see Campaigns ➲58) The time to get this technique out is in the week or two leading up to a performance, when your piece is already in **great shape**.

...and don't try it too *late*

A dress rehearsal the day before is a **hiding to nothing**. If it goes well, there's no relief, because it's *supposed* to. But if it goes badly...

Whenever you're running a dress rehearsal, you should leave yourself enough time to be able to **do something** about any problems you discover. Otherwise there is no point in discovering them...all they'll do is worry you.

The only 11th hour Dress Rehearsals that you should be considering are OPENINGS AND ENDINGS⮌215, both of which are bite-sized enough to repair if there really are any last minute problems. But even then, it's usually best to leave well enough alone—trust the practice that you've done on this earlier to carry you through. (See CLOSURE⮌80 and ONE WAY DOORS⮌208)

Ask for feedback

Your dress rehearsal audience might not be musicians, but **they know what they like**. Should the middle

section go faster? Were the soft passages soft enough? Too soft?

You'll get lots of different opinions, and you certainly don't have to act on all of them. But if everyone there is telling you that they **couldn't hear** the end of the piece, then you should project the last page a little more on concert day.

Make the truth easy to tell

For the most honest feedback, have your audience *write comments down*—this helps combat the "it

was really nice" sappy-lollipop-non-feedback that many people feel compelled to give if they're actually talking to, well, a *person*.

Give them a sheet with two columns:

- Elements to **keep**

- Elements to **consider changing**

This will give you a **more accurate picture** of what you need than the traditional "good points vs bad

points". Marking a passage for "change" doesn't mean the playing was bad—it just means that the listener imagined a better way. (Or *thinks* they imagined a better way)

It also helps non-musicians overcome their natural reluctance to label *anything* as bad, when they don't know anything about music.

Get it while it's still warm

The audience's reaction is important, but even more important is your **own assessment** of what just happened.

With every second that passes though after the end of the performance, your sense of how you really played will grow increasingly fuzzy.

So while the audience is busy writing their own feedback, **write some of your own**—you can quietly review it later.

If you're using cosmetics...

They should also be present in the Dress Rehearsal. Cosmetics will only save you if they're skillfully applied, and well rehearsed—and

like everything else you're planning to do on concert day, you need to have tried them out under pressure first.

See COSMETICS➲94 if this all sounds a bit mysterious...

Scheduling Dress Rehearsals

If you really want to make Dress Rehearsals feel official, then mark official dates for them in your COUNTDOWN CHART➲99. That way, if you know you have a concert in 12 weeks, then you would **also know** about the dress rehearsals that start in 10 weeks. Preparing for the first of those dress rehearsals will then ensure that you're concert ready *two weeks ahead of schedule.*

Once the dress rehearsals are on your countdown chart, you'll have all that time to be thinking about them, together with **daily reminders** that they're coming up—which adds enormously to the legitimacy of the occasions.

All helps add to the pressure generated by your concert simulators. And it gives you plenty of time to organize an audience to match.

Recording Dress Rehearsals

If you've got recording gear of any sort, you can learn even more from your Dress Rehearsals by being able **re-live** them afterwards. Instead of having to be completely reliant on your memory as to what actually happened, you can listen to the **action replay**, and hear for yourself.

You can also use recordings of multiple rehearsals to make accurate **comparisons**, and to be sure that the way you *think* you sound is the way you *actually* sound.

See RECORDING YOURSELF➲270 for more information on this.

Engaging Autopilot
The dangers of practicing without *thinking*

Megan has just **finished practicing** for the day. "Sounded like you were working hard in there", says her father. "So **tell me**—what did you get *done* today?"

What indeed. At that point, Megan realizes with a shock that she **actually doesn't know**... she's been practicing for almost an hour, *but can't remember anything that happened.*

But still, an hour is a lot of practice. **Does it really matter** that she doesn't know how she spent the time?...

IF YOU'VE JUST finished practicing…but have **no memory** of what you actually did during that time…then there's a different word for what you were *really* doing in there. And it's not "practicing".

You were on **autopilot**, and it's a PRACTICE TRAP➲236 that almost every student falls into at some stage.

Autopilot means switching on your brain **as little as possible**—usually just enough so that you can play your instrument without accidentally swallowing it or starting a fire—but apart from that, you're not really supervising things too closely.

Notes will be played. Pages will be turned. But you'll only be **dimly aware**, because your **brain** is **somewhere else**.

Don't confuse it with practice

Working like this is fine for **filling half an hour with sounds**. They could even be the sounds of your pieces. But it certainly **won't help you solve problems**, or improve that tricky bit on page 3.

And it's absolutely, definitely not going to have you ready for your next lesson—any more than daydreaming while you **doodle** on your **homework book** is getting you ready for school tomorrow.

Practice of the Undead

Here's the really **spooky thing** though:

The whole time you are on autopilot—even though your brain is off—you will still **be able to play**. In fact, you might even be able to play quite well. It's similar to the way a **chicken** can still walk around even after its **head** has been **cut off**.

The end result is that your playing is the same **mindless practice** the **Undead** would do if ghouls had music lessons, which is one of the reasons ghouls don't have symphony orchestras.

And it goes unnoticed…

There's another problem too. If you're really lost in your daydream, you might "practice" for **quite some time**—well beyond the daily minimum that you might have been set. And you know what happens then?

Your **parents** might actually **praise you** for all this nonsense.

"You work so hard" they'll say proudly.

What they really should say is **"Hello? Hello?"** while they poke you in the forehead.

(We'll look in a moment at how you can **give yourself a poke** like this)**…**

...by *almost* everyone...

Even if you and your family **don't notice** that you've been running on autopilot, there is someone who will quickly find out that your practice has been a **mindless mess.**

Your **teacher.**

When your lesson rolls around, the fact that you've "done half an hour every day" **isn't** going to **save you,** because a week of autopilot practice usually sounds the **same** as if you **haven't practiced at all.**

In fact, it can have you sounding *worse.*

Autopilot is a great way to **reinforce mistakes** you never even knew were there—and an even better way to plant and **fertilize brand new ones.**

The end result is that you can spend plenty of time working, but have **nothing** to **show for it.** Keep that up, and you won't feel like practicing at all.

So what can you do about your autopilot practice? How do you pop your daydream bubbles?

> # Autopilot is a great way to reinforce mistakes *you never even knew were there*—and an even better way to plant and fertilize *brand new ones...*

Startling your autopilot into disengaging

If you want to **switch off** your autopilot, you have to **interrupt** irrelevant thoughts before they take over.

To do this, you're going to need to **create a shock** for yourself. Something loud, and **unexpected.**

Find a **kitchen timer**—the noisier the better—set it to go off after 5 minutes, and start your practice.

If you fall victim to autopilot, the time will **pass quickly,** and your first reaction when the alarm goes off will be "what the **heck** is **that?**"

At that point, it's **not just an alarm.** It's really saying "Hey **dopey!** Focus!" Set it again, refocus, and get on with the task at hand.

When you eventually find that instead of interrupting a daydream, the timer is interrupting your practice instead, set the timer for 10 minutes instead of 5. It's a sign that the **cure** is **starting to work,** and your first steps to a bigger world of sustained concentration.

In fact, your aim is to gradually extend the set time until there's **no need** for the **wake-up** call at all.

Random checks

The aim this time is not to startle you, but for you to have to **describe** what you've been doing.

The plan is for a family member to come and tap you on the shoulder at **random**, maybe once or twice in each practice session—at which point you need to be able to **tell them** two things:

• Exactly **what** you're trying to **fix** right now

• How you're **going about it**

If you're **fuzzy** about either of those two things, then your autopilot is at least **partly on**—which is a sign that you need another tap on the shoulder again soon. If not, then they should **increase** the amount of time before the next visit.

Again, the aim is that eventually you **won't need** visits like this at all. And you'll be amazed at how much **faster** you get through your practice tasks.

Work to targets, not times

When you're running on autopilot, there is absolutely **no link** between how long you've been practicing and how much better you're getting.

Because of this, time is a **terrible measure** of your progress. (In fact, time is *always* a terrible measure of your progress—see CLOCKWATCH-ERS ➲76)

So instead of practicing until a certain amount of time has passed, **set yourself tasks** that you have to get through—*and then practice until they're done.* (See SESSION AGENDA ➲305)

With this shift in the rules, you'll be **heavily punished** for running on autopilot—simply because your practice session won't ever come to an end. Remember, until your todo list is complete, you're **stuck** there.

But the flipside is also true. As soon as you've completed and tested your tasklist—*even if only a few minutes have passed*—you can stop.

This means you have a powerful incentive to concentrate, because the reward is less practice. You can then use that time for something else entirely, or surprise your teacher by getting more done than they asked for.

Record your progress

A great way to detect and shut down autopilot is to keep a BREAK-THROUGHS DIARY ➲46. Because you will be making a brief **note** of every new achievement, autopilot sessions will **reveal themselves** immediately—*because your entry for the day will be blank.*

Sometimes it will be blank because autopilot meant that you **didn't achieve** anything. Sometimes it will be because autopilot meant you **forgot to record** details. And sometimes it will be because autopilot just stopped you from **noticing** anything you *did* achieve.

No matter the reason, it's a sure sign *you* weren't flying the plane. Which means you'll have no idea where it's been going all this time.

Further help

There's loads more help on avoiding autopilot—check out the "Staying Focused" section in the USHER ➲27.

Exaggerating
Imprinting important points by overstating them

B illy has a **long list** of changes he's supposed to make to his piece. None of them are especially difficult—the problem is going to be **remembering** them all.

There's no need for Billy to worry though. There's something he can do to ensure that each requested change becomes **impossible to forget...**

...although it means that his practice is going to sound a little...

...umm...*unusual*...

Whether you're simply using pencil marks, or COLOR CODING⟳84, it doesn't take long before your music is **covered with reminders**:

- *Make these staccatos shorter.*
- *Keep this pp genuinely quiet*
- *Don't forget the double sharp!*
- *Raise your wrist as you play this*
- *Change pedal here*
- *Use three consecutive downbows here*
- *Take a quick breath between these notes*
- *Project the melody more*
- *Keep these sixteenth notes even*

None of these items are necessarily difficult to get right, but remembering the **entire list** can be a problem.

A LESSON REVIEW⟳178 can **help cement** them in your mind, as can using a FRESH PHOTOCOPY⟳151 and making the markings yourself.

There's **another trick** you can use though. It's going to make your practice sound a little **weird**, but it's going to be *very* hard to forget these corrections once you're done.

Creating a lasting impression

The aim of this practice session is to **exaggerate** each of the items on your list to a point where it sounds like you're **creating a parody.**

So if one of the pencil marks on your score was a **reminder** to "Observe this accent", then observe it you will...and then some.

If you're a violinist, this means a crunch and a **cloud of resin** that would set off fire alarms. A saxophonist would blurt that note until their eyes are bugging out and the neighbors start thumping the walls.

A great ugly overplayed accent? It's a **strange thing to do.** Which is precisely the point:

Because it was strange, you'll remember it.

Hard wired for weird

Our brains are designed to **filter out** and **quickly forget** the **same old** same old. But they're wired to keep strong—and often permanent— impressions of things that are out of the ordinary.

And the **weirder** the event, the **more likely** you'll be to remember it.

Every time you **go shopping**, you pass **hundreds of people**. You won't remember their faces, what they wore...it all gets **stored** under "no need to remember this" (Your brain would quickly **blow up** if it couldn't do that)

But some years ago, at a shopping center, an old lady that I didn't know came storming over towards me, yelling something that I couldn't understand. She was holding a packet of chips...which she then clapped violently against her other hand to burst in my face.

She then disappeared back into the crowd, ranting as she went, leaving me with a shirt covered with chips, and a curious crowd of onlookers. To this day I have no idea what her problem was, or why I was targeted.

But since that doesn't typically happen to me when I shop, the encounter stuck in my memory. I can still see her clearly.

Create your own oddities

Moments of weirdness like that aren't just going to **happen** when you practice —you need to **create them**.

If, in our previous example, you accent the living daylights out of that note, you'll remember forever afterwards that the note needed to be stressed.

Obviously you **won't perform it** like that, but you're not practicing to learn *how* to play an accent—you're practicing to **remind yourself** to insert one in the first place.

The aim of exaggerating is to turn these reminders into out-of-the-ordinary behavior from you, but

> # Our brains are wired to keep strong—and often permanent—impressions of things that are out of the ordinary...

behavior that is **based directly** on whatever the reminder was asking for. Hence the over-the-top accent. Let's take a look at how this might apply to some of the items in the list at the start of this chapter:

"Make these staccatos shorter"
Sounds like a **challenge** to me. There's a subatomic particle called a **neutral pion** that decays in 84 billion billionths of a second—your job would be to make these staccato notes **disappear even faster.**

Anybody in the room listening to you play these notes should **think** they've heard something...but somehow **not be sure...**

This is going to take some effort and experimenting on your part—in the process, you'll **cement** in your

mind the idea that **these notes** are supposed to be **short.**

"Keep this pp genuinely quiet"
You need to be able to win a Who Is The Quietest competition against a slipper-wearing koala that's meditating in a soundproof room.

You'll quickly discover that it's quite hard to do this, but **ten minutes of trying** will be enough for you to forever associate this section with quiet playing.

"Don't forget the double sharp!"
This is a little trickier. You **can't exaggerate** this in the same way that you handled the staccato and pp passages. That double sharp is either ON or OFF, there's no **degrees** of those two **states.**

But you can accompany playing the double sharp with unusual levels of **fanfare** and **attention**. Pause just before the double sharp, choose a **crazy voice** (Dobby the House Elf? Eeyore? Chewbacca?) and enunciate "DOUBLE SHARP!"

Then play it slowly and deliberately.

Repeat the passage a few times, pausing every time before the double sharp, and using a **brand new voice** each time to announce its arrival. The worse the impersonation, the better. The louder the better.

It sounds stupid. It *is* stupid. **That's the point.** You'll remember it *because* it's stupid.

In fact, after just two such voices, it will be almost impossible *not* to remember that double sharp now. (and your family is going to be very, very worried about you)

"Draw a quick breath between these notes"
On concert day, you'll take a short, discrete breath that is unobtrusive and allows the melody line to continue unbroken.

But today—because you're practicing the breath just to **remember** that it's supposed to be there—you're going to draw the great shuddering gasp of the final moments of a buffalo that had chain-smoked it's whole life.

This is exactly the sort of breath you *don't* want to take on concert day, but right now, see how much noise you can make with it.

And again, repeat the passage a few times.

This jammed-vaccuum-cleaner-meets-Darth-Vader inhale is an **absurd** way to handle that passage. You won't breathe like that on concert day.

But you will *remember* that a breath is **due** at just that moment.

And then dial it back down
All this craziness is designed to help **imprint** the issues in your mind—and that's **all** it's designed to do. This is not a blueprint for how to improve passages or perform with conviction—like so many of the practice techniques in this book, it does one thing very well, and almost everything else badly.

Once each issue is imprinted, **abandon** the exaggerations, and **back it up** with some practice designed to **fine tune** delivery of each issue.

The idea is that now you know you're supposed to play in a certain way, you've got to **switch** your attention to playing that way **well**.

So having worked out exactly **when** that breath is supposed to appear, you'll then spend some time working on the breath itself. Only this time, you'll practice it until you really can deliver it without anyone noticing.

Excuses and Ruses

Why you'll never really fool your teacher if you haven't practiced

S am has had a **good week.** Not "good" in the sense of "lots of practice". Good in the sense of lots of computer games, beach, friends and television.

In fact, he **hasn't opened** his music all week.

He's not too worried though. He **knows a few tricks** that will mean that his teacher will never know he didn't practice—and if **that doesn't work,** he has a long list of excuses ready to go.

Sam, it *won't* work. **Here's why...**

I<small>T MIGHT BE HARD</small> to imagine, but once upon a time, a **long time ago**—when horse-drawn carts clattered through gaslit streets — your **teacher** was a student too.

Here's what they don't want you to know about that time though:

No matter how they lecture you at lessons *now*, there would have been weeks *then* when they **didn't practice**, and then had to come to the lesson **unprepared**.

Shocking, but true.

Now don't smile like that. This is *not* good news for you.

It simply means that whatever excuses you try to use for not practicing, your teacher will be **on to you**.

Not because they're a better person than you. *Because they used **exactly the same excuses** when they were a student.*

You'll be as transparent to them as a four year old—face, hair and clothing caked in chocolate, arm still

stuck in the cookie jar and a mound of wrappers at their feet, **denying** that they've been eating sweets...and **then** saying that maybe they might have eaten just *one*, but by *accident*. (And it was their *sister's fault*)

What's ahead in this chapter

This chapter will take you on a tour of all the **Classic Excuses and Ruses** deployed when students haven't practiced. It's designed to make you blush, because it's a collection of tales that *you* may have told, and swindles you may have attempted.

Don't feel **too bad** though. These same tales and ruses are uses by students the world over. And

remember, they were the same ones used by your teacher.

Your job is to read through them, acknowledge your guilt in the past...

...and then **read the rest of this book** so that you don't need to resort to such weaselings in the future.

The two options

Ok, so let's imagine that you haven't practiced, and that you're trying **not** to get into trouble. Hypothetical, I know—it's not like that would ever happen to *you*. Ahem.

At this point—with the lesson about to start—there are lots of tactics you can try, but they really can be grouped into two families:

Option 1: Deflection

These techniques are designed to **prevent** your teacher from **discovering** the lack of practice in the first place.

If you're successful, then you won't *need* to make an excuse, because you're teacher will never know about your slack week. Brilliant!

How do you do this? We'll look at some common methods in a moment, but have no doubt—none of these tactics will even come close to fooling your teacher.

Option 2: Excuses

Instead of deflecting, this tactic is based on **freely admitting** that there hasn't been enough practice, but then giving Compelling Reasons for the lack of activity. So rather than a sleight of hand, it's a **plea for understanding**—that circumstances beyond your control have quite simply made practice impossible.

The idea you're trying to sell is that you're a *victim*. That you shouldn't be spoken to harshly. You should be *pitied*.

Again, we'll take a look in a moment at some of these common excuses, and why no teacher is going to seriously buy them.

Classic Deflection Tactics

Ok, so you haven't worked as you should this week, and have decided on **deflection** as your way out. The idea is that you'll be trying to **steer** **the lesson** so that your teacher doesn't get a chance to ask for what you haven't done.

So what are the classic deflection tactics? And why are they ultimately doomed to fail?

The Prattle Defense

This tactic takes advantage of the fact that your lesson is a **limited length**, and is a favorite ploy for chatterbox students.

The plan is that if you can spend the entire lesson **talking**, you might not even be *asked* to play the unpracticed sections. There just won't be time left.

Students who use this tactic start the lesson by talking about something—anything—and then **not pausing for breath**.

"You'll never guess what happened at school today, well let me tell you about it, first Amy and Rachel turn up late, saying that Michelle had been in a bike accident, except that it wasn't true, all that happened was that she...

Music book is not even out of the bag at this point, much less on the stand.

...had a flat tyre, and then Mrs Morris gave us a test that none of us were expected, and my dad is going to be so mad when he sees what score I get, although we don't...

The teacher keeps trying to say "hello" to the student, but...

...get the test back until Wednesday, and who knows, maybe I guessed

well, and anyway you should SEE Jennifer's hair, no way I would have paid for that cut, it's crazy, besides you should have heard what Sandy did, I was so surprised, well maybe not totally surprised, but I wasn't expecting it completely in any sort of total way..."

Tick tick tick. Keep this up, and the whole lesson will pass.

Well, that's the idea. It rarely works that way in reality though.

How a teacher might defend against this: They'll listen patiently to this nonsense for a minute or two. Then you'll simply be interrupted, and they'll segue into your piece for the week. It's really not hard, and unlike you, they've had plenty of practice.

Game over.

The Obscure Help Ploy

Again, this takes advantage of a ticking clock, but this time, you're hoping your **teacher** will do the talking.

So instead of prattling, you'll start **asking questions** about things in the score—complicated questions that you know are going to **take time** to explain:

"I've always wondered about the differences between mordents, inverted mordents, half-inverted mordents and...

if you make something up, you can really confuse them...

Spanish mordents and isosceles quarter-trills...I was wondering if you run through each of them, and could find me a couple of examples of each in your own music library?"

How a teacher might defend against this: Sensing a deflection, they'll *defer*, with a statement like this:

"That's an interesting question. I'll need a little time to look up the answer—I'll get back to you next week. In the meantime, I want to hear your etude"

Game over.

Iceberg tip scam

No questions or chatting this time—instead this tactic relies

on showing a sudden **fascination** with a **very small part** of your piece.

This very small part happens to be the only section that you had **actually practiced**. But it's in good shape. So you'll stop at the end of that section each time, ask a question or two, and then try the passage again, with the recommended improvements in place.

The aim is to spend the lesson showing off and working with this one good passage in your piece, and then hope your teacher assumes that the **rest** of the iceberg **matches the tip**.

How a teacher might defend against this: This tactic relies on the teacher *agreeing* to all these endless loops. Sooner or later, they'll say "No—I think we're done with that bit for today".

What then?

That's right. Game over.

Mock Shock

This tactic is called on when you've been unsuccessful in using up all your lesson time, and it's obvious that you **will** have to play unprepared material after all.

Students employing this tactic will play badly, and then **protest** *"It didn't sound like this at home!"*.

They'll **feign amazement** that things could be going so wrong so suddenly.

Nice idea. But you're not fooling anybody—you're teacher has seen it many, many times before.

How a teacher might defend against this: After the initial disaster, you'll be given the benefit of the doubt, a chance to settle,

and then an invitation to try it again. Your teacher will remind you that it's only natural that sometimes the first couple of attempts in a lesson can be a bit rough.

But they'll also remind you that by the fourth or fifth attempt, you should really be showing *some* sign that you know what you're doing. Otherwise it would be pretty clear that you never knew it in the first place.

Game over.

Casting doubt on instructions

Another tactic that is used in the event that the Wind-Down-The-Clock type tactics didn't work.

But unlike the feigned amazement of Mock Shock, this time you'll feign **indignation** and **confusion** at having been asked to play this bit at all.

The protest will be that you **didn't know** that you were supposed to practice this. That you've been ambushed with it now, and so of *course* it doesn't sound good.

How a teacher will defend against this: Written instructions. Very hard to continue the protest when the actual instructions say otherwise.

They'll point to the page, and ask you to read the instructions out loud.

Game over.

"Let's work on <u>this</u> instead"

Another tactic designed to **sidestep** having to play what you were supposed to. It usually involves the student bringing with them another piece—usually an **old** piece—and suddenly and mysteriously wanting to spend lesson time on that instead...

There's nothing mysterious about this at all though. And your teacher certainly won't be mystified.

How a teacher might defend against this: They'll listen to it for a bit, not wanting to discourage what might be a genuine interest.

But they'll quickly work out what you're up to, in which case they'll change channels on you:

*"You've done some good work with that. Yes, I want to hear it again... but in a couple of weeks' time—let's move now to **this** weeks' work though"*

Game over.

Classic Excuses

So deflection is not as effective as it sounds—like Wile E Coyote chasing the roadrunner, the reality never seems to match the plan.

The problem is that if deflection is not going to work, then it will be quickly obvious that you haven't practiced. At this point, you would have to resort to excuses—all

designed to prove that it was **completely understandable** that you hadn't worked this week. That you're a **victim**, in need of understanding.

Yeah, right. Let's take a look at some of this hooey.

Overloaded week defense

The idea here is to prove to your teacher that your week was **filled with assignments and deadlines**, and so practice was impossible.

Sounds fair enough. In fact, it might even be true.

But guess what. You'll *always* have lots of assignments. That's part of being at school. You can't wait until they stop before your

practice starts—otherwise your practice will never start.

What really kills this defense though is not just logic. It's that your teacher will have had experience working with students who are **much, much busier than you**—and yet somehow found time to practice. In fact, it's often the busiest students who practice the most consistently.

So your teacher is really not going to be sympathetic to the overloaded week defense...

...unless you can make them aware *in advance*. That's then a whole different story. If you genuinely have a high-stress period at school—say an annual **exam week**—then give your teacher a **heads up** about it *before* the event. They will usually adjust your practice load to suit.

If you really do feel that your weeks are too busy for you to practice, then you should check out the chapter on TRIGGERS ➲347. You've quickly discover that you've got more time than you think.

Impossible conditions defense

This excuse is based around the idea that conditions had **conspired against you** somehow. It might involve pointing out that you had visitors, or that renovations meant that your usual practice room was unavailable.

The reality is though, none of these things were *genuine* barriers. Obstacles perhaps—they might have made it more difficult to practice than normal—but certainly **not impossible.**

Find alternatives. Practice at school. Borrow an instrument. Look for a different practice room in the house. Spend more time doing Scouting, Tabletop Practice or Scribing – techniques that don't require an instrument or practice room, and therefore dodge the obstacle entirely.

So unless your flute was **stolen** in the same week that a **hurricane** destroyed your house, while a separate **skiing accident** left you with **two broken arms,** and both your parents were on **jury duty,** meaning that you had to spend most of the week looking after your **nine younger siblings,** give this defence a miss. Nobody will be impressed by it.

Missing resources defense

This time, the protest is that practicing was impossible because of the **unavailability** of key resources. You couldn't find your music. Your metronome broke.

Excuses of this sort would carry weight, if only the problems you were outlining weren't so easy to fix or work around.

And if that **sounds unfair,** ask yourself this:

If you had been guaranteed $100,000 and an extra weeks' holiday this year if you had been able to practice anyway, would you have found a way?

See? It *was* possible. You know it. Your teacher knows it. So who exactly is buying all this?

The "I was rudderless" defense

This argument is based around the idea that you were **perfectly willing** and **able** to practice this week, but that you **didn't know** what you were supposed to do. And so you did nothing.

A variation on the Casting Doubt On Instructions tactic, this defense is **no defense at all.** If you genuinely were confused about what you're supposed to be working on—*and had any intention of ending that confusion*—you would have contacted your teacher midweek.

So you obviously either **didn't care** too much that you were confused...or you **weren't really** confused in the first place. Either way, it doesn't look good.

Of all the excuses and ruses here—none of which work—this one doesn't work the **fastest.**

In short...

Excuses and ruses don't fool anyone, make you look bad, age your teacher prematurely, and require a **lot of effort on your part.** In fact, it takes substantially *less* effort to gently go through your to-do list between lessons...

...and get things done.

Experimenting
Testing different interpretation options

Michelle can play right through her piece easily, and rarely makes mistakes. But there's **one problem**.

It's *boring*. Boring to play. Boring to listen to.

"I don't know what else to do" she thinks "Maybe it's just a **boring piece...**"

As we'll see, it's hardly ever the *piece* that's boring. But how is Michelle going to **discover** the excitement inside?...

EXPERIMENTING IS a creative way to practice that can help **old** and **tired** pieces become **fresh** and **surprising**. Sometimes *very* surprising.

The whole adventure is based on **three ideas**:

1) That there are **countless different ways** that you could play any passage in your piece...and that so far, you only will have tried a fraction of those possibilities.

2) That some of those possibilities will be **more effective** than others.

3) That because you've only tried a fraction of these possibilities so far, *the best options are probably yet to be tried*...which means they are waiting for you to discover.

So go discover them. Which is why you're going to need to Experiment.

"I wonder what if..."

When you run your Experiment, you'll be playing each passage in your piece in *as many different ways as you can*, while **listening** carefully to the results.

During this time, your favorite question is going to be:

"I wonder what if..."

"I wonder what if I were to push through to the next phrase, instead of holding back like I normally do?"

*"I wonder what if I made these staccato notes **really** short, instead of the current non-legato approach?"*

"I wonder what if I brought out the left hand in this passage?"

"I wonder what if I delayed this crescendo by another measure, and then made it steeper?"

Don't just **wonder** "what if" though. Go **try** each of these things, see what you think.

Don't prejudge...

Some of the best ideas you'll ever use can sound silly until you actually try them. So when you're creating your "I wonder what if?..." possibilities, keep an open mind.

Even if you're 99% sure your "what if" is a bad idea, **try it anyway**—

you'll be amazed (and delighted) by how often you are wrong.

...but be guided by the score

Perhaps the only exception to prejudging is where your idea **openly contradicts** the composer's markings. If the tempo indication is Largo, then you should probably discard "I wonder what if I played this opening at a cut-time prestissimo"—**even if** this otherwise slow movement sounds exciting when delivered like a caffeine-filled hummingbird playing an etude.

That having been said though, composers are **not** always automatically the best interpreters of their own music—just as there have been some brilliant interpretations of Shakespeare that **openly defy** the marked stage directions.

If you genuinely have discovered that a section is breathlessly exciting if you **refuse** to crescendo at all, despite the marked crescendo, then so be it—although you might want to run it past your teacher first (See the note below on a "Don't Mess With This" list)

Even the bad results help

Your experiment won't exclusively uncover **treasures**. Sometimes you'll try an "I wonder what if..." and realize very quickly that it was a **bad idea**. But that doesn't mean you've **wasted time**.

For example, if placing a **strong accent** on the first measure of each bar ended up making the melody sound ploddy and insincere, then it's worth knowing that. You've moved a **step closer** to discovering the best delivery of this phrase...by taking a step **away** from a *bad* delivery.

> # You probably shouldn't experiment with the notes themselves, but just about everything else is on the table...

The power of sampling widely

If you were interviewing candidates for a job, you've got **twice the chance** of finding the right person if you interview four people than if you only interview two.

This is why companies that interview two hundred people for a job end up with such **fantastic staff**—they have a *hundred* times the chance of finding the right person as a company who only interviews two people.

The same holds true for your performance. If you've only ever tried to play a passage one way, then you'd have to be **very lucky** for that to just happen to be the best way.

But if you've tried a dozen different models, then on concert day, we're

not just hearing what you came up with **first**. *We're hearing the very **best** out of all the options you considered* —and the more you considered, the better the best is likely to be.

Elements to experiment with

So what can you experiment with? You probably shouldn't experiment with the notes themselves, but just about everything else is on the table:

Dynamics. Not just which dynamics and where, but *shapes*. So if you're planning a crescendo to run over three measures, is it going to **steadily** get louder throughout, or is most of the crescendo going to **happen in a rush** in the final half measure? There's a huge difference between the two—you won't know which to use until you experiment. And then when you're done, try it with a *de*crescendo.

Articulation. Placement and intensity of accents, staccatos etc. For example, are you going to treat those indicated dots as staccato, staccatissimo, or simply non-legato? And will they all be **uniform**, or will they **evolve** as the passage moves forward?

Time dependent elements: Choice of tempo, steadiness of tempo, rubato. If there's a dramatic moment in the piece, try **delaying** it, then try **anticipating** it. Then try it bang on time. See which feels most compelling. Similarly, experimenting with different tempos for the piece as a whole.

Technique related elements: What happens if you breathe differently? Or hold your hand higher? Or lower? Or maintain more tension across the bridge of your hand? Or less? Every physical change you make will have some sort of impact on ease of delivery and your sound—make lots of changes, pay attention to what happens as you do.

Find a better move

There's a saying in chess that once you've found a **good move**, wait, and find a **better one**. The same is true of your musical decisions.

So even if your experiments so far mean that you've found an exciting way to get neatly from the 3rd to the 4th variation in your Theme & Variations, you might find an **even more** exciting way if you run a few more tests.

It can be hard to achieve Closure ↻80 with Experiment practice sessions—in fact, the whole process can become a little addictive.

Keep a "can't decide…" book

If you find you're **torn** between two possible ideas, make a note of the options and the section they apply to. Have your teacher then act as the umpire at your next lesson.

Get a "don't mess with this" list from your teacher

While experimenting theoretically allows for any possible combination of dynamics, articulation and rubato, there will be some areas of the piece where your teacher will have Non-Negotiable ideas. That this passage *needs* to be pianissimo. That those notes in measure 14-18 have to be just as staccato and biting as you can manage. Consider using Color Coding ↻84 to clearly mark those elements that you shouldn't experiment with.

But even in sections where your dynamics are non-negotiable, you can still experiment with your posture, and the extent to which principle beats are accented. And whether or not this section will be rigidly in time, or maybe feeling like it's hurrying forwards slightly…

…the point is, even in the most proscriptive sections, you'll have plenty of room to be able to tweak elements that aren't specifically mentioned.

Which is great news, because working like this is a ticket not just to *creative* and *interesting*, but *revelatory* practice.

Fire Drills

Training to cope gracefully with onstage mistakes

G abriella has just watched her best friend **mess up** at her end-of-year recital...and **cover it** up so well that most of the audience **couldn't tell.**

"I don't know how you keep so **calm**" says Gabriella "I would have fallen to pieces..."

"I **haven't always** been able to do this." says her friend. "In fact, I've actually done some **training** in secret on just this issue..."

Secret training? To shut down mistakes as soon as they appear? Is that something Gabriella...or you...could do too?...

Here's a shocking **truth** most students try to hide from: *no matter how much practice you do, or how good that practice is, you still can't guarantee that things won't go wrong on stage.*

"What if I mess up?" is the big question that **makes students so nervous** before performances. You'll be told "everything will be fine", but the answer actually is "you almost certainly *will* mess up, at some point".

Students try to **save themselves** from this by practicing harder. To *prevent* the mistake. That makes sense, but as any fire-fighter will tell you, it's **only half** of what's needed.

Foundations in prevention

Apartments and office blocks are **potential disaster zones** in the event of a major fire, and so a lot of thinking has gone into how to **prevent** such infernos.

Because of this thinking, certain building techniques and materials have been **outlawed**, others have been made **compulsory**. Electrical systems are routinely checked,

corridors and basements are kept free of combustible material. The result is buildings that, while not fireproof, are certainly **much less likely** to become infernos.

The focus clearly is on **preventing** a fire in the first place—very similar to the idea that you'll practice harder to prevent mistakes in your performances.

But, unlike musicians practicing, building fire plans **don't stop** at prevention.

But ready for the worst

While fire prevention is certainly an important start, there's a second question that is focused on too:

What if—despite all our best preventative measures—there actually is a fire?

Once the fire appears, plans for prevention are no longer going to help. The fire is already here.

But before we wail "Oh the humanity!" and update our wills, there's something important to remember:

A fire in of itself is not a disaster.

It's what happens now in **response** to the fire that will determine whether it's a minor mishap, or a front page tragedy.

Because the stakes are so high, this response is not left to chance. It's **rehearsed**.

You've taken part in such rehearsals. They're called **fire drills**, and they make sure that in the event of a fire, everybody associated with the building will **know** exactly what to do.

Residents or workers have a **preset** evacuation path to preset evacuation points. They know to leave belongings and just *go*. They know who on their floor is in charge of getting everyone out. They know where to meet outside. They know the safest, fastest way to get there. The fire department, police and ambulance services will be notified. Rolls will be called at the evacuation points. Fire doors will be closed.

It's a complex sequence, but in the event of a real fire, this would happen **smoothly and automatically** —because it had been practiced.

And so the strategy is in two parts:

1) To do everything humanly possible to **prevent** a fire in the first place.

But also:

2) To have a **rehearsed harm-minimization response** ready to go in the event that there *is* a fire.

Remember, a fire is not a disaster. But unless you've rehearsed your escape plan, what happens next might be.

Drills aren't just for fires

The same thing is true when you're performing:

A mistake in of itself is not a disaster.

It's what happens next that counts.

But here's the thing. Musicians usually don't practice "what happens next". There's no fire drill.

So if something goes wrong on stage, they're in trouble, and worse still, they haven't practiced a way to get *out* of trouble.

No wonder musicians get nervous. With no "what if something goes wrong" plan, you've only got **one hope**:

Not making any mistakes. Ever.

And I'll tell you right now—even if you read this book from cover to cover, and then practice 12 hours a day—that's pure fantasy.

Fire drills for performers

There are plenty of tactics you can use to get yourself out of trouble onstage, but like anything else, if you want to do that well, you have to practice it.

So let's imagine that you're onstage, and you've just played something that is definitely NOT in the score. What can you do?

Drill #1: Teleport Points

You will have been told before to "just keep going" in the event of a mistake. It's a **good idea**, but it's not always so easy to do.

If what you've played is enough of a mess, you can become completely **disoriented**, and it can be hard to picture clearly any moment in the piece that you could keep going *from*.

In such cases, you might find yourself having to resort to the **worst** of all "just keep going" locations—back at the **start** of the piece.

For you to be able to deftly **teleport** to a **nearby** passage though, you need to have taken care of three things in the practice room first:

1) You need to have worked out where these teleport points are. These are places in the music that you can pick up from completely cold—just as surely as you can pick up from the start.

2) You need to have rehearsed starting suddenly from each of these places, so that you can picture any of those points *and* jump there instantly.

3) Once you can safely jump to *any* point, you need to **practice being able to jump to the *nearest* point.** To do this, you're going to need to have a mock disaster—play for a while, then deliberately play some nonsense.

Then ask yourself "Quick—where is the nearest teleport point?". Then stop playing the nonsense, and teleport.

What this means is that if you **trip** on concert day, you won't necessarily **fall**.

Yes, it's better not to have made the mistake in the first place. But if your teleport skills are well drilled, you'll be able to jump out of trouble **so fast** that the audience will wonder if you were ever *in* trouble.

What about your accompanist?
Fair question. Your accompanist won't magically be able to **anticipate** that you're going to teleport, so expect things to be a little bumpy when you first arrive.

However, if you keep playing from that point with authority—ignoring your accompanist completely—a

good accompanist will amaze you with how quickly they'll jump to where you are too.

Why can they do this? *Because a good accompanist will have had plenty of practice at teleporting over the years*—both in the practice room and onstage. As long as you stay the course once you've teleported, they'll be fine.

Drill #2: Beautiful nonsense
Ok, so you're lost on stage, but you think you can find your way again, and won't need to teleport. This means that you'll be fumbling around for the right notes for a while. That doesn't mean you have to play these fumble-notes *badly*.

A key to minimizing the impact of a mistake is for everything to be **as normal as possible** while you're playing it. But the problem is, when mistakes happen, students can go into a minor panic, and then things are definitely *not* normal.

So there's the original mistake, but it's now being **compounded** by the performer turning off dynamics, forgetting about phrasing, abandoning tone quality control—everything except life support gets shut down while they try to recover.

All for some wrong notes.

As a result, even people in the audience who are tone deaf—heck, even people in the audience who are just plain deaf—will have a sense that something is wrong. Too much has changed.

Wrapping the mistake well

The thing to remember is this:

The worse your mistake, the more beautifully you need to play. Wrap these wrong notes in compelling dynamics, sensitive phrasing and deliberate articulation. Make sure that the only thing that has gone wrong is **what** you played, not **how** you played it.

At the end of the concert

If you wrap your mistakes well enough, the comments from the audience at the end of the piece will not be about your lapse (believe it or not, most people won't even know!). At worst you might hear "That Beethoven certainly writes some eccentric music at times, but oh my, wasn't it well played!"

You can then smile a little smile, and you can make it up to Beethoven next time you play.

But it won't just happen

Like teleporting, wrapping mistakes takes practice. So in the practice room, the next time you mess up, instead of stopping and going back to fix it, try to keep going—riding out the wrong notes by playing them as beautifully as you can.

Drill #3: Improvise to safety

Being able to play **nonsense convincingly** is a start, but even better is to be able to play **convincing nonsense**.

In other words, instead of just **fumbling** for notes while you figure out what's next, you would be **improvising** something that *sounds like it belongs to the piece.*

Don't panic—you don't need to have the improvisation powers of a Beethoven or a Bill Evans to make this rescue work. Remember, you're **not** trying to **win a grammy** with the result—you're simply trying to get yourself **out of trouble.**

The aim is to produce an improvisation that is more believable than the random fumbling you were going to do otherwise.

Become a style mimic

The key is not in the notes you choose, but in ensuring that **other musical elements** in the piece make sense.

So **for example**, if the passage was made of gently flowing triplets, then your nonsense notes should also be gently flowing triplets. Doesn't really matter *which* notes—the fact that the rhythm is continuing like this will have most people **believing** that everything is as it should be.

If instead the passage you were playing was built from staccato eighth notes, then that's what you'll play. You'll play whatever—but as staccato eighth notes. ▸

You might not be matching the notes correctly, but at least you're matching the style.

What about the notes too?

Mimicking the style of the passage is the majority of the swindle. The rest is being able to select notes that feel like they belong too.

Discussions about musical rhetoric and melody construction fall well outside the scope of this book, but you **don't** actually need to be as **sophisticated** as that to make this work.

In fact, it's another instance where simply being **on top of your scales** will really help. (See Fitness Training ➲146). If you know the key the passage is in, then select notes from that scale. Combined with the style being continued, you'll end up with something that is **surprisingly believable** from the audiences point of view. Perhaps a little...odd somehow...but believable nonetheless.

But DO try this at home first...

While these very basic principles of improvised rescues are easy enough to understand, it's **not** easy when you first try it. So if you want this skill as a safety net on stage, you have to have spent time developing it in the practice room.

To practice this, choose sections of the piece, and then make up your **own version** of that section—your notes, but keeping true to as much of the style as possible.

If at first, all you can manage is random notes in the same tempo, then that's a **great start**. Next time, you might be able to continue the tempo, **and** mimic the rhythm too.

The time after that, you might be able to handle notes at the right tempo, continue the same rhythm, and keep the **same phrasing**. It's all **fiction**, but the more time you spend practicing it, the more **convincing** your fiction will be.

Drill #4: Poker face

All your cover-ups will count for nothing if you react to your slip by pulling a face...or worse still, as a student of mine once did onstage, by swearing loudly.

It's **natural** to want to react, but you can't afford to handle every mistake by behaving like someone has just **stood on your foot**. All that will do is have the audience *looking* for a mistake—even if they hadn't noticed it yet.

Again though, if you want to have a poker face for mistakes on stage, you have to work on maintaining the facade in the practice room too.

To practice this, set yourself a whole week where you observe your own reactions to messing things up (you'll mess up a lot of things in a whole week, so you'll get plenty of practice). Notice how you tend to react, and then tone it down so that even those closest to you wouldn't be able to tell.

Drill #5: Symmetrical mistakes

This technique is a **good** one for concerts, but **probably not** a great idea in an exam. Some teachers may not agree with it at all, but it has saved me on many occasions, and more than a few of my students too.

The tactic **takes advantage** of the fact that music is often made from **patterns**—there are sequences, question and answer phrases, and straight up repeats (just to name a few).

This means that if you are **listening** to a performance, and you hear something a **little strange**—but it does not happen again anywhere else in the passage—it is reasonable to assume that it was **probably an error**. Usually a glaring asymmetry in an otherwise symmetrical passage will be perceived as a mistake—much more so than merely a wrong note.

So, **repeat your mistakes**.

You heard right. Make them **symmetrical**. If you split a note in the first part of a phrase, split it in the second part too. But split it beautifully. Make it sound like it was *supposed* to be a grace note.

And you will have a room full of people who will think that just perhaps it *might* have been a grace note. This is **much better** than a room full of people who all know you just messed up.

Likewise, if you jumped a fourth rather than a fifth in the melody the first time, do it the second time too. It might produce an unusual harmony—don't hide from that, actually linger on it. If you do it

beautifully enough, you will fool the people who don't know the piece, and have the people who *do* know it wondering whether you were simply working from a different edition. Remember, just as with your Beautiful Nonsense and Poker Face deliveries, things done **with conviction** are credible.

Obviously you can't apply this technique to **all mistakes** (if you get carried away during your aria, and accidentally slip off the stage into the orchestra pit, don't deliberately throw yourself into the percussion section again during the following recitative.) But for **minor errors**, this is a great cheat.

Practicing this at home

Again, you need to have done this behind the scenes **before** it's going to work reliably for you on stage.

The idea is to declare a practice session as being a Symmetrical Mistake session. Throughout that time, any error you make, you need to **duplicate** in any similar phrases.

You need to be careful with this though—you don't want to **ingrain** those errors. Practice this

skill sparingly, or to be safe, with pieces that you're **not** planning on **performing**. (Duplicated mistakes get stronger, remember—see CEMENTING➲64)

The ultimate reward

Of course, fire drills are not designed to be a **substitute** for learning the piece properly. You should be PRESSURE TESTING➲249 your pieces thoroughly long before performance, so that you're not expecting trouble in the first place.

But the real benefit of having run fire drills is not that you'll be able to cope with mistakes on the day—*it's that you **won't** be as **afraid** of mistakes happening.*

And because you're feeling less anxious, you'll be **less likely** to make mistakes in the first place.

So the very act of practicing fire drills hugely increases the chances that you'll **never need** to use them...

Fitness Training
Behind-the-scenes practice to help **all** your pieces

Casey has a **special** sort of preparation that she does—in addition to her regular practice.

None of it is on her teacher's *Please Cover This Week* list, but it's helping Casey to **play better**, practice **less**, and learn pieces **faster** than most other students.

What's her secret? What is this special training that she does? And how can you **do it too?**...

IF YOU WERE a **professional athlete**, your training would consist of **much more** than just practicing the **elements** of your game.

You would expect a soccer player to run plenty of drills on passing, dribbling, shooting, tackling, heading and taking penalty kicks. These are the **elements** that are on show in each game, and any football player obviously need to have **first rate skills** for these areas.

However, what's *not* so obvious is some of the **other work** that the fans in the stadium **never** directly get to see.

This training happens behinds closed doors, and most of it wouldn't seem to resemble soccer.

There's work on flexibility, endurance, sprint training, strength and conditioning. They'll work on their nutrition, their sleep habits, and their mental preparation. They'll study tactics, create strategies, scrutinize opposing teams and players, and review past performances of their own.

The fans will never know. But the *player* will, and it will have a positive impact on every game they play.

The invisible advantage

All of this behind the scenes work is part of the soccer player's "fitness"—a term that goes well beyond how puffed they get if they're running to catch a bus. The soccer players never get a chance to **directly show** all this work—it's not like they're going to have to **run** five laps of the field and then **drop for 30** pushups as part of Saturday's big match.

But the **entire regimen** means they come into each game as a fully prepared and well-rounded player—difficult to wear out or injure, smart about how they handle their opposition, and with their bodies in the best possible shape for peak performance.

None of this **happens by accident**. In fact, most professional teams have members of the coaching staff **dedicated specifically** to this behind-the-scenes training.

It's that important.

Fitness training for musicians

What's this got to do with music? When you're practicing, it's **tempting** to spend all your time on the "visible" items. The pieces for your recital. The passage your teacher asked you to polish.

That's a **bit like** the soccer player only working on kicking and passing. Just as there is essential behind-the-scenes training for the soccer player, **musicians** have their **own fitness** work they need to do too.

This fitness work won't **directly** get you ready for next lesson or recital. In fact, you won't ever get a chance to show this training to an audience.

But increasing your **musical fitness levels** will have a huge impact on your playing—and perhaps most importantly, on your practicing too. Let's take a look at **three** of the most common fitness training elements you'll face, and just why they're so important.

1. Scales and technical work

You'll never see "D Major Scale" scheduled as the **opening item** in your recital. But your scales fitness work will have had an **enormous impact** on whatever piece you actually *do* play—from the time you first read through the piece, to the performance itself.

Scales and technical work are an example of **prepractice**—developing skills now that you can call on in pieces later. So how does all that prepractice help?

Learn new pieces faster

If you already know D Major scale, the fact that your piece is *also* in D Major means that you have a **huge head start** when you are learning it. You will be **expecting** particular notes and particular fingerings, and you will

be **right most of the time**—saving you plenty of reading time.

What if you were that comfortable with **every key**? You'd have a head start for **every tonal piece** you ever play.

Instant expertise at scale-based passages

Those big runs at the beginning and the end of your piece? No need to practice those if they're in D Major—you had done the practice **in advance** by becoming good at the scale behind the scenes.

Which means that the runs can sound great on concert day, *even though you may have spent almost no time working on them directly.*

More precise and powerful passage work

Of course, not everything in your pieces is going to appear as a **straight scale**. There might be a tricky run on page 3 that doesn't *directly* quote a scale you've worked on, but the time you had spent on scales in general meant that your "chops" are in good shape.

End result? You would have been able to master that passage with **much less practice** than somebody who didn't have the scales background—again, because the scales work you did a year ago ended up being **prepractice** for the piece you're doing now.

Help with memory lapses

That **horrible moment** at the end of your performance—when you couldn't remember whether the C's in the final run were sharp or not—was saved by the fact that you knew the whole run was based on a D Major scale.

So you thought of that single fact, and just let the passage happen. The C#s would tumble out automatically, because they were always there in your scales work too.

The more figurations your fitness training includes, the better

Part of the aim of scales work is so you can look at a brand new passage and say "I've done that before". Or at least something very like it.

Obviously then the greater the variety of figurations you've covered in your scales fitness work, the more often you're going to be able to say "I've done that before" when you tackle new pieces.

For that reason, you don't want to **limit** your scales practice to always delivering the same scales in the same way. Start on different notes, with different rhythms, at different speeds. Work on broken chords and arpeggios as well as scales. And **factor in** sudden direction changes, so that your scales are not always just up or down.

All this variety will help **mirror** what you're likely to encounter in reality. For more information, check out the chapter on DESIGNER SCALES ⟩106.

Scales Bootcamp
skālz bŏŏtkamp, *noun*

The fastest, clearest way to get to know your scales, and then master them.

Philip Johnston

If you're a pianist and want to *permanently* get on top of your scales, then you can quickly and ruthlessly beat them into submission with *Scales Bootcamp*.

The guarantee is that if you complete all the listed Achievements for any scale, you'll *never* need to practice that scale again (!)

You can take a tour of the book and see how it all works at:
www.insidemusicteaching.com

2. Sightreading

Scales aside for a moment, every piece you ever learn to play will be **new** at some stage. When your piece is a newborn like this, **how fast** things progress is **limited** by how well you **read**.

For this reason, good sightreading is not just a party trick. It's a **discount voucher**, that promises big savings of your most precious asset: *Time*. In fact, it can enable you not just to minimize, but to **eliminate** the figuring-out-how-to-play-this stage of practice, allowing you to **concentrate straight away** on actually polishing your performance.

So while other students are still **busy slogging** through new notes, you'll already be speeding the piece up, injecting dynamics and adding your own performance stamp.

3. Theory

Theory is **not** just about filling in **worksheets** and **causing yourself pain**. Similar to solid scales, a good understanding of theory will allow you to make assumptions about what's coming up in scores you've never met—and be *right*. It's nothing short of a Learning New Piece Accelerator.

So if I'm learning the first movement of a classical Sonata, I know that the centre section is likely to be built from **short snippets** of the opening theme, running through a bunch of different keys.

Why? *Because I know what a development section is.* I know when in the piece it's likely to appear, how long it's likely to last and how busy things are going to get—even though I've never played or heard the piece before. All I really need is confirmation that it's a sonata, and the name of the composer. My theory knowledge will usually **do the rest**.

But there's more. Not only can theory help you solidify pieces you already know, it will allow you to **neatly describe** what's already in your piece, making it much easier to **remember** otherwise complicated passages.

So instead of a passage just being masses of flats that you have to

wade through, a little theory knowledge can go a long way:

Ah! 1st inversion Gb Major broken chord—then same again in the relative minor.

You won't have to read those notes after that. Nor will you have to remember them. Armed with that description, you could **re-create** the entire passage.

Don't wait to be asked

The students who are the most musically "fit" are not always those with the **most demanding teachers**. It's those students who demand the most of **themselves**.

Because you won't always be asked to **show** these fitness elements in lessons, you won't get extra credit for working on them. As a result, it can be very tempting *not* to work on them at all—after all, who will know? *You'll* know. Music fitness is prepractice for thousands of pieces you haven't even met yet, and it will help **lift** your playing to heights that regular practice alone could never reach. You'll also be

able to **learn new pieces** much **faster** than you ever thought possible.

In short, if you do the training, you'll be armed with the equivalent of brand new **musical super-powers**.

Still not convinced? If nothing else, remember this:

*Fitness Training a ticket to **less** practice.* Every minute you spend now on music fitness training will save you an hour in the future.

I'm sure you'll think of good things to do with all that time you save.

If you want to get moving on your fitness training, there are plenty of theory and aural drills online at **www. insidemusicteaching.com**

They're **randomly generated**, so they're never the same twice, and **self marking**, so you can see where you went wrong. (Or admire how clever you are)

Fresh Photocopies

Creating your own custom scores, tailored for practicing

Simone's score has reached the point where there are **more pencil markings** than **notes**. There are circles and reminders, and then reminders *with* circles around them...

She's tempted to get out an **eraser**, but is worried about losing months of feedback.

Then suddenly she realizes. "I've been **such a dope**" she thinks. "There's a much **easier way** to handle all this"

What was her **new plan**?

R EMINDERS, NOTES and **markings** are inevitable additions to any score, but **managing** them can easily get out of hand.

The **traditional method** is to dump everything on the single copy that you own. So from day one, every correction, suggestion, overlooked dynamic, tempo marking and segment division will all be written on the same document.

While this **sounds efficient**—after all, every note that has ever been made about this piece is all in one place—it actually causes plenty of problems.

Why single scores don't work
It may well be that there are a **hundred different things** that you need to remember in your piece, but having them all **yelling at you** at the same time is not the way to notice them all.

If all your notes are going on a single copy of the score, that score is going to become **horribly cluttered** with reminders. Open any page of a piece you've been working on for

a few months, and you'll see what I mean.

COLOR CODING➲84 is one way to relieve some of this, but even that is going to be limited by the score's scarcest resource—*space*.

The problems don't just stop at clutter though.

Old news
All of those markings may have been relevant at **some stage**, but that doesn't mean that they're still relevant *now*.

For example, a circle around a key signature change, with a note saying "Bb Major!" may well have been

useful in the **first week** you had this piece, but is just **deadweight** information the day before you actually perform the piece. (I'm assuming that by then, the key signature change will be well and truly known to you!)

As a result, not only does your score become cluttered, *it becomes cluttered with information that has a **use-by** date.* Unfortunately, the markings themselves **don't magically disappear** on that date. (Yes, you can erase them...but do you?...)

So making all your marks on the same score creates both clutter and a backlog of out-of-date information. Sounds bad enough. But there's worse to come.

One marking, one vote

With a **single glance** at your cluttered everything-is-circled score, if there is a reminder on page 2, and then another on page 3, *they'll appear to be equally important.* They're both circles. One marking, one vote.

That doesn't always reflect reality though. It may be that the reminder on page 3 is **critical** to all future practice on this piece, while the marking on page 2 was merely a **possibility to try**. However, since they're both clothed exactly the same way—pencil markings on your score—there's nothing that immediately tells you one is more important than the other.

As a result, of the hundred markings on your score, the **Essential** and the **Probably-Can-Forget-This** dine at the same table—along with, as we saw above, the **Not-Relevant-Any-More**—and they're very hard to tell apart.

The end result is that while your score will be covered with advice and information, all you'll see is "blah blah blah". Doodles, scribbles and concentric ellipses that you'll quickly learn not to notice.

The solution...

...is surprisingly simple. Instead of trying to cram every note ever made into the same score, you're going to **distribute** all these notes through **lots of copies** of that score.

That gives you the opportunity not only to have fewer markings on each score, but to **group** markings according to type.

To prepare the way for all this, whenever you get a new piece, the very first thing you should do is make yourself a **stack of photocopies** of that piece. Not to pirate the piece, but so you now have a dozen or so **fresh working copies**.

You then keep those copies handy when you're practicing, and will **choose** your copy based on the type of work you're about to do.

This now enables a small but very **powerful change**:

Writing notes on one copy will still leave the other copies clear.

So no matter how much you write on copy#4, it won't make the tiniest bit of difference to copy #7.

As we'll see, that's going to open up a huge range of new possibilities in your practice room.

Uses for Fresh Photocopies

So apart from helping to minimize clutter on the page, what are these photocopies *for*? Try these ideas for starters:

Notelearning Copy

This is the copy you would use for your **initial work** with a new piece.

Anything you discover as part of SCOUTING➲299 you'll mark on here, together with anything that will help you learn the piece faster (such as actually **writing in** the letter names of multi-ledger-line notes, or the **counting** under any complicated rhythms)

This is also where your **teacher** will mark any wrong notes, fingering errors, clef changes—the "oops, you missed this" mistakes that are typical of the early stages of a new piece.

Why would you want a special photocopy for this? *Because most of this information will only be relevant when you're first learning the piece.*

That's ok—none of your other photocopied scores will feature these particular reminders. As a result, you can feel free to make as many notes as you need.

Planning copy

You'll use this copy to help you plan out your practice for the week.

You're not writing reminders of any sort on here, or corrections—instead, you're labelling **what** you intend to cover, and on **which day**

No matter how much you write on copy#4, it won't make the tiniest bit of difference to copy #7.

As we'll see, that's going to open up a huge range of new possibilities in your practice room.

of the week you'll be covering it. That way, instead of having your plan in a separate notebook, you can actually have it right there on the music that you'll be working from.

So, after reading your practice instructions for the week, you might label the opening 12 measures as being for **Monday**, and write "Memorize" above them.

Tuesday might be marked above the development section, and the instruction might be "Double check accidentals". Tuesday might also be marked above the final page, with the instructions "Bring

up to 120 BPM" and "Detail trawl" (See Details Trawl➲110)

You'll do the same for the other days of the week, taking care to match all of this to the outcomes your teacher needed from the week.

In this way you end up with a **clear blueprint** for the week ahead—you keep it handy to help you answer the question "what did I have to get done today?" (See Session Agenda➲305)

Of course, the instant the week is over, the plan **becomes obsolete.** But that's ok—the beauty of using copies is that you can use another fresh copy for the *next* week.

Issues from Last Lesson copy

Corrections and notes from your most recent lesson are *always* going to be current and relevant—it makes sense to have them all in **one place**, readily **accessible** and **quarantined** from your other notes.

Instead of allowing such notes to **get lost** amongst months of old notes on your one-and-only-score, bring a fresh photocopy to each lesson, and as your teacher makes points, *mark them on the score.*

The score then acts as a highlights reel of that lesson, making it much easier to conduct a LESSON REVIEW➲178.

This photocopy is **reusable**. Next lesson, you would erase any points that are no longer issues (because you had fixed them), while any that are still lingering will still be part of *next* week's list.

Interpretation copy

This is quite unlike any of the photocopy scores so far, and acts more as film-director's notes. Instead of being concerned with what to play, it's where you sort out *how* to play.

You're not writing corrections of any sort on here, but instead **recording ideas** for **interpreting** the piece.

You'll mark in dynamics, rubato or articulation details that you are considering—and then, after you've run EXPERIMENTS➲135 to find out whether they'll work, you'll either **erase** that idea, or mark it in **ink**.

This copy is all about helping you answer the question "I wonder what

if...", and then being able to record the results of such wondering.

Over time, it will become a comprehensive description of exactly **how** you plan to deliver the piece—the end result of hours of trying different possibilities, and then noting what worked and what didn't.

Alternative version Copy

Sometimes choosing between different interpretation possibilities can be agony—especially if you like all of them.

In such cases, you can use fresh photocopies to create **several different** interpretation takes on the same piece—similar to a director filming several different endings to a movie.

These directors will sometimes choose between those endings by **screen-testing** them with focus groups. You can choose between *your* different versions by bringing the interpretation copies with you to your lesson—your teacher can take it from there.

Acceleration Copy

This copy won't help you at all with interpretation, but it can help you track progress in the development of another important skill.

You'll often have practice campaigns based around **speeding up** passages—you would use this copy of the score to record the results of techniques such as METRONOME METHOD⊃195

Typically, this type of fresh copy will be **covered with numbers**, reflecting the tempo each section is currently up to—a bit like a **scoreboard** that shows your progress towards getting the piece up to speed.

Keep it handy, get it out whenever speeding up is one of your Tasks For The Day.

"Ready" list Copy

You **don't have time** to practice everything all the time—as you work it's going to be important to start building a list of sections that **don't need** further practice. (See CLOSURE⊃80)

This copy allows you to mark what will be a **growing collection** of passages that no longer need attention from you, and it's a great feeling whenever you are able to add something to this score. It's almost as if the passage you are marking has "graduated"—the simplest way is usually to highlight the passage in green.

The aim is that by **concert day**, the **entire piece** would be highlighted like this. It's then a great way to get a snapshot of the health of a piece—if most of it is already marked on you "Ready" list score, then it's in great shape.

Stripped Copy

This is a **special photocopy** of the score that has had all the dynamics, articulations, tempo markings and other details **removed**. You can do this by using whiteout on a copy, and then photocopying that copy—the whiteout shouldn't be visible.

This copy is a great way to **test your knowledge** of the details in the score. Your job would be to **write in** as many as you can from memory—or, armed with a list of all the details, place them in the correct locations. See DETAILS TRAWL⊃110 for more on this.

Lesson Agenda Copy

During the practice week, you'll come up with questions and issues that you'll want to **take up with your teacher** at the next lesson. (See LESSON AGENDA⊃171). Instead of adding such notes to an already cluttered score, you can **reserve** one of your photocopies to help you remember all these things—whenever a question occurs to you during the week, simply mark it on the score.

You can then take the score with you to the lesson.

Like the *Issues from Last Lesson*, this is a photocopy that you can **reuse**—simply erase the notes at the lesson as you cover them with your teacher.

Anything that was not erased, you can cover next lesson. (You won't always get through everything... your teacher has their own agenda to get through too.)

Thematic Copy

Intended for use with Thematic Practice➲330, any markings you make on this score will be confined to addressing a **single issue.**

So you'd have one score dedicated to dynamics, another to legato playing, another to projection and so on. Keep them **in a file,** and then every time you were focusing on a particular theme, you would use the score dedicated to that theme.

If you were working on rubato, for example, then you'd get out your rubato photocopy—on there would be all the notes you had ever made about rubato, and space to record results from today's work on that issue.

Restoration Copy

If you're **returning to an old piece** after an extended absence, it can be hard to break the old habits (see Restoration➲289).

One way to help things feel fresh is to ensure that you're not working with the **Same Old Copy** with all the **Same Old Pencil Markings** that you used to use. You'll quickly end up playing it the **Same Old Way.**

Work instead with a fresh copy, stripped of all previous reminders. It forces you to work out things like fingerings and dynamics from scratch—since you're now older and wiser than last time you played this, you should come up with better solutions.

A copy for every occasion

Unless you want to look like the picture below, you're probably not going to use **all** these ideas every time you practice.

But even having just a couple of fresh photocopies in the loop can help you **focus** your practice — which is really the point.

Choose the issues that are most important, and then create copies for the practice techniques that will target those issues. So if you're speeding up a piece, then it makes sense to have a copy for Metronome Method. If you need to run a details trawl, make sure you have a Stripped Copy.

Like this **whole Practiceopedia,** use what's useful, ignore what's not.

Horizontal vs Vertical

Knowing when to change your practice direction

Bianca has just **changed teachers,** and she's very confused.

Her **old** teacher told her to tackle her pieces **one section at a time,** and only ever to focus on a few measures at once.

But her **new** teacher wants her to treat each **piece as a whole,** telling her that practicing in segments creates a segmented performance.

How can **two trained musicians** have such different ideas? **Who** is right? And **how** can you **tell?**

FORGET ABOUT THE battle between Coke and Pepsi. Or Macintosh and PC. There's a much **bigger showdown,** between two traditional approaches to **practicing**, and it's raging in millions of music studios across the world.

Here's the question that's **causing all the fuss:**

*When you're working on a piece, should you work on **one segment** until it's concert ready before **starting the next**...or should you gradually polish the **piece as a whole**?*

So if your piece is in four sections, and you could **measure progress** in degrees of readiness ranging from A (Concert ready!) through to E (Absolutely no idea), would you:

• **work on section 1** until it was worthy of an "A"...

...and then **work on section 2** until *it* was worthy of an "A"...and so on

OR

• Take the piece as a whole **from an "E" up to a "D"**...

...and then from a "D" to a "C"... and so on.

Two completely different ways of working, each with their own champions and critics.

But which is better?

Before we open the envelope, let's take a closer look at both nominees.

Labelling the contenders

The rest of this chapter will refer to the first technique as being **"Vertical"**, because it picks on a narrow part of the piece, and then works **in depth**. It's almost as if it **sinks a mineshaft** into the segment, trying to extract as much as it possibly can.

Once that shaft has mined everything there, you'd sink **another** mineshaft in a different segment.

The second technique is **"horizontal"**, because your work is spread widely across the whole piece. So instead of sinking a mineshaft, you'd use a bulldozer to **shave 50 centimeters** from the entire landscape.

You'd collect any diamonds that were uncovered, then you'd shave another 50 centimeters on your **second pass**...and so on. It's not as deep as using mineshafts, but it covers a much wider area.

Practicing *vertically*

To practice this way, the first thing you'd do is divide your piece into segments—in effect, you're marking out where the mineshafts will be.

So you might have one for the **opening eight measures**. Then another segment that takes you **up to the repeat**. Then another that goes as far as the **key signature change**...and so on until you're creating a segment for the coda at the end of the piece.

Doesn't have to be in order

You will be working on these segments one at a time, but there's **no rule** that says you have to start with the *first* segment (see SHOOTING THE MOVIE➲315).

The point is that whichever segment you start with, you **don't move on** from that segment until it's in **good shape**.

Advantages to working this way

• **Rapid improvement:** Because you're working on such a small section, you'll notice it getting better quickly.

• **Maximum reps in minimum time:** With the end of the segment only being 10 seconds away from the beginning, when you're

CEMENTING➲64, you can repeat the passage 30 times in only 5 minutes.

• **Wide coverage of issues in single practice sessions:** If you're working with THEMATIC PRACTICE➲330, you'll be able to get through a lot of different issues in a short time—because the passage you're polishing doesn't take long to play.

And traps for the unwary...

• **Uneven coverage:** If you miscalculate your preparation, and find the concert upon you before you're ready, you'll have passages that are excellent side by side with passages that you've *never practiced at all*. Try covering *that* up on stage.

• **Lack of unity:** With all your focus having been in segments, sometimes the piece can *sound like lots of segments*—instead of a single entity.

• **Bottlenecks:** Because you don't move on to another segment until the current segment is polished, *if you get stuck with a segment, everything stops*. All the other segments waiting in line will be looking at their watches and fretting about whether they'll *ever* have a turn.

Practicing *horizontally*

No segments this time. Instead, you'll be working on the **whole piece**, one issue at a time.

So you might start simply by **listening** to the whole piece, and following the score (see SCOUTING ↪299). Then you might set yourself the goal of being able to **tap the rhythm** of every part of the piece.

After that, you run a series of (very) **slow motion playthroughs** of the whole piece. On each pass, you'll find that you remember things from the previous playthrough, and your playing will grow more confident.

It doesn't mean no-stops

If you're tapping the rhythm of the entire piece, and you have trouble on page 3, it's not as if you have to **skate straight past** the problem because you're "working horizontally". You would still **stop** and work on that section until you could tap the rhythm.

But then you'd move on—and that's the key difference between this approach, and working vertically. If you were **working vertically**, having fixed the rhythm in that passage, **you'd fix something else** in that same passage. In fact, you'd continue to fix things in that passage until there was **nothing left to fix**.

Working **horizontally**, once you've taken care of the issue-of-the-moment in that passage, you **move straight on** to the next passage.

Advantages to working this way

• **"Big Picture" view** : Right from your very first practice session, you'll be forming impressions about the *whole* piece, not just the segment-of-the-day.

• **Even coverage:** On concert day, there's no risk of having uncharted territory in your piece. Why? Because from day one, you've been practicing the whole piece every time.

• **Easier to plan:** Because you meet the whole piece straight away, you'll also know straight away about passages that are potential problems. As a result, you can start factoring them into your work immediately, rather than being ambushed by them three months into the campaign.

• **No bottlenecks:** You don't need to wait until section 3 is perfect before you tackle section 4. Every part of your piece is not only accessible immediately, but is always on your agenda.

And horizontal traps...

• **"Harbour Bridge" syndrome** The Sydney Harbour bridge is constantly being painted—the reason is that there's so much to cover, that by the time you get to the end, the beginning needs painting again.

Particularly if your piece is enormous, working horizontally can sometimes mean that by the time you get to the end of the piece, *you can't remember all the issues you sorted out at the beginning.*

Which means you have to practice them all over again.

• Insufficient reinforcement
The temptation when working horizontally is always to keep moving forwards, never lingering on a passage for too long. This can mean that improvements can be merely **temporary**—there was never enough repetition to truly CEMENT➲64 them.

This isn't a flaw in the idea of working horizontally, so much as it is in how people *execute* that idea. Remember, you're allowed to stop and cement an improvement whenever you like.

• Feeling of less rapid improvement. When you work horizontally, you're *spreading the work for any given passage over the entire campaign*—which means that it can take the entire campaign to get that passage concertworthy.

In other words, don't expect dramatic improvements in a passage from one day to the next.

So if you're a person who needs to get from E to A+ as fast as possible, this is not the technique for you. Focus on single segments and work vertically instead.

And the winner?...
That's just the thing. As is so often the case with long running debates, there is no clear winner.

But that's not a license to choose whichever you like. *There are too many drawbacks to each to adopt either as your only solution.*

So what are you supposed to do?

Yins, Yangs and examples
Instead of fighting over which approach is better, use them as a **team.**

That way, instead of having to **choose** between the strengths of the two sets, **you can have it all.** Rapid improvement AND even coverage. No bottlenecks AND many reps in a short time. Easier to plan AND wide issue coverage in a single practice session.

Because the **strengths** of working vertically are the **weaknesses** of working horizontally—and vice versa—the two techniques actually **dovetail** beautifully.

The trick is in knowing when to use each:

• If you were SCOUTING➲299 at the very **start** of a campaign, you would normally work **horizontally**—that way you get a comprehensive overview of the piece.

• If you encounter a **problem passage** at any stage, you'd usually work **vertically** as you tame it. Boot Camp➲43 and Clearing Obstacles➲72 are both **trouble-shooting techniques** that require the vertical practice philosophy of focus-on-one-passage.

• If instead you were seeking to **identify** problems, then a scanning technique like BugSpotting ➲53 would require you to **sweep horizontally** through the piece.

• If you've just been working vertically to solve a **tricky technical problem**, then it would make sense to go through the rest of this piece horizontally to find all other instances of this type of passage. Not only does provide a logical flow to related passages, it will also **reinforce** the work you've just done.

• If you have a **performance looming**, then you might run the ultimate in horizontal practice—a Dress Rehearsal ➲115. But when the time comes to **polish your opening** into something truly compelling, then that's going to be a vertical exercise. (See Openings and Endings ➲215)

> **Because the *strengths* of working vertically are the *weaknesses* of working horizontally—and vice versa—the two techniques actually dovetail beautifully.**

• If you **suspected** that your piece was gradually getting faster, then you would normally work horizontally as you play through the piece with the metronome.

• If you're making use of One Way Doors ➲208, then unless it's a *very* short piece, you'll be forced into working vertically

So this question of horizontal vs vertical practice is **not** one that you **resolve once**, and then apply to your work for all time. You have to ask yourself again afresh *every time you start a new practice session*—and the answer will vary, depending on the problems you're trying to address, and the practice techniques you're planning on using to solve them.

It's always frustrating to read "It depends" as the answer to a question...but for some questions, it really *does* depend.

But if you're prepared to embrace **both** horizontal and vertical practice—and be **smart** about when you use them both—you'll have a huge advantage over students who only use one.

Isolating

Stopping problems from interfering with each other

R oslyn's new piece is progressing **very slowly**. Three weeks of practice, and it's nowhere.

"I'll never learn this" she glooms. "If I'm not messing up the **notes**, or the **bowing**, then I'm making **rhythm mistakes**...there's just too much to cope with at once..."

"You know something" says her teacher "I think you've just revealed why there's a problem in the first place. **Replay** your last sentence, and **think** about what that says about your practice..."

What had he spotted? And how can she turn this around?

Y OU'VE PROBABLY never seen a DOM before. It stands for **Difficult-O-Meter**, and it's a gadget that somebody should build so that **every musician** can have one. (You can see a DOM in the picture on the right.)

What's a DOM for? It's the world's first **difficulty-rating** machine. Simply tell it the name of any activity—musical or otherwise—and the Difficult-O-Meter will accurately evaluate how difficult that activity is for you, assigning it a **score out of 10**.

"1" means easy. "10" would be for something that is **almost impossible**. Most activities will be somewhere in between.

This means that if you ever wanted to know whether it's harder to **sink a basket** from the free-throw line, or get a **tennis serve** in, just ask DOM. He'll tell you.

Or if you're wondering how hard it is to **water-ski**? Ask DOM. Or how tough it is to make an **origami pelican?** Ask DOM. He can't tell you *how* to make the pelican—and certainly can't make one himself —but he can confirm that it gets a

"4" for difficulty if you want to **try it yourself.** (An origami Sydney Opera House would be a "5".)

Ok, so far DOM is useful for **settling bets** and creating interesting trivia. But what makes DOM so **useful for musicians** though is what it will tell you when you start asking it about *combining* activities.

As we'll see, when you start asking it to rate the difficulty of doing **two things at once,** a whole new range of scores appears. And since playing a piece normally demands doing more than one thing at once, the **implications for practicing** are enormous.

When challenges combine

Let's imagine that you've just switched on DOM, and have asked it to give "*Hopping on one foot*" a difficulty rating. Hopping really isn't so tricky, so DOM comes back with a 2 out of 10.

Let's also imagine that you have asked it to rate "*writing your name*". DOM pauses for a moment while he accesses the information, and then gives a 1. Very easy.

But what about "writing your name WHILE hopping on one foot"?

Now that's a whole different thing. This **combined challenge** is definitely harder—but how much harder? Maybe it would be 2 (hopping) + 1 (writing your name) = 3?

Nope. Not even close.

DOM comes back with a 9.

If you think that score is a **little high**, get yourself a pencil and paper, and **try** the writing-while-hopping challenge for yourself. You'll quickly see that DOM knows its stuff.

This means something **very strange**

has happened:

The total difficulty is greater than the sum of its parts!

This doesn't just apply to hopping and writing your name. This idea is a **key concept** in your practicing—and it's a common cause of all manner of practice disasters. Let's take a closer look at some of the **skidmarks** that lead to the wrecks...

...When pairings collide

Whenever you're practicing, you'll have a long list of elements you're trying to get right:

- Correct notes
- Rhythms
- Dynamics
- Phrasing
- Articulation
- Posture
- Tempo Control
- Choice of tempo
- Rubato
- Legato
- Projection
- Fingering/bowing/tonguing
- Pedalling (for pianists)
- Intonation
- Tone quality

...all worthwhile elements, and there are many, many more.

You could **ask DOM** about any one of those items, and the rating is probably not going to be too bad.

But here's the thing. Some pairs of elements on this list **shouldn't be worked on simultaneously**—particularly in the early stages of a CAMPAIGN ➲58—*because they interfere with each other.* Just like hopping and writing shouldn't be paired up, because the two tasks combine badly.

The end result of such bad combinations is **practice** that produces **no progress.** Let's take a look at some **classic examples...**

...*new notes AND new rhythms...*

Part of dealing with a brand new piece is to work out the **correct notes,** as is sorting out what's going on with the **rhythm.** If you asked DOM about your plans, it might give the following ratings:

"work out the correct notes"	2
"work out the correct rhythm"	3

Nothing too scary about that.

But if instead you had asked about working out the correct notes **and** the correct rhythm *at the same time*—**combining** the two challenges—the DOM rating would be **off the charts.**

Why? Because the **needs** of the two challenges **collide** head-on.

Unless your sightreading is in great shape, reading notes in a new piece requires **flexibility** with time. There's nothing unreasonable about that—this time flexibility is there so that you can **slow down** or **stop** while you double-check tricky ledger lines or accidentals. In short, it's so you **don't play nonsense**.

However, if you're insisting on the **rhythm** being right too, *then you won't have that flexibility*. Getting the rhythm right means that you will have to deliver your notes **on** time, **every** time, **ready or not**...

...and sometimes, you just **won't** be ready.

When that happens, you've got two choices, and neither option is good:

Bad option 1) Play your **best guess** when the note falls due—*and live with the fact that some of these notes will be fiction.*

Bad option 2) Take the **time** you need to guarantee correct notes—*which will distort the rhythm.*

Either way, because the way the demands of the two challenges collide, you'll only be getting one element correct at best. **Unfortunately though**, students who start new pieces with this particular pair of elements often end up getting **neither** right.

...making repairs AND full tempo...

If you're a violinist practicing an etude, there will be a point in the piece's development when you'll be considering taking the work **up to tempo** for the first time.

There might also be a point at which you might need to be practicing in some significant **bowing changes** from a recent lesson.

Again, as **separate challenges**, these are both manageable. But if you try both these things at the same time, then something *has* to give. Full tempo makes it **impossible** for you to give the new bowing the consideration it needs, which usually means reverting back to what you had been doing anyway. (See SPEEDING ⟩320)

The **flip side** is no better—**slowing** to accommodate the demands of the new bowing will make playing at full speed impossible.

End result? The collision between the two incompatible tasks **cripples both tasks**, meaning that despite practicing, *you'll turn up to next lesson with the same problems in place as the lesson before.*

...or for pianists...

Perhaps the clearest way to see this syndrome in action is the classic trap of the piano student trying to play an unfamiliar piece **two hands together** straight away.

The DOM rating for each hand individually might only be 3 out of 10, but *combined* the score can be high enough to fry DOM's circuits faster than you can say "why won't this bit get any better?"

So when a piano teacher is **begging** for separate hands, it's not because they **enjoy the sound** of only half the piece at a time. They're trying to **save** you—and the piece—from overload.

...and countless others

Whenever you have two tasks where the demands of one **compromise** your ability to cope with the other, then you've got a **collision** in progress.

When it does happen though—and it will—there's only one question you need to ask:

What are you going to do about it?

Avoiding collisions

Collisions through bad pairings are a constant danger in the **early stages** of any campaign, but remember—*it takes two to collide.*

So to avoid collisions, wherever possible, you should be working on **one element at a time.**

Because musical elements tend to be **intertwined** though, separating them like this is not going to happen automatically—it requires a special sort of practice.

The technique is known as **"Isolation"**, and allows you to master individual skills without them being corrupted by other elements competing for your attention.

It starts by **asking yourself** "what exactly is it that I'm trying to fix here?", and then **rearranging** your practice so that you're fixing that... *and only that.*

So it's not about what you do practice. It's about what you *don't*.

Let's take a look at a few examples:

Isolating Rhythm

If you have a brand new piece, and you need to work out the rhythm, then that has to be your focus—*to work out the rhythm.* To then ensure that this task is then not colliding with tasks such as "trying to figure out notes", *don't even play notes....*

...just **tap** the rhythm. You don't

even need your instrument. That way, there is nothing else **competing** for your attention or **making demands** that compromise your rhythm delivery. It's just you and the raw rhythm, isolated, and played in it's most basic form.

Because the practice is then so focused, you'll quickly be able to tick off this rhythm as having been dealt with, and move on to something else.

Isolating notereading:

Similarly, if you have a **sequence of notes** you are unsure of, then it's **madness** to try to figure out that sequence with the rhythm and tempo intact too.

Instead, you would **isolate** the notes, by simply playing them through in order, *taking as much time as you need for each one.* It's much like a **dancer** walking slowly through the steps of something new—they don't try to put it in time to music, or make the movements at full speed until they are completely clear on the **sequence** of movements.

This doesn't mean rhythm and tempo are suddenly not important—it just means that you're fighting **one fire at a time**.

Isolating dynamics

At first glance, this seems tough to isolate. After all, how can you rehearse dynamics **without** actually playing the notes and rhythms in the piece?

It's not as hard as you might think though. The point of the session is not necessarily to *play* the dynamics—it's to **become clear** on which dynamics belong to which part of the piece.

As a result, you can easily isolate this element by **conducting** the score. Put your instrument away,

> # It starts by asking "what exactly is it that I'm trying to fix here?", and then rearranging your practice so that you're fixing that...and *only* that.

stand in front of a copy of the music, and start waving your arms as you read through the music, and hear the piece in your head. The bigger the dynamics, the bigger your gestures.

So a **pianissimo** passage would have you barely moving. The **crescendo** that follows would see you increasing the size of your movements, while a **sforzando** would produce a sudden big arm jolt.

In this way, you can run complete **dynamics-only** practice sessions.

You're going to have to respond appropriately to every dynamic marking that appears in the score. But because you're not actually **playing** anything though, *there's*

nothing else to focus on apart from the issue at hand. It's just you and the dynamics.

Half a dozen conducting sweeps through the piece like this, and you'll have completely transformed your knowledge of what the score asks for—even though you haven't played a single note. (See also DETAILS TRAWL➲110)

Isolating rubato

Rubato is another element that gets **sabotaged** when combined too early with other elements.

Your **intention** might be to gently push a passage forwards, but uncertainty about fingering (for example) will ensure that the whole passage **hesitates** instead. So those intentions might have been good, but your lack of mastery over key elements in the music makes it **impossible to deliver** on those plans.

Like the dynamics check though, you **don't need** to be playing anything to rehearse the ebb and flow of tempo in your piece. Simply conduct the score again, as you listen to the piece in your own head. But as you do so, *use your conducting to clearly indicate all planned variations in tempo.*

That way you have **separated** your rubato rehearsal from the mechanics of actually delivering the piece—so if there are still unresolved problems with delivery, it won't get in the way.

Recombining

Although isolation is an important practice technique, you can't work this way **all the time**. After all, on concert day you obviously have to be able to handle ALL those elements simultaneously.

Unfortunately though, you can't change the fact that the **combined** DOM rating of **colliding skills** will always be higher than the sum of the **separate skills**.

But if you take the time to ensure that each of the skills have been **isolated**, and therefore **mastered separately**, something unexpected happens.

They no longer collide when combined.

Think about the first example for a moment. Delivering the rhythm correctly collided with working out notes, because you had to **pause** to work out notes. You needed **flexibility** in time that delivering the rhythm correctly wouldn't allow.

But once you **know** the notes, *there's no need for this extra time.* You'll be able to find them without having to stop and think—which means that it's now **fully compatible** with delivering the rhythm too.

What you've effectively done is **reduce** the DOM rating of each separate skill **so much** that even the **inflated** combined rating is **manageable**. So instead of two ratings of a 4 producing an impossible 15, you've now got two ratings of a 1 producing a 5...

...it's still more than the sum of its parts. It always will be. But it's now a number you can **work with**.

Perfect matches

Not all pairs collide like this—in fact, some issues are **easier** when combined.

For example, if you're a pianist, learning the fingering along with the notes will help you learn the notes **much faster**, because you'll be able to call on **muscle memory**. You'll be able to "feel" which note comes next, as well as being able to see it.

And—despite the warnings in this chapter—some students actually report the same thing when handling rhythms and learning notes at the same time. Somehow the rhythm ends up being "attached" to the notes, and helps them retain new notes more easily.

The point is not to label particular pairs as **always** being "bad" or "good"—it's to be alert to the possibility that both types of pairs exist, and to make use of isolation when you need it.

As with every other technique in this book, isolation is a **tool**. Pull it out when it's needed, keep it on the shelf when it's not...but always keep it handy.

Lesson Agenda

Setting aside issues to raise at your next lesson

The part of each lesson that Luke **hates most** is when his teacher asks if there's anything he needs **help** with.

No matter what he says, he always thinks of things **afterwards** that he *wishes* he had said.

"It's a very easy problem to fix" says his teacher "But it's not something you can fix at the lesson. You have to fix it in the **practice room**."

What? Surely it's a lesson thing? What was the teacher's **plan?**...

Music lessons are *supposed* to be a **team effort**. Your teacher gives you advice and feedback at the lesson. You go home and prepare **between** lessons, knowing that if you have any trouble, you can always **ask for help** at your *next* lesson.

But here's the problem: *students don't always ask for help.* Sometimes because they **don't want to,** but usually because they **forget**. With up to six days between an at-home practice problem and the next lesson, it's no wonder.

It doesn't have to be this way though. Just as you would for shopping list items, or important phone numbers, if you *really* need to remember something, there's **only one way** to handle it...

...you have to write it down. Not sometimes—**every** time. Which is why you should never practice without having your **lesson agenda** nearby.

Creating your lesson agenda

You don't need to **wait** until there is a mid-piece **calamity** to add to this "please help!" list. Whenever you

encounter something you need help with—a **weird symbol** in the music, a passage you **can't play**, a rhythm you **can't work out**—*make a note*. It's not enough just to say to yourself "I should remember to ask about that next lesson"...because you might *not* remember.

You then **bring these notes** to your lesson, and go through them with your teacher one by one.

In this way, things that **bug you** at home don't just stay at home. They become part of the **lesson agenda,** so you can get the help you need.

Using a reverse notebook

One possibility is to **set up a book** like the one your teacher writes in each week—except that instead of your teacher writing notes for you, you're writing notes for *them*.

You'd **write the date** for the week at the top of a blank page, and then any notes for the lesson agenda would go **underneath**.

Because these notes are all going in the **same place,** as long as you don't lose your book, your notes will be safe too. Keep it by your music stand, and then all you have to do is remember to **bring it** with you to **each lesson**.

Spike-file it

A **less formal** alternative to the reverse notebook is a **spike filer** (It's the same gadget that a lot of restaurants use to collect orders). Just jot down the note or question you had on a scrap of paper and slap it on the spike filer once you're done.

When lesson time comes, simply **bundle up** everything that's on the spike-filer and bring it all to your teacher's studio.

Sorting them by priority

It's important to make your agenda comprehensive, but your lessons are **quickly** going to become **impossible** if you turn up every time with 75 different agenda items that you expect your teacher to address. **Remember**, your teacher will have items of their own that they want to get through too.

As a result, you need to **accept** that it might not be possible to deal with every single problem that you recorded—which means that you want to start with the most pressing issues, not just those that you **happened to record first**.

You're going to need to use a variation of the TRIAGE➲342 technique to determine what the most critical issues are, but two indicators of high priority are:

- Issues with **multiple occurrences** during the week. If you were tripped up by the same ornament in five different practice sessions, then a discussion about ornamentation is needed next lesson.

- Issues that affect **broad sections** of the piece. Even if an issue seems unimportant, if it appears in three of the five pages in your piece, then it's time for intervention.

Before you lodge an item...

...ask yourself what advice your teacher is *likely* to give you. And then **try that out**.

Why? Because you **shouldn't be listing** items that are only problems because you haven't been prepared to **try** likely solutions yet.

So if you have a rhythm that you can't work out, and you can all but *hear* your teacher suggesting that you try **writing in the counting**—and you haven't done that yet—then **go do it**.

Even if that doesn't work, it's still worth trying to **fix things yourself.** A lot of agenda issues are only issues because you haven't practiced them the **right way** yet—before you dial 911, check this book for any techniques that perhaps might still help.

Typical agenda issues

- **Unfamiliar signs**, notes or terms
- Bowings/fingerings that just **don't make sense**
- A **rhythm** you can't work out
- A passage that, despite practice, is **not improving**
- Any sort of **pain or discomfort** when you're practicing
- A performance **idea** you're considering that is contrary to score indications
- Any passages that just **feel "flat"**, despite your best efforts
- Sections that you just **can't play in time** with the metronome
- Passages that **still sound "wrong"** even though you've double-checked notes and rhythms
- A marked fingering or bowing that you're **considering changing**
- Passages that you simply cannot get **up to speed.**

Lesson Preflight Check

Finding out if you're on track for next lesson

There are three days to go until Cameron's lesson, and he's **not even close** to being ready.

The problem though is that he has **no idea** this is the case. He'll find out he's not ready the same way he always does...with a **panic attack** on the day of his lesson.

It doesn't have to be this way. There's a **special practice session** he can run **once a week** that can rescue all of this...

IF YOU WAIT *until* your lesson to **find out** whether you're ready for your lesson, then that's usually a **sign** that you're *not* ready.

Why? Because a **big part** of being ready is not just **having** everything done...

...it's **knowing** that you have everything done.

It's being able to **confidently say** to your teacher:

"I know exactly what you needed me to do this week, and I've completed all of it."

Rather than simply

"I've done plenty of practice this week, I should be ok"

(If that second statement **sounds fine** to you, then you need tip a bucket of ice over your head, and then **read the chapter** on CLOCK WATCHERS ⟳76)

So **how will you know** that you're lesson ready?

The Preflight Checklist

Pilots don't just jump in the front seat of their Cessna, turn up the stereo and take off. They need to be 100% certain that everything is working as it should first.

Of course, there are **two ways** they could find out.

They *could* take off, and test things out in **mid-air.** (Not a good idea)

Or they can run right through a checklist **before** they go anywhere:

> Landing gear. *Check.*
> Flaps. *Check.*
> Onboard navigation. *Check.*
> Fuel. *Check.*
> Brakes. *Check.*

Which is exactly what *does* happen. And there will also have been a whole lot of **other tests** run by mechanics long before the pilot even got in the plane.

The end result? As the wheels leave the tarmac, the pilot can **confidently say:**

> *"Everything's ready"*

Don't find out in mid air

You'll certainly find out **at your lesson** whether you had completed all your practice tasks or not. In fact, your teacher will normally dedicate the first few minutes of your lesson to **checking exactly that.**

But that's a bit like finding out in **mid-air** whether your plane is ready:

> Landing Gear. *Check.*
> Flaps. *Check.*
> Onboard navigation. *Check.*
> Fuel. *Empty.*
> Brakes. *Check.*

Whoa! What was **item four** again? What would be so frustrating here is that fuel would have been a **very easy** thing to fix...if only you'd

noticed it before you took off. Not so easy at 20,000 feet.

That's exactly how **uncompleted practice items** work too. Most tasks that you had left undone you probably could have easily covered with a small amount of practice...if only you'd known.

Timing is everything

We'll have a look at **how** to run your Preflight Check in a second, but a more important question is working out **when** it should take place.

It needs to be **late enough** in your practice week that you've had a chance to actually complete your practice tasks—however, it needs to **leave enough time** before your lesson that you can still catch up on any tasks that you discover aren't ready.

It's no good running a Preflight Check **twenty minutes** before your lesson. (Sure, it's *technically* "preflight", but it's a bit like running a check while you're hurtling down the runway)

Similarly, a Preflight Check after only **one day** of practice will usually

just confirm that you've still got lots left to do. (C'mon! It's only 24 hours into your practice week—of *course* there's still lots left to do!)

Normally I recommend a preflight check on the **fifth day** of your practice week. By then, you should be just about finished all your practice tasks—but if the Preflight Check **goes badly**, then you still have **time** to make good.

Essential equipment

It might be **more complicated** for real pilots, but there's really only one thing you'll need for your Preflight Check:

A comprehensive list of everything your teacher needed you to get done this week.

You're then going to **run through** every item on that list—*every item* on that list—and PRESSURE TEST ➲249 it.

So if your list included the requirement that you be able to play page two of your new Sonatina from memory, then **at some point** in your Preflight Check you need to be able to do **exactly that**.

Remember, anything you don't check for now, your **teacher** will be checking for **at your lesson**. So it will definitely be noticed—the only question is **when**.

The whole point of the Preflight Check is to notice things while you can still **do something** about them.

If the Check goes badly

Sometimes these Preflight Checks can reveal that you're **nowhere near** as ready for your lesson as you **should be**.

That doesn't mean **game over** though. It just means you have to play some serious offense in the final quarter.

You'll be amazed how often a burst of **intelligent work** after a Preflight Check can take you from *nowhere-near-ready* **to** *wow-my-teacher-is-going-to-be-so-impressed*.

Remember, your Preflight Check doesn't just come back with "ready" or "not ready". It will **also let you know** exactly *which* practice items are not ready. In this way, that final quarter burst of practice is not just more practice—it's also **better targeted** practice.

You can then spend **most** of your time on the items that are **least ready**.

Show your teacher

When your teacher asks how your practice week was, you won't be limited to just giving them an **adjective**:

> "It was *good*."
> "I did *lots* of practice"

Tell them instead the **results** of your Preflight Lesson Check, the Pressure tests you passed, together with **when** the check took place.

Why Preflight Checks can go badly

Preflight Checks are **very good** at helping you understand **how ready** each practice item is, but not so good at helping you understand *why* some items are not ready.

You'll need to **respond differently**, according to the true cause:

1) Not enough practice

Practicing is certainly not about how much time you spend, but it does **take time** to get through all your tasks. So if you know that the reason for the bad Preflight Check was "insufficient practice", then you need to schedule **additional sessions** for the remainder of your practice week.

2) Working on the wrong things

See the chapter on Practice Traps ⟳236 or Engaging Autopilot ⟳120 for more on this. In the meantime, consider using Session Agendas ⟳305 and Blinkers ⟳38 to keep you **focused** on the tasks at hand.

3) Choosing the wrong practice techniques

The type of practice you need to do for a "please speed up page X" is very different from preparing for "Please rework the fingering in measure Y". If you don't **match** your practice to the task, you won't be ready for your Preflight Check...or your lesson.

4) Poor closure skills

When you're practicing, you *have* to know when it's ok to stop, because overpracticing practice tasks can be just as bad for being lesson-ready as underpracticing.
   See Closure ⟳80 for more help with this..

Lesson Review

Ensuring last lesson is fresh in your mind while you work

Maria's teacher told her that there were Five Really Important Things To Remember about her new piece.

The problem is that she can only remember **three** of them...and she's **not so sure** about one of those.

Although Maria is far from being scatterheaded, this is **not the first time** this has happened.

Is there anything she can **do differently**...so that she's not always practicing only **half** of what's needed?

I T MIGHT NOT always feel like it, but even the least busy lessons are **packed with information**.

Sometimes this information will only affect tiny moments in your piece.

Consider using your 3rd finger instead of your 4th finger on this note.

And sometimes it will be **global**:

You've ignored the key signature for the whole piece! You now have 243 B flats to insert.

At the time you're told these things, you'll nod, and tell your teacher "ok". It's **not** like the information is **hard to understand**.

But *understanding* the information is not the problem. The problem is *remembering* it. Especially when it's one of many, many things you were told.

The shopping trip
Let's imagine that you've been asked to do some **grocery shopping**.

"Here's what I'd like you to get" you're told "we need milk, eggs, cat food, broccoli, sausages, washing powder, beans, more pegs for the clothesline, butter, breakfast cereal and a frozen chicken."

Like the points made in your lesson, it's certainly not hard to understand. But **remembering** it all?...

If your brain is anything like mine, by the time you're **halfway to the shops,** your head will be **scrambling things:**

"Milk, eggs, sausage powder, a chicken for the clothesline, a frozen cat...broccoli?...um, what was the other vegetable?..."

When you come home, you'll have bought 5 of the 11 things you were supposed to...and another 10 things that were **never on the list** in the first place.

The **same thing** will happen to your **lesson information**.

With every day that passes, you will remember less and less of what happened.

Don't believe me? Try the next exercise...

The Blue List
Right now, go and get yourself a **blue pen** and a **sheet of paper.**

Back already? Great. Now write down **every point** you can remember being made last lesson.

Take as long as you need.

When you're finished, put the sheet of paper **somewhere safe**...and then make sure you **take it with you** to your *next* lesson.

The Red List

At that next lesson, if your teacher has to **remind you** of a point they made last time—and that point is *not* on your blue list—then don't just nod and say "ok".

You need to *add* it to your list.

But you add it in *red* pen.

Chances are, as soon as your teacher makes a Red Pen point like that, you'll **smack yourself** in the forehead and think "How could I have forgotten that???"

Even **more frustrating** is that often these Red Pen points are things you could have **easily fixed**...if only you could have remembered.

Your pass mark

Once the lesson is over, quickly **count up** how many red pen points there were.

There is only one **acceptable total**:

Zero.

Anything higher means that your brain is **leaking** valuable information...and wasting time. The longer the list, the bigger the leak.

So what can you do to stop leaks like this? It's actually quite easy. You're going to stop them before they start.

Early blue lists are longer

Here's something that's a little weird:

If you created your Blue List straight after a lesson, it's going to be much longer than if you create it half way through the week.

Why? Because your **recall** of the lesson will be at its **strongest** straight after the lesson...and then will **diminish** with every **passing hour.**

With 168 hours until your next lesson, that's a **lot** of diminishing.

It doesn't *have* to deteriorate like this though. There's a way to **stop** the information from **fading**, and it's something you should do **every**

week before you practice.

Stopping the decay

The **key** to stopping information disappearing is to *reinforce* it.

And the earlier, the better. **Don't wait** until midweek before you try this, otherwise the **damage** will already have been **done**.

Instead, start by making use of the **trip** home. Before your car pulls into your **driveway**, you need to have listed all the points that were made at your lesson.

You'll find that because your lesson has only just finished, these points should still be **fresh**, and should **come easily.**

It doesn't sound like much. But **two very important things** will have happened then:

1) These points have appeared a *second time.* Your brain will **notice this**...and the information will be less likely to fade as a result. ("Again?" your brain will think "Hmmmm....maybe this is important after all")

2) You forced yourself to *actively recall* the information. This will **forge pathways** in your brain that will ensure that you can recall the information again in the future. (Our brains are clever like that)

Contrast that with what happens if there is **no review.**

1) Your brain hears the information once, at the lesson itself. But it hears **lots of things** once, and to keep you sane, helps you forget most of them.

2) Your brain is **not required** to call on that information. And so it files it under "Probably not needed". Like something you put in an unlabeled box and stick in the attic.

And then just like that unlabeled box, *you won't be able to find that information when you need it.*

Which is a **fancy way** of saying that you will have **forgotten it.**

A second dose
If you really want to ensure that nothing fades, then you might want to have a further top-up on the **day after** your lesson.

Again, your job is to list as many points from your lesson as you possibly can.

Your brain will really have got the message now that this information is **worth filing**, and making accessible. And so you'll remember it.

Remembering is a good start...
...but it's *only* a start. These Lesson Reviews will help you recall all the points that you needed to work on, but it's now still **up to you** to actually do that work.

Browse this book to find the practice techniques that will help you deal with each of these points, and then go knock them off one at a time.

Measuring your progress
Every so often, run the Blue List/ Red List exercise again. While Lesson Reviews don't guarantee that there will never be Red List items, they do guarantee to **radically shorten** those lists.

Which means your teacher can spend less time telling you about things that you really already know (but had just filed badly)...and instead can surprise you with new ideas.

Level System
The astonishing power of tiny steps

Paul is **staring down the barrel** of a brand new, and very long concert etude. All he can see is a **dozen pages** of angry looking notes, and no way of learning them all.

All this, and the first performance in **three months**.

"Forget size" says his teacher "Building a wall a **hundred miles** long is no different from building a wall a **foot** long. Either way, your job is not to build a wall—*it's to lay bricks*. One brick at a time."

Very sagelike. But how can it help Paul in the practice room?

SOMEBODY SHOULD tell music publishers that pieces really should come with **instructions**. Not telling you how to play the piece (there are already plenty of instructions like that), but how to **learn** it in the first place. A step-by-step guide that takes you from **never seen it before** to **ready to perform**.

That way, when you're practicing, all you'd need to know is **which step** you're up to. Read the guide, it will tell you what's next.

So if it says the next step is to listen to the recording of page 2, then **that's what you do**. If it says it's to come up with a good fingering for measures 24-31, then that's your next job.

None of these steps by themselves might seem like much. In fact, any one of them might only take a few minutes to complete. But **added together**, they'll deliver the piece for you—guaranteed.

Of course, such instructions **don't exist**. That's OK though.

You're going to **create** them.

Creating your own instructions

The idea is that you're going to turn the big task of learning your new piece into **many, many steps**:

- Each step should be **completable** within a few minutes.

- Steps that appear early on your list will help **prepare** you for steps that appear later

- The steps will start easy, and **become more demanding** as you near the end of the list.

- Your steps should be **varied**—mixing up the type of practice you do, and the musical elements you focus on.

Having done that, you'll **number** these steps. So the very first thing you'll do is Step 1. Finish that, and it's time for Step 2...and so on.

We'll have a look in a moment at **what these steps could be**, but the important thing to understand is that by the time you reach your final step (which might be step 100 or more!) your piece will **be in fantastic shape**.

More than just a guide though

These steps are more than just an instructor that tells you what to do next. They can also tell you—with a single number—**how close** your piece is to being ready.

So if you have 80 steps, and you've completed 20 of them, you're a **quarter of the way there**. By the time you've done step 41, you'll be more than half-way.

In this way, they're not just steps. They're actually **levels of proficiency**. When you are at Level 60 (the 60th step), you will be MUCH better at this piece than when you were only at Level 18.

This means that when your teacher asks you how this week was, you can actually answer with numbers:

"Great! My etude is now at Level 48 - only 15 Levels to go"

Your job each week will be to keep moving forward through these levels.

> # The important thing to understand is that by the time you reach your final step, your piece will be in fantastic shape...

Gradually making levels harder

The hardest part of all this is to create Levels that **gradually ramp up**—from very easy initial challenges, right through to highly demanding Levels at the very end.

So how can you tailor your challenges to make them easier or harder?

Just how long is this segment?

Early levels might only require you to play a single phrase.
eg. Be able to play measures 12-18

Later levels will require entire pages, movements, or eventually, the whole piece.
*eg. Be able to play through the **entire development section***

Scout... or play?

Early levels are more likely to be based around scouting challenges—eg. listening to the recording, circling accidentals, working out bowings
*eg. **Listen to the piece** right through five times, following the score as you do.*

Later levels are more likely to involve actually playing.
*eg. Be able to **play the piece** from beginning to end*

Can I stop and think?

Early levels won't have rigid requirements for must-be-in-time-with-no-stops, so you'll have time to stop and think if you need to.
*eg. Be able to play through the opening 12 measures—**breaks are fine**.*

Later levels will often run with a metronome, so you are forced to play on time, every time
*eg. Opening 12 measures, 120 bpm, **no gaps or stops**.*

Look ma, no music

Early levels will allow you full access to the score
eg. Be able to play through the second variation

Later levels will require you to play from memory
*eg. Be able to play through the second variation **without the score***

Toughness of testing

Early levels might only require you to play something through once with no mistakes
eg. Be able to tap the rhythm in measures 40-54 without error

Later levels might require several consecutive playthroughs without error, or the use of other PRESSURE TESTING ➲249

*eg. Be able to tap the rhythm in measures 40-54 **five times in a row**, without error.*

Pressure requirements

Early levels will see you complete all challenges in the privacy of your practice room, with no consequences:

eg. Be able to play page two twice in a row without error

Later levels might involve audiences, and penalties for messing up.

*eg. Be able to play page two twice in a row with a **family member watching**. **Any mistakes**, and you make their bed for a week.*

Tempo

Early levels will see you either playing with a free tempo (so you can stop and think), or a **comfortably slow** tempo.
eg. Be able to play the coda at 60 bpm

Later levels will require tempos that go even beyond performance tempo.

eg. Be able to play the coda at 180 bpm

Later levels might also require tempos that are **uncomfortably slow**, so that you have plenty of time not just to think, but to **doubt**...

eg. Be able to play the coda at eighth note = 80

Split focus

Early levels will allow you to focus entirely on the task at hand

eg. Be able to play page two right through without error

Later levels will test your ability to deliver passages automatically, by giving you something else to focus on at the same time.

eg. Be able to play page two right through without error, while you count backwards from 200 by 7s.

(The arithmetic involved isn't hard, but if there's anything about

page two you're unsure of, either your performance will **fall apart**, or your backwards counting will **stop**...try it and see.)

An example

So how might this all fit together? Let's take a look at an example.

Let's imagine you had a new piece —*Theme and 4 Variations*—and let's assume that you happen to be a piano student.

How might your levels look?

Before you start to play anything, you should run through some SCOUTING➲299 levels:

☐ **Level 1**

Listen to the recording while you follow the score (six times)

☐ **Level 2**

Be able to **identify** which variation is which when the recording is started from a random location

☐ **Level 3**

Write in the names of those high **Ledger Line** notes in variation 4

☐ **Level 4**

Mark all key signature and tempo changes

☐ **Level 5**

List everything about this piece that is going to be **easy**

☐ **Level 6**

Be able to **describe** the characteristics of each variation

Next, you might decide that it's worth **mastering the rhythms** that are at the core of each variation. Notice that by simply tapping the rhythm, you're ISOLATING↪164 it from other elements, so you don't get confused by notes as well.

☐ **Level 7**

Be able to **tap** through the rhythm of the **main theme**

☐ **Level 8**

Be able to tap through the **rhythm** of **Variation 1**

...and so on right through to

☐ **Level 11**

Be able to tap through the rhythm of **Variation 4**

After that, you might decide that since it's a theme and variations, it's going to be important to be thoroughly on top of the **theme**.

To make sure you don't **fluke** any of these levels, you might also insist on being able to demonstrate any level **twice in a row** before being able to tick it:

☐ **Level 12**

Be able to **play through** the notes of the theme (Right Hand only). **Take as much time** as you need between notes, don't fuss about rhythm.

☐ **Level 13**

Be able to play the theme with the **correct rhythm** (Right Hand only)

☐ **Level 14**

Be able to play the theme with the correct rhythm and the **metronome** (Right Hand only, any slow speed you like)

☐ **Level 15**

As for Level 14, but this time at 3/4 of full tempo

Right hand theme is in pretty good shape by now, time to take a look at **left hand**. Because it's made from different material, your Levels will be slightly different:

☐ **Level 16**

As for Level 12, but for **left hand**.

☐ **Level 17**

Be able to play through the sixteenth note Alberti Bass left hand part as quarter note **block chords**.

☐ **Level 18**

As for Level 17, but **from memory**.

☐ **Level 19**

Be able to play through left hand **as written** from memory. (No more block chords)

☐ **Level 20**

Be able to play the left hand of the theme with the correct rhythm and the **metronome** (any slow speed you like)

☐ Level 21
As for Level 20, but this time at 3/4 of full tempo

Ok, so let's take a moment to see what you've **accomplished so far.**

You've **scouted** the entire piece, so that you know exactly what to expect from the campaign ahead.

You have also done some **intensive work on the theme**, so that you know it:

- Separate hands
- Correct rhythm, with metronome
- Each hand from memory
- Up to 75% of full tempo

It's now time to put it **two hands together.** But rather than attempting that straight away, you might create some levels that get you used to not being able to give each hand your full attention.

☐ Level 22
Be able to play the right hand, while your left hand taps a repeating rhythm.

☐ Level 23
As for Level 22, but vice-versa

Now that you've tasted—and coped with—having to do **two things at once,** you might as well play what's actually there:

☐ Level 24
Be able to play through the theme two hands together. Don't worry about maintaining a constant tempo—take as much time as you need.

And now making the **requirements tougher,** as you did before when you

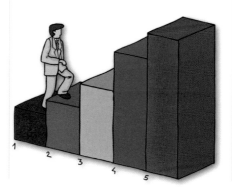

were working separate hands:

☐ Level 25
As for Level 24, but with a **metronome** running (your choice of slow speed)

☐ Level 26
As for Level 24 but **from memory.**

☐ Level 27
As for Level 24 but **at 75% of full tempo**

Rounding things off now for the theme with some seriously **tough tests** (see PRESSURE TESTING➲249)

☐ Level 28
Two hands together, with the metronome, **5 times in a row** with no errors (any slow speed you like)

☐ Level 29
As for Level 28, but at **75% of full tempo**

And now to **prove it's ready** for your next lesson:

☐ Level 30
Record a note-perfect, 75% of full tempo performance of the main theme. Email the recording to

your PRACTICE BUDDY ⟳226 as evidence of your accomplishment.

Your theme should certainly be in good enough shape to **show your teacher** next lesson—all from having taken these microsteps that are Levels.

You could then create similar Levels for each of the variations, so that they're ready too.

The power of constant ticks

Most students **already break up** bigger pieces into smaller tasks, but the mistake they make is that these tasks aren't nearly **small enough**.

If you can't complete a task within one practice session, it's **too big**. It should have been several tasks instead.

So while 30 Levels just to get the theme ready might **seem like a lot**, it means then that *most Levels will only take a few minutes to complete.*

This is **fantastically motivating** when you're working, because you are always within reach of a new goal. It's exactly the same "one more

turn" mentality that makes some **computer games so addictive**—the designers will ensure that there's always a new reward waiting for you, if only you just **keep playing** a little longer...

It also means that you can have the satisfaction of **ticking off** several levels in every practice session.

You'll be able to see your piece regularly progressing, as your Level climbs ever higher.

Calculating your ETA

Whenever you fly commercially, pilots are able to accurately provide an (E)stimated (T)ime of (A)rrival, based on your speed, the distance still needed to travel, and any weather considerations.

Levels provide a very tidy way to

answer a **similar question**:

How long is it going to take me to get this piece ready?

If you created **100 Levels** for the piece, and you're getting through **1 Level each day**, it's going to take you 100 days to complete the piece—just over **three months**.

If instead you're getting through **10 Levels every day**, then it's only going to take 10 days to complete the piece—just over **a week**.

So based on your daily Level average so far, you can **calculate how long** before you're done with all the levels.

When you see what a huge difference just a **few extra Levels per day** makes to your ETA, it's a powerful incentive to do a little extra practice. (See TURNAROUND TIME⟳352)

Setting better instructions

Level system is **only as good** as the levels you **set** for yourself. Like every other practice technique, the more you use it, the more effective the tool will become.

But if you want to get things off to a good start straight away, there are four common problems for inexperienced level-creators:

• *Setting levels in the wrong order*

It's no good if Level 8 relies on skills that you won't develop until Level 12. For every Level on your list, just check that you haven't listed a pre-requisite for that Level to come *afterwards*. For example:

❑ **Level 15**
Be able to play the right hand, while your left hand taps the rhythm of its part

❑ **Level 19**
Be able to tap the rhythm of the left hand part.

At best, you'll get to Level 19, and realize that you've already covered this back at Level 15. At worst, you'll get **stuck** at Level 15 while you try to figure out what really is the Level 19 task anyway.

• *Making the jumps too big*

If a Level is too tough, then you'll get **bogged**, and nothing after that Level will get done. So if the jump to your next Level feels like

> # Most students already break up bigger pieces into smaller tasks, but the mistake they make is that these tasks *aren't nearly small enough...*

it might have been too big, add some stepping stones to get you there—turning a 14 into a 14a, 14b and 14c:

❑ **(Original) Level 8**
Be able to play page 2 through with the metronome at 60bpm

With stepping stones inserted:

❑ **Level 8a**
Be able to play **first three** lines of page 2 through with metronome at 60bpm

❑ **Level 8b**
Be able to play **remainder** of page 2 through with metronome at 60bpm

❑ **Level 8c**
Be able to play **whole of** page 2 through, no metronome, no errors.

❑ **Level 8d**
Be able to play page 2 through with the metronome at **60bpm**

• *Making the <u>initial</u> Levels too hard*

Nothing will kill your progress faster than feeling that everything is hopeless right at the start of the campaign. Create some **gentle Levels** to begin with, just so you can get some **quick runs** on the board—that way you're creating an atmosphere of "can do" rather than "uh oh".

Again, it's something that computer game designers understand—you're usually in for **easy progress** and plenty of **encouragement** at the very start of the game, while the boss levels are saved for the end.

• *Using exactly the same Levels for every piece.*

This would be fine if every piece had exactly the same demands. But if you have a piece that is **nothing but triplets** from start to finish, and another where there are **no two measures** with the **same rhythm**, then at the very least, the rhythm Levels for both pieces should be different.

The second piece is going to need **plenty of extra Levels** dedicated to rhythm, while the first might not need any at all.

So Level System cannot be a one-size fits all. *In fact, no practice technique can be one-size-fits-all.* You've always got to tailor it to suit what's in front of you.

Don't look *up*

Mountain climbers are told not to look down...when you're running Level System, it's critical that you don't look *up*.

The jumps between Levels themselves might be small, but it can be disheartening to know that while you've completed 25 Levels already,

there are still 85 Levels to go.

Your job though is not to do 85 Levels. It's only ever to do the *next* Level.

Take care of it, then ask "what's next?". The Level System will have laid out the answer for you already... just keep taking it one Level at a time.

And then at the end of the practice session, look *down*—you'll often be amazed at just how far you've come.

Practice Buddy Levels

Another approach to Level System is to have your PRACTICE BUDDY⟳226 **create your Levels for you**—you'd do the same for them.

You lose some control, but it also keeps the levels fresh, because your buddy will set very different Levels from those you would have set for yourself.

Sealed instructions

If you really want to make it impossible to **look up**, then only reveal each Level as you complete the level before.

So once you've completed Level 2 that your buddy set, you get to see Level 3—*but you'll still have no idea what Level 4 contains*...or in fact, how many Levels there are. A great way to keep you **focused** on what's immediately in front of you. (And you have to trust your Buddy not to have set you 14,998,335 Levels)...

Marathon Week

Pushing yourself to find out what's really possible

Victoria is in a state of **shock**. Her teacher has just given her a brand new piece—6 pages long—*and a week to learn it.*

"But..." she protests "I mean...I can't...it's 6 pages long!...how am I supposed to...?"

What she's trying to say is that normally it would take her at least **a month** to learn something this long. Her teacher **knows this** though...which is exactly **why** this deadline was created.

Too little time to prepare way too much? Is that going to help Victoria? You bet—in fact, it's going to change the way she practices permanently...

A S A PERSON WHO is all fast-twitch, I'm no fan of **long distance running**—in fact, if somebody asked me whether I thought I could run **5 km** without stopping, my **automatic reaction** would be "no way!".

But I wouldn't really be **telling the truth**. If it was clear to me that in order to **save someone's life**, I had to run *10* km without stopping, I'd **find a way**.

You would too. Just ask **Pheidippides***.

We operate every day with **assumptions** about what's possible and what's not. But most of these assumption are not even close to what's *actually* possible—they're just based on what we're used to and comfortable with so far.

Your practicing is **no exception**. You'll have your own set of beliefs about what you **can** and **can't** do, and **how long** it will take.

And guess what?

You're wrong.

Your *perceived* practice limits

Let's imagine you've been given a **brand new** piece of music. You've also been asked a **question**:

How long will it take for you to be able to play this from memory?

And so you'll look at it, **comparing** it with pieces you have successfully completed in the past. You'll also **weigh up** your own confidence with memorizing.

Based on that **thinking**, you should be able to come back with an answer. Three weeks. Three months. By the end of the year. Whatever.

Let's imagine now that the question was **turned around**. Instead of:

"How long will it take you..."

let's imagine you were asked

"What would you have to do to play this from memory in one week?"

That question doesn't concern itself with the feasibility or otherwise of the goal. Instead, it forces you to **start thinking creatively** about how you could make it happen.

At that instant, something **magical happens**. Faced with having to spend time thinking about how to bring this miracle about, a part of you will start to believe that the miracle is possible.

From that point onwards, it *is* possible.

The power of "how can I...?"

You can unleash this magic on your own practice by taking two simple steps:

1) To state a goal that **seems outrageous**, and well beyond anything you've done before.

2) Instead of asking "Can I?" (which would normally trigger an automatic "no!"), you would **reframe the question** as "*How* can I"

This gives your brain a different task entirely. Instead of being asked to **label** the challenge as "possible" or "impossible", it's been asked for **help** to make a target happen.

Your brain is very, very good at handling requests like that. As human beings, we're hard wired to come up with creative options for "how" in the face of tough odds. (Just picture how creative you would suddenly become if you were marooned on an island.)

So once you've been given the deadline—even though it's tight—if you ask yourself "how", your brain *will* come back to you with possibilities:

"Ok. So this needs to be ready in 7 days. Perhaps I could...

A)...CREATE **two additional practice sessions** each day. This will mean that I'll be doing as much practice in *one* week as I normally would in *three*—a great head start.

B)...TRACK DOWN a **recording** of the piece, and listen to it while I do my homework, in the car, while I exercise...whenever. Make it a part of me (see RECORDINGS➲277), so that I'll be able to spot errors instantly, and read faster.

C)...ASK my teacher to put me **in touch** with a student who has **already played** this piece. Then contact the student to ask for ad-

vice. (see PRACTICE BUDDY➲226) If there are parts of this piece that they think won't take much work, I want to know about that now.

D)...SCHEDULE an **additional lesson** midweek. I can talk with my teacher about my plan, and get help with my progress so far.

E)...TAKE the score with me to school. Use some **free periods** for SCOUTING➲299 and DETAIL TRAWLING➲110. If I can sneak into the music room at lunch-time, I might even be able to get some practice done too.

F)...SCOUR my Practiceopedia for any practice techniques that might help specifically with learning a new piece in a short time. I don't want to **find out afterwards** that there was a great idea I could have tried...if only I'd known...

G)...SCHEDULE a LESSON PREFLIGHT CHECK➲174 during the week, so that by half way through the week, I can ensure I'm **halfway there.**

H)...NEGOTIATE with my sister to cover my chores this week,

in return for which I'll cover hers next week. I can use the additional time to capture some additional practice.

I)...**DIVIDE** the piece into five segments, so I can accurately create SESSION AGENDAS➲305 to cover the whole piece, and still have **two days** to spare.

You'll find that once you start making a list like this that it will become big quickly—and that you'll feel oddly **energized** and **optimistic**. It's not just a fluffy "I believe, therefore I can"...you've actually created an action **plan** to make it possible.

In short, the "How can I" question works because it's a **fertilizer for optimism**, forcing you to focus on solutions, rather than the magnitude of the problem.

Test yourself: Marathon week
To fully appreciate the power of "How can I", you need to experience it for yourself.

For that reason, once a year—every year—I would set my students a

> ## Once you've tasted the fact that you can learn *five* pages in a week, it's very hard to go back to only doing *one*...

Marathon Week. In this week, they would be given a practice task that would normally fill a month...but it all had to be **ready in seven days**.

Their job was to use "How can I" to come up with a plan, and then make the impossible real.

Sometimes they got all the way to their target. Sometimes they fell short. But *every* time, they covered more in a week than they ever thought possible.

Which meant that they always emerged from the week with their **assumptions** about their own limitations permanently **transformed**. Once you've tasted the fact that you can learn five pages in a week, it's very hard to go back to **only doing one**.

So the ripples from the Marathon Week go well beyond the week itself. It **changes the answer** to the question:

"What am I capable of?"

Aren't you curious to find out what the answer to that question *really* is?

Create your own
You don't need to wait for your teacher to set you a week like this. **Choose a time** when demands from school are relatively light, and then **set yourself** an Impossible Target.

Ask yourself "how can I", and follow your own recommendations just as hard as you can. Then enjoy the astonishment on your teacher's face when you present your work next lesson.

Metronome Method

Sneaking up on full tempo

Eric's piece is marked *Presto*. The **only problem** is that the fastest he can actually manage it is *moderato*—and that's on a good day.

"This piece is **SO fast**" he tells his teacher "I know it will sound great **if I** can ever **get there**, but..."

"Not if. *When*" interrupts his teacher. "Here—take a look at this..." and she **writes some instructions** in his book. "Think you can do that?"

Eric reads it, thinks for a second, then **smiles** and **nods**. What does his teacher **have in mind**?

Eric's problem is not the speed itself—it's the **distance** between what he **currently** can do, and what he needs to **end up** doing.

The mistake he's making is picturing that distance as some sort of **impossibly large jump.** His worry is that if he can only currently cope with only 80bpm, how will he ever cope with *180?* That's over 100bpm away! Nobody can jump that far!

That's **right** Eric. *Nobody can jump that far.*

At least not in **one jump.**

I live in Canberra, the capital of Australia. It's around **250km from Sydney.**

Could I jump from Canberra to Sydney? Not in one go (as I write this, even the current world long jump record is 249.92 km too short for that)

But if you give me **lots of little jumps...**

Let's take a look at how this idea can **save Eric,** and get your pieces **up to speed** too.

The practical joke

Let's imagine that Eric was comfortably playing at 80bpm, but that while he was busy doing that, you **played a trick on him.** You nudged his metronome—without him seeing you—up to 84bpm.

What would happen?

Don't hold your breath waiting for a "Hey! What's going on!" from Eric. Chances are *he won't even notice.* The difference in speed between 80 and 84 is so slight that even if you're listening for it, it's **hard to pick.**

Not convinced? Go get your metronome, **try it** for yourself. You'll see what I mean.

So any piece that you cope with at 80, you should also be ok with at 84.

There's no reason for things to stop there though—we're **not done** tricking him yet. If he can cope with 84, then after a few minutes, you could sneak in again, and bump it up to 88. He won't notice that increase either. Or the one after that. Or the one after that.

And in this way, you can help him

sneak up on speeds that he never thought he'd be able to manage—including full tempo.

Boiling the frog

I'm not about to test it for myself, but I have read that if you put a frog in boiling water, it will **jump out**—but that if you put it in lukewarm water, and *gradually* increase the temperature, it will eventually **boil to death.**

Such is the power of gradual increments from a safe start. If you can keep the increments **small,** and be **patient** before making each increase, then you turn some small numbers into some very big numbers.

But the key word here is *gradual*. For your practical joke on Eric to work over and over again, you need to **be patient**. If it's only been a **couple of minutes** since the last speed increase, then he will probably **notice** if you try to add another 4 beats per minute so **soon**.

You need to give him time first to completely **acclimatize** to the new tempo. Like the frog getting used to the new water temperature.

That way, when you bump the metronome up to 88, *he will be comparing it to 84*, rather than part of him still **remembering** what 80 felt like (A comparison like that won't necessarily go so well, because 8 beats per minute really is something he might notice.)

Temporary Ceilings

Eric might not be *noticing* that you're increasing the speed, but if you kept the process going long enough, sooner or later he obviously **won't cope**. Otherwise, using the logic of "just keep adding 4", a speed of 100,000bpm is eventually possible. (In fact, infinite speeds would be theoretically possible!)

> If he can cope with 84, then after a few minutes, you could sneak in again, and bump it up to 88.
>
> He won't notice that increase either. Or the one after that. Or the one after that...

In reality though, what will happen is that he'll **hit a ceiling**—a speed beyond which trouble appears.

That doesn't mean game over. If it sounds as if he's struggling with the demands of the new tempo, *then you just don't increase any further...yet.*

This willingness to **sit patiently** at **red lights** is critical to the success of Metronome Method. The increments in the method might all be *gradual*, but they only ever happen when the practicer is **completely comfortable** with the speed they're already tackling.

Remember though, the more

experience Eric has with **successfully coping** with his ceiling speed, the more likely it is that just *another 4 bpm will become possible...*

In which case, Metronome Method is off and running once more.

Of course, this is not for Eric...

Yes, enough with Eric already. The point of all this is that you can use exactly this process to speed up **your own** pieces—the only difference being that you'll **know** when you've made a speed increase.

You still start from a **safe** and comfortable speed. You still make the increments **too small** to feel. You still allow time to **acclimatize** to each new increment before moving up again.

You still only ever increase the speed if you're **coping** with the existing speed. And if you want to remove any possible **psychological barriers,** then increase the speed without looking at the metronome (just **look away** when you turn the dial or move the slider)

It's just that instead of pulling this tempo swindle on someone else, you're pulling it on **yourself.**

Knowing when it's ok to go *up*

It's all good and well to talk about moving up to the next speed when you're coping with the existing speed...but what does "coping" with the existing speed mean?

There's a simple way to answer this, but there's a little **groundwork** you need to have done first.

Before you ever start any sort of Metronome Method, you should always be able to play a **slow motion version** of the passage that is **performance ready** in every way *except for the final tempo.* (See Prototypes◗257).

This prototype version is then going to act both as a reminder of what your standards are, and as your **canary in the coal mine.** As you gradually speed it up using Metronome Method, it will give you an early warning of any danger—not from gas, but from excess speed.

How will it warn you? *The quality of your delivery of the prototype will suffer.* You won't be able to play those sixteenth notes as evenly as the original prototype. Or you won't be able to control your intonation

so well. Or you'll have trouble handling the staccatissimo passage. Or the fingering might prove unreliable...

Little wobbles like this are a **plea** from the prototype itself:

"Please, can we not go any faster just yet. I'm not quite on top of the speed we're already doing...."

Your answer to that plea always has to be "Sure...take all the time you need."

But then, as soon as it *is* coping again, you bump up the metronome...and look again for any further warning signs.

So Metronome Method might well be about **incremental** speed increases, but that doesn't imply that it's about **regular** speed increases. Unless you're successfully handling speed X, trying X+4 is just giving you **less time** to handle a problem you already weren't coping with.

Worse still, because of the repetition that is inevitable with Metronome Method, if you're increasing speed despite problems, you'll also be Cementing➲64 those problems. You'll end up with a **mess**—it will be a fast mess, but a mess nonetheless.

Snakes and Ladders Variation

Using **traditional** metronome method as outlined above, as soon as you reach your speed ceiling, you **stay** at that speed...until you can cope, in which case you go faster again.

It's based entirely around only ever **moving one way**—up—but then pausing the ascent at the first sign of resistance.

Snakes and Ladders Metronome Method is an alternative you might

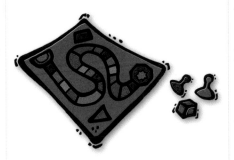

want to try, and it works a **little differently**. After every playthrough, you simply ask yourself "How did that go?".

If **everything was fine**, then you'd bump the metronome **up**. If your prototype was compromised at all—even in the smallest way—then you'd bump the speed **down**.

At the end of the practice session, **record** the tempo you were **up to**.

When you start your next Snakes and Ladders Metronome Method for this section, *that's the speed you'll start at.*

So if your practice session started at 80bpm, went up as high as 140bpm, but then finished at 124 bpm, then next session would start where you finished—at 124 bpm.

You **don't** get any time to **acclimatize** to each new speed—instead, your protection from overheating is that the speed can actually come *down*.

You'll then **yo-yo** up and down (in fact, some practice sessions, you'll end up lower than when you started), but unless there are serious problems with your prototype, over several weeks your speeds will usually **trend upwards**.

When Metronome Method doesn't deliver

Sometimes you'll find that your current ceiling is well short of your target speed, and **won't seem to budge**.

There's an entire section in the Practiceopedia Usher➲19 devoted to speeding up pieces—Metronome Method is one of just many practice techniques that can help you get where you need to go. Far from being competing options, they're actually designed to be used in **combination**...so like every practice technique in the book, Metronome Method is part of a team.

Not wanting to practice

How to deal with the biggest practice crisis of all

It's now been **two weeks** since Chris has done any practice at all, and he's not doing a very good job of **hiding** it.

His **parents** are giving him a hard time about it. His **teacher** is giving him a hard time too. He doesn't want to quit lessons, but just wishes that practicing would **go away**.

What can be done? In fact, can **anything** be done? Or is his practice...and ultimately his lessons too...**doomed**?

I T'S GOING TO HAPPEN at some stage. To you, to the student who has their lesson **straight after you,** and the student who comes after *that.*

It's happened to every member of **every symphony orchestra** in every city on the planet, to the **conductors** who direct them, and the **soloists** who headline their programs.

And it doesn't stop there. Oh no.

It's happened to **your teacher,** to their teacher, and their teacher... right back to the **first person** who every played your instrument.

No matter who they are, e**verybody** who has ever played a musical instrument has had days—heck, sometimes *years*— where they really **didn't** want to practice.

The interesting question is *why...*

...because hidden in the answer is the **cure.**

Before we start looking at possible answers and cures though, let's take a look at the not-so-smart way the problem is **usually handled.**

Just get on with it?

Music teachers and parents aren't just going to sit idly by while you sit idly by. They're going to tell you to just "get on with it"—to close your eyes, pinch your nose, then **swallow the medicine anyway,** it's good for you.

But here's the thing. Even if you cave in—and practice anyway because you know you're *supposed* to—something vital still hasn't changed:

*You still didn't **want** to.*

You're acting out of a **sense of duty,** which is commendable—you'll probably make a fine **astronaut** one day—but it hasn't changed the fact that you and practicing still aren't getting along.

When you don't want to practice, the **critical** thing to change is **not** whether or not you practice (the "just get on with it" approach).

The thing to change is the fact that **you didn't *want* to** in the first place—which means understanding *why* you don't want to. Otherwise you're treating the **symptoms,** but not the **disease.**

Naming what puts you off

From time to time, I'll hear students say they **don't like** being involved in **sport,** and are upset because it's compulsory at their school.

The statement "I don't like being involved in sport" doesn't really tell me anything useful though, *because sport is such an enormously **diverse** concept.* It includes everything from extreme mountain bike riding to croquet, sumo-wrestling to chess. It can be **hit-and-giggle** or it can involve preparing for the **Olympic Games**.

So there's no way they're basing their statement on a comprehensive consideration of *all* sports. What they really mean is that from their limited experience with sport so far, there are *elements* present in *some sports* that turn them off.

Perhaps they don't like being out of breath. Or having to give up part of their weekend. Or they're afraid of contact injuries.

What they need to realize though is that it's still possible to play sport, and **avoid** these perceived downsides. They just need to **choose** better.

Choosing better? How?

Let's take the examples one at a time:

• If they don't like being **out of breath**, it doesn't automatically mean *all* sports are off limits. Maybe indoor soccer or long distance running are **not good ideas**, but ten-pin bowling or billiards are just a couple of many alternatives.

• If they don't like **losing their weekends** then cricket is a bad choice*. But if that's their main objection to sport, then swimming is one of many sports that will normally leave their weekends intact, as most of the training happens early in the morning.

• If they're **nervous about contact injuries,** then rugby or ice-hockey are sports to avoid, but not all sports involve high speed collisions with people bigger than you. Figure skating, athletics and volleyball are just some of many sports that have almost **no chance** of contact injuries.

So they could write a comprehensive **complaint list** of all the sporting issues that annoy them and **still** find a dozen sports where these complaints are just not relevant.

The same thing is true of practicing.

---

* In case you're not familiar with the game, a full cricket Test Match takes *5 full days to play*, while even the "short" version of the game still takes **8 hours**. It still remains one of my favorite sports though. (I always wanted to play for Australia. It's just that they never pick me.)

It's not *all* of practicing you don't feel like. It's **bits**. Transform those bits—or dodge them entirely—and practicing is a brand new game, and something you might not mind so much after all.

In other words, if you don't like it, don't just do it anyway. *Change* it.

So what *exactly* don't you like?

"Practicing" is too general an answer to be helpful. Just like "sport", "practicing" can be **many different things.**

Some methods of practice are **loaded** with those elements that you don't enjoy. But other techniques will be completely clear of those bugbears.

For example, if you **hate learning new notes**, then that sort of practice will drive you nuts—and have you avoiding practice. But working on speeding up a piece that you can *already play* might be fine.

In fact, if you have some weeks where you **do** feel like practicing, and some where you **don't**, it's not necessarily a sign that you're flaky—instead, it's often because of the different **type** of practice that each of those weeks requires.

As soon as you can be **specific** about your dislikes, you're well on the way to curing your don't-want-to-practice blues. Instead of not practicing, all you need to do is **modify** your practice so that it *no longer contains the element that was annoying you*.

Or at least contains much *less* of it.

Let's take a look at some common irritations, and changes you can make to eliminate them:

> It's not *all* of practicing you don't feel like. It's *bits*.
> Transform those bits—or dodge them entirely—and practicing is a *brand new game...*

There's no let up...I'm so sick of having to practice every single day...

You're right. That sounds terrible—no breaks, no holidays, just a hamster on the practice wheel for the rest of your life. But guess what...

...it doesn't have to be this way.

There's absolutely **no rule** that you must practice 365 days of the year. And there's **no evidence** to suggest that musicians who practice without breaks are better for it.

If the fact that practicing seems **never-ending** is what's driving you crazy, then there's an easy fix:

Switch to a practice timetable that has rostered days off.

It might be every **fifth day**. Or it might be every **Tuesday**, simply because on that day your schedule is filled with other things.

But the **big change** is that you'll always only be a few days away from a break of some sort. As anybody who **works on a Friday** will tell you, knowing the weekend is coming up is sometimes enough to keep you going.

Alternatively, days off might be something that you can **earn**. The idea is that each week you can **stop practicing** as soon as you are ready for your next lesson...*no* *matter when in the week you reach that milestone.*

In other words, if you get through your work quickly and well early in the week, you earn yourself a **mini-vacation**.

Apart from giving you the possibility of some downtime, the earn-your-days-off system is also a huge **incentive** to practice intelligently and hard at the start of each week.

The important thing to realize is that despite all this time off, there's **no damage done.** When the lesson comes around, your teacher can hear that you're ready. This is on top of the fact that during the week before, you had two days to relax. Everybody wins.

Remember, your **job** when you practice is *to be ready for your next lesson.* It's not to notch daily tally marks on your prison wall.

My parents are on my back over practicing—they always nag me...

Yeah, well they'll tell you that they **wouldn't have to** if you practiced once in a while...

...which you might, except that they always nag you...Joseph Heller would be grimacing. I'm not getting into family therapy here, but there is a way you can write yourself a **ticket out of this loop.** There's a little dealmaking you need to do first though.

Your parents' part of the bargain is to **say nothing** to you about your practice during next week. A whole week. No matter what you do...or don't do.

And as long as you are then ready for your lesson, they can't

say anything **the week after that either**. So you have the power to extend this zone of silence. Of course, if you *aren't* properly prepared on lesson day, then **all bets are off.** Nagging will be back, and with reinforcements.

This deal though is a **fantastic opportunity** if you're keen to get your parents off your case. All you have to do is be ready for your lesson each week, and you won't hear a peep from them...but how you get there is up to you.

Just picture it. **When** you practice is up to you. **How** you practice is up to you. **How long** the practice sessions last is up to you. As long as you can deliver the goods on **lesson day,** all is ok.

Once you've **had a taste** of the freedom that working this way brings, you won't want to **go back.** Which means that you'll have a powerful new reason for being ready every week...

...and of course, to achieve that, you've got to practice hard.

Good outcome all round.

It's so BORING...every practice session feels the same.

Uh oh. This probably means that every practice session *is actually the same*...in which case you'd have to ask yourself "how on earth have I allowed **that** to happen?"

Apart from being boring, the needs of your pieces change from day to day—**a one-size-fits-all** approach is not going to get the job done.

If you're **not sure** how to add new ingredients to your practice, there's a whole chapter in this book dedicated to VARYING YOUR DIET ⟳360 Or for a more **extreme approach**, try the chapter on RANDOMIZING ⟳262

But at the very least, if you start **matching** practice techniques to the changing needs of your pieces, then that **guarantees** that every day of practice will be unique. You'll never have two days with exactly the same requirements, which means that you'll never have two days with exactly the same practice.

In short, if you're bored because your practice is always the same, **it's your fault**—but it's also very easy to fix. You'll find it much easier to look forward to practicing when you don't feel like a worker on an assembly line.

I hate learning new pieces...my reading is not great and a page of music takes me forever...

Slogging through new notes is never fun. In fact, if that's **all** practicing ever consisted of, then most people would quit.

But it's **not** all practicing consists of. In fact, it shouldn't even be *most* of what practicing consists of.

Learning new pieces is just **one part** of your practice campaign (see CAMPAIGNS ⟳58)—you'll still have older pieces to speed up, make reliable or memorize, and upcoming performances to polish for.

If you hate learning new pieces, one way to make your practice less painful is to make sure that your practice contains a **mix** of different practice types. The logic is that if I *have* to eat **soft-boiled liver**, then I want other things on my plate too.

But if you **really dislike** this phase of practicing, there are steps you can take to minimise it...or even eliminate it altogether.

• First of all, running a thorough SCOUTING ⟳299 mission **before** you practice the piece will get your notelearning off to a **flying start**.

• Using LEVEL SYSTEM ⟳182 can then help turn the **colossal job** of learning the new piece into a series of easy-to-digest steps.

• Even better though is to decide that it's time to **transform your sightreading.**

Why? Because if your sightreading is in good enough shape, *you won't have to learn the notes at all....*

...you'll be able to play them **first time.** (See TURNAROUND TIME➲352).

I just feel like I don't make any progress...there's lots of pedalling and no forward movement.

Check out the chapter on STALLING➲325 for help with this—but be assured that you're certainly not alone in feeling this way from time to time.

Untreated though, this is a **dangerous disease.** If you lose faith in practicing's ability to improve your playing, you'll stop practicing....

Let it continue for too long, and *you'll stop lessons too.*

So if your practicing is not working, it's essential to find out why—and then to **change** how you work. You're either using the **wrong practice technique,** or using the right practice technique **incorrectly.**

But before you diagnose yourself with this disease, it's worth keeping a BREAKTHROUGHS DIARY➲46 for a couple of weeks—sometimes you'll discover that you're not really stalling at all.

I'm sick of having to play things over and over and over again.

Whoa...back up a second. Playing things over and over and over again **doesn't sound much like practicing** to me. Practicing with heavy repetition is known as CEMENTING➲64, and certainly has a place as a later stage practice technique—but it's one of

hundreds of other techniques available to you in the meantime.

Not only is spending all your time cementing a boring way to work, it's also a very *bad* way to work. You'll be **trapping** all sorts of nonsense in the cement, and then will have to schedule extra practice later to *un*cement these errors.

If you're making the "I'm sick of having to play things over and over and over again" complaint, then you're spending most of your time using the **wrong tool** for the **wrong job.** Read through the rest of this book, try some alternative techniques. You'll quickly discover that the over-and-over-and-over again brand of practicing is only a small part of a much bigger practice universe.

It takes too much of my free time

Then find a way for it to take *less* time. Consider this:

You might not enjoy **chopping wood**—again, because it eats into your leisure time. *But how much leisure time is eaten depends on the tools you use to do the job.*

If you're trying to chop wood with a shovel, then you better **clear your diary**—you're going to be there all day, and tomorrow too. Chop with a brand new and sharpened axe though and you could be out of there in minutes.

The time taken also depends on *how you use the tools*. So if you have a brand new and sharpened axe...and you use it to **saw away** at the log, then you're still going to be there for a long time.

Practicing does take time away from other things, but remember that when most students practice, they end up using a **lot more time** than they needed. It's not the requirements of the task that's time consuming—it's the inefficient way that the task is **handled**.

So before you declare that the job takes too long, take a moment to check the tools you're using, and ask yourself:

Is there any way I could get the same results in a fraction of the time? (You bet there is—see the chapters on TURNAROUND TIMES➲352 and MARATHON WEEK➲191)

My piece is boring

First of all, make sure that you haven't confused "boring" with "I'm just sick of it because I'm not making good progress".

The true test is to listen again to the recording—or have your teacher play it—and then ask yourself this:

If by magic, I could sound like that right now—no work required— would I enjoy playing this piece?

If the answer is **yes**—and once the work factor is taken out, it often is—then the piece is not the issue. You just need to find a way to get **faster results** with it (have you checked out LEVEL SYSTEM➲182 yet?)

If the answer is **no** though, then unless the piece is absolutely **essential** to your development, or compulsory for a **life-changing** competition, talk to your teacher about ditching it.

Remember, the reward for all this practice is that you get to play the piece well. But if it's a piece that you just don't like...why would you go to all that trouble? If I practiced

juggling every day for the next ten years, I'd be really good. But knowing that doesn't motivate me to practice juggling—I've got no interest in being able to juggle.

The **single best thing** you can do to motivate yourself is to find a piece that really fires you up. If you've discovered something that you want to play badly enough, you won't even **notice** the amount of practice you do to get there.

More help with this issue

Not wanting to practice is a complicated practice disease. Reinventing what practicing involves is a great start, but there's **plenty more** you can do.

There are ideas scattered throughout this book that can help, but you can find **everything you need** in one place in the "Not Wanting to Practice" section of the PRACTICEOPEDIA USHER➲17.

So there's **help all around**, but in the end, you've got to be ready to fight this battle. Your lessons are depending on it.

One way doors
Eliminating the need for constant revision

As far as Tristan is concerned, there are **two types** of practice. There is the "learn **new** things" type of practice. And there is the "**revise** what you've already done" type.

There's only **one problem.** With four long pieces to work on and plenty of scales, he's **using up** almost all his time on the **second** type of practice. And the more new things he learns, the **longer** the "revise" list gets.

He resolves to do **more** practice. His teacher tells him he should actually be doing *less*. Surely that **doesn't make sense?**...

I T DOESN'T MATTER how much you resist, practicing always seems to end up **revisiting** work you've already done. Which means that the passage you practice **today** is something that you'll also practice tomorrow, and the **day after that**.

And the day after *that*. And so on, into **next week**, and perhaps even **next month**.

Sometimes all this revision is important. Some passages are genuinely **difficult enough** that dozens of practice sessions are needed to get the job done. Others require revisits because they rely on a level of "playing fitness" that you have to maintain, and which **fades** with lack of use.

For passages like these, constant revision is not just explainable, it's **essential**.

But there are plenty of passages that do not fall into either of those categories. If, for example, a passage is sounding good, you're clear on what you're doing, and you're finding it easy...

...why would you waste time *revising* it?

Sounds self evident. But it's not what happens.

The revolving door approach

Many students revise *all* their passages *all* the time—terrified that if they were to leave even the easiest passage for 24 hours, it would start **springing leaks**. It's almost as if the only thing that keeps passages healthy is **constant checkups**.

So check up on it they do, like anxious parents **ringing the babysitter** every quarter hour just to make sure that "everything's ok".

Much to nobody's surprise, whenever they run a check-up like this, everything *is* ok with the passage. No leaks. No fires. All sounding good, **just like the last time** they played it.

Viewed like this, the whole needless-revision process doesn't look like *practicing* so much as like *superstition*—a ritual that you undertake to ward off demons that might afflict your otherwise healthy piece.

There's a **much better way**, and you won't believe how much time you'll save.

Revisionless Practice?

This chapter aims to end all this **unnecessary revision** by suggesting an idea that will seem **radical** to many students:

That it's possible to work on a passage **once**, work on it **well**...

*...and then **not** need to work on it again.*

Whether that sounds crazy to you or not, think of what it would mean if it *were* true. You no longer would have to find the time to revise every passage in every piece you play. In fact, the only passages slated for regular review would be those that **genuinely need** the attention.

Everything else would be labeled as "Practiced well, and ready to go"— almost like it had been stamped by the factory inspection team.

Fantasy? No way. In fact, as your pieces get longer and more demanding, you **won't have time** to work any other way.

Let's take a look at how it works.

The one-way door experiment
The best way to understand this method is to try it for yourself.

Choose a passage from one of your pieces that you would rate as being "easy", but one that you still tend to practice regularly.

You're about to dedicate a **special practice session** to this passage, during which you'll be free to practice it however you like.

*But then that will be the **last time** you're allowed to practice this passage for a month.*

Seriously.

So once you declare the practice session "finished", it will be as if you have passed through a **one-way door.** If you listen carefully, you'll hear it lock behind you. You can't go back to fix anything, or just quickly "check up" on how the passage is doing. It's done—*you're* done—and you need to move on.

It's a small change, but with enormous consequences, almost all of them good.

The "later" trap
Let's imagine you have chosen your passage, and are about to have **one practice session only** on it, before putting it out of reach for a month.

Before you start work though, remember this:

You can't just continue to practice the way you always have, and then expect not to have to revise.

Why? Because your constant revisions in the past also had a legitimate hidden purpose. It was **covering you** against the possibility that you *might not have practiced the passage properly in the first place.*

So more than just mere revision, these additional sessions are also there to tidy up anything you missed—or messed— first time around.

This safety net approach sounds like a good idea, but it can **wreak havoc** on your practice standards in those early sessions.

Think about it for a moment. Being able to constantly review means that you have an **inexhaustible supply** of additional practice sessions.

Because you *know* you've got all those additional practice sessions up your sleeve for later, *there's no pressure to get everything right now.* You don't need to check things too carefully in the **first session**, because you can always check them again in the **second**.

And so your practice can be **sloppy**. You can misread rhythms, omit rests, invert dynamics. Near enough is good enough because you're revisiting it again tomorrow, and the next day, and the next...

But what if you knew that you were **not** going to revisit it? Not tomorrow. Not ever....

When going back is not an option

Here's what makes the one-way-door technique so **confronting**, and so effective:

Anything you overlook or don't get around to now, is not going to get done. Ever. There is no "later" to put it off until.

Knowing that, your whole practice world is thrown into a spin—and your **expectations** of yourself during

that one and only practice session *have* to skyrocket.

Ask yourself this. Let's imagine that you had a performance in a week's time. It's not a difficult or a long piece, but it's a piece you've **never seen** before.

Now imagine that due to a school camp, *the only day you can practice is today.* One practice session only, no going back afterwards. After that, the next time you'll play this piece will be **at the concert** itself.

Now before you ask, you also need to imagine that there's no way of getting out of this concert. It's something you **have to do**...it just so happens though that the success or otherwise of the performance will

come down to one practice session. Picture the **changed demands** you'd have of yourself in that practice session—remember, it's the *only one you've got:*

- Wouldn't you concentrate harder?
- Wouldn't you check the score more carefully?
- Wouldn't you insist that rhythms are worked out more carefully, and delivered with more precision?
- Wouldn't you be more rigorous in applying Pressure Tests➲249?
- Wouldn't you be slower to declare a passage to be "finished" or "good enough"?
- Wouldn't you be less likely to waste time on sections of the passage that you can already play?

*And isn't **any** practice technique that's going to lead to all these outcomes worth trying?*

One-way-doors isn't just a technique to help prevent unnecessary passage review. It's also a kick-start to *sharpening* your practice in the first place. **Extreme circumstances** that can help you discover reserves of concentration and precision that you never knew you had...because you never needed them all in one place before.

The practice Budget Committee

Despite all this though, the idea of ignoring passages for a month at a time can still **sound scary** to many music students.

But the question you need to **ask yourself** is this:

If your one-way door practice was thorough enough in the first place, *what on earth would you use those extra practice sessions for?*

Let's imagine that those practice sessions cost $100 each, and you had to justify the **budget expense** to a **committee**. They would ask—and fair enough too—*"since you claim to have covered this passage in great detail in a prior practice session, how do you see these additional sessions making further improvement? And if there* **is** *improvement to be made, what was the area in your initial practice that was deficient? Either way, haven't we just blown $100 somewhere?"*

Ouch. Seems they have a point.

There's good news though, even if the committee is smirking as they test out the "Veto" stamp on each other's forearms. You don't *need* the extra sessions in the first place. They only ever would have been for **reassurance**.

The passages that stick in your head—and under your fingers—do so not because of how many times you play them, or how frequently you check them, *but because of how clear your picture is of them.*

Sometimes it takes plenty of repetition to get you there, but make a picture clear enough, and no amount of time will clear it away (when was the last time you "practiced" saying the **alphabet**? Or spelling your **name**?)

So if your command of a passage fades with time—and particularly if it fades *quickly*—then that's just a sure sign that *you never knew it that well in the first place.*

Which means you shouldn't have locked the door on it when you did.

Knowing when it's ready

Closure⤴80 for One-Way-Door practice items is particularly tricky. Remember, you don't get a second shot at it, so before you actually go through the door and lock it behind you, you need to be *very* sure that you're all done with what was in the room.

How? You need to run some serious quality control testing, using Thematic Practice⤴330, together with Pressure Testing⤴249. Look for the ideas in those chapters that frighten you the most, double them, and then try *those*.

That way, when you do sign off on the section, you can do so knowing that:

- You've covered all the **essential musical elements**
- Your good playing of the passage was **not just a fluke**
- Your picture of the passage is **clear** (See also VISUALIZING ➲364)

Once you've done that, close the door, and move on with confidence.

What if it's *not* ready in a single session?

It's certainly not game over—in fact, it will happen to you a lot when you

use this technique. You'll simply run out of time.

Don't panic. There are a couple of things you can try.

1) Downsizing

One option is to **start smaller.** Your first attempts at one-way door practice should be with passages that you genuinely regard as being easy—so you can focus on the **process**, rather than be fretting over how built your enemy is.

Work the passage hard, test it...and then **leave it alone** once you can pass those tests.

Try it again in a few weeks' time, see how much has stuck.

Once you've experienced success working with some easier passages, you can try it on the harder stuff.

B) Extend your preparation

Another option is to **return to the passage in your next practice session**—not to revise anything, but to continue getting the passage to a point where you *can* sign off on it.

Effectively you would be treating this all as a **single practice session** that just happened to be interrupted by (say) school and a few hours' sleep.

It's not cheating. The essence of the one-way-door technique is **not** that it happens in a single practice session, but that it's **one-way.** So once you've signed off on a passage—no matter how long it took you to get that passage ready— you don't look back.

That principle **still holds** for passages that may have taken **several practice sessions** to prepare in the first place. Whenever they're ready for the first time—*even if that took a dozen practice sessions*—then you should be able to safely leave them for a month, and still know how to play them.

So it's about eliminating a **security blanket**—the constant need to check up on yourself—not teaching yourself how to cram the preparation of a concerto into half an hour.

So would you ever revisit a "locked" passage?

Yes, but only if **something changes**. Perhaps you've learned the neighboring passages too, and it's time to **integrate** the original passage into a greater whole. Or perhaps you've decided on a **brand new tempo** for the whole piece, and now need to speed the passage up.

Or the **performance** is starting to approach, and you need to run a series of Dress Rehearsals↪115.

So there will actually be plenty of times when you play this passage again. But none of them will have been "just trying it to see if I can", because like **drinking seawater**, no matter how many times you relieve yourself, you still won't be satisfied.

Don't forget...

Like all your practice techniques, you'll get **better** at this. The more you use one-way-doors, the more comfortable you'll become with the idea that practicing is not necessarily an exercise in **high-maintenance**. You'll start to trust that a well-learned passage can go for several weeks with no practice at all, and *still* be in great shape.

In fact, you will sometimes be able to play pieces that you haven't

practiced for years—if they were works that you truly knew thoroughly.

What will you do with all the spare time?

Now that you don't have to waste all your time constantly revisiting healthy passages?

You can handle **more pieces** at once. Or **slash** your Turnaround Time↪352 for individual pieces. Or spend more time on **behind the scenes** Fitness Training↪146. Or use Tightening↪337 to **discover elements** in these healthy passages that actually could use some improvement.

You could also strengthen your picture of all your pieces using Visualizing↪364, or explore more possible interpretation options by running additional Experiments↪135...

...or you could simply **take a break** occasionally. With the sort of intense no-compromises work that one-way-door practice demands, you will have earned it.

Openings and Endings

VIP attention for the most important parts of any performance

Raquel has a performance looming, but her teacher has given her a **very strange** practice instruction.

He wants her to spend almost all her time on just **two sections** of the piece—*sections that she can already play well.*

He's pointing to the **beginning** and the **end**, but she can't see **how** she can do any more with those...or **why** she needs to. What's she missing?...

Sir Thomas Beecham once commented that as long as the orchestra begins and ends together, the audience really **doesn't care** what happens in between. I'm not sure all audiences are that forgiving, but experienced conductors know just how much **depends on** those dozen or so measures that **bookend each concert.**

The **beginning** is important because it's the audience's first impression. Mess it up and the audience will quickly stop paying attention to you, as they start re-reading their programme, hoping that your tempo is brisk and that you don't observe any repeats.

Similarly, the **final measures** are vital because they are the **applause trigger**, and the last thing the audience **remembers** about your performance. It's a little scary how easily audiences can be manipulated into **clapping like crazy people**, just because the ending was dynamite, but it's certainly a phenomenon that good performers exploit.

But great beginnings and endings don't just happen. You've got to **engineer** them—which means

setting aside some practice sessions dedicated to just that.

Fort Knox Secure

First things first though. Before you start engineering anything, you need to ensure that those beginnings and endings are **completely secure.** Moments of *"what on earth comes next?"* are one kind of problem when they strike **halfway** through a performance, but they're an absolute **calamity** if that's how your performance starts or ends.

Of course, with any sort of performance coming up, you should have thoroughly Pressure Tested ⮌249 your whole piece

anyway, but the openings and endings should come in for some **special attention** when you do. There's two ways you can do this:

1) By pressure testing the openings and endings **more frequently** than you test anything else.

2) By making the **demands** of those tests **tougher** than you normally would for other parts of the piece. So if you normally run a test with a three-in-a-row requirement attached, you'd bump that up to *five*-in-a-row for your starts and ends.

Doing this won't make the opening or ending memorable. It won't make anyone weep, or leap from their seats. But you've guaranteed that at least these crucial moments **won't embarrass you.**

Which means you're now ready to start adding some serious polish— knowing that what you're polishing isn't white-anted underneath.

Cold starting

Professional tennis players are allowed time to **hit up** before they start the match—and even then, it can sometimes take a set or more before they **settle** into their game.

Unfortunately, there are **no hit-ups** for you when you perform. You can't "just try" the opening measures a few times onstage to settle yourself down. Aside from the tune-up, as soon as you play *anything*, your performance is underway.

This means you have to become **very, very good** at cold-starting — *because it's the only sort of start you're going to get.*

Even if you're playing a concerto —and the orchestra is starting *for* you—your **first entry** is still something that you have to be able to **hit the ground running** for. You can't feel your way for a while, adjust to the light and conditions and then try to catch the eye of the conductor so you can say "ok, I've got it now… can you get everyone to **shush** so that we can take it again from the top?"

Running Cold-Start Simulations
Cold starting is not something that can only happen on-stage. It's a skill you can **develop** in your practice room by running **Cold Start Simulations.**

These simulations are **not** going to look much like the **rest of your practice**, because you're only going to be able to run each simulation **once** in a practice session—right at the very beginning.

You can't do multiple "cold starts" in a row (after the first one, they're not cold any more). You also can't rehearse "cold starts" after you've been playing something else for half an hour already.

So with your opportunities for such simulations being limited, whenever you've got a concert looming, *every practice session should begin by starting a performance of one your pieces.* That's when you'll be at your coldest, and the **first half dozen phrases** or so are all you'll need.

There's nothing magic about this. Running simulations doesn't **save** you from having to cold start in the concert. (*Nothing* can save you from that) It just means that the experience **won't be unfamiliar** to you.

Tempo setting
When you choose a tempo at the start of the piece, the rest of the

performance is **counting on you** to choose well.

Choose something **too fast**, and you're setting yourself up for accidents in upcoming tricky passages.

Choose something **too slow,** and the performance will feel labored, with melodic lines that are impossible to sustain.

Of course, students don't **deliberately** choose crazy tempos. It happens when they haven't had **enough practice** at choosing tempos in the first place.

Which of course is not something that's going to happen to *you.*

Developing tempo-sense
Getting the tempo right may be crucial, but we're not all born with an inbuilt sense of what 63 bpm is. If you want to learn to choose appropriate speeds, *you have to practice choosing appropriate speeds.*

That starts by **finding out** what the appropriate speed is. The next time you're playing the piece at what feels like an optimum tempo, **measure** the speed with the metronome, and write down the number.

This is your reference point—put it in a safe place.

Then, whenever you run a Cold Start Simulation, you won't need to **wonder** whether the speed you chose is right or not. You'll know—because you can **easily compare** what you played with that metronome setting.

Sometimes you'll hit it. Sometimes you won't. But the more often you **aim** at it, the better you'll become at hitting it when you need to.

Your tempo instincts will become progressively more tuned until you can eventually produce something very close to the optimum tempo **on demand**, and under pressure.

Preplaying

This is mostly to save you from any **ready-fire-aim** mishaps during your performance.

The idea is that you'll normally have a bunch of things you need to remember while you're playing. That

you were going to **project more** at the opening. That you were going to **understate the rit** before the repeat, but **exaggerate the rit** before the coda.

These are things that you need to remember *before their moment arrives in the piece*. Otherwise, when you *do* remember them, the sentence in your head will start with an "ooops".

The very **best time** to give yourself these reminders is just before you

start. That way it's close enough to showtime that you won't forget, but not after the event. It's similar to the coach of a football team giving **last minute instructions** before the game gets underway.

But if the **first time** you try to recall such instructions is on-stage, you'll forget things. Preplaying—your pre-performance self-talk— is an **essential** part of your performance, and like any other essential part of your performance, it should be **part** of your practice. The reminders you need to give yourself should flow as naturally as the notes that follow.

It's an anywhere, anytime thing

The great thing about practicing Preplaying though is that you don't have to be in your practice room at the time. Next time you're stuck on a **bus,** or in one of those lines in the supermarket that **won't move,** see if you can accurately picture everything your upcoming performance needs to contain. Do this a few times, and the reminders will **leap straight out** at you on concert day itself.

Keep it positive

Preplaying is not just a lecture to yourself though. You should be trying to create *a mental picture of you getting these reminders right.* Saying to yourself "I hope I don't mess up on Page 2" is NOT preplaying. That's **sabotaging.** However, picturing yourself staying relaxed on page 2 *is* preplaying, and exactly the sort of thing that's likely to deliver page 2 well for you.

You won't always find such positive pictures easy to create. Which is exactly **why** you need to practice it. (See also VISUALIZING ➲364)

Getting into character

If you want the piece to convey a sense of **optimistic majesty,** then you've got to be feeling that way before you start. If you want the piece to be **lonely and anxious,** then that's where a part of you needs to be too.

The chapter on PAINTING THE SCENE ➲222 talks more about the impact of scenarios on your playing, but getting into character like this is **no easy thing** if the first time you try it is on stage. Like an actor preparing for a role, you need to **rehearse the switch,** so that you can turn on the emotion instantly, and with conviction.

Yet another facet of practicing that has absolutely nothing to do with notes. (A lot of the best parts of practicing don't).

Applause triggers

Ok, so the beginning of your piece can **determine what happens** with the rest of your piece. You've got to be able to start cold, find the right tempo, give yourself the perfect Preplay messages and then get into character for the performance itself.

But the power of the *end* of your performance is perhaps even more impressive. It determines not just **when** the applause starts but **what type** of applause it is, and **how much** there's going to be.

In fact, the only way to have **more control** over the applause is if you were allowed to actually **conduct** it.

Endings and applause types

There are some **dramatic endings** that can produce instant and enthusiastic applause—the "bravo" applauses. Conductors will often play up the big V-I-V-I-V-I looping cadences at the end of orchestral works, turning the final stretched out tonic into nothing short of a bring-the-audience-to-their-feet triumph, with the applause starting even before the final note has ended.

At the **other end of the spectrum**, there are endings where the spell woven by the almost-inaudible final phrase is so complete that nobody wants to interrupt the silence. This applause will start almost hesitantly, and then grow quickly in volume and warmth—almost like house lights slowly going up again. There are countless flavors in between, but the important thing is to take a look at the end of your piece from the **audience's point of view**. Then ask yourself—*how do you imagine them reacting?*

Unlocking the solution

The very worst thing you can do is to allow the ending to just *happen*, with nothing special to stick in the audience's mind. It's like slapping a "The End" title up at the end of a movie to cover the fact that you don't really have anything meaningful to say.

So if your piece has an **unexpected final note**, make it *really* unexpected—do everything you can to have the audience anticipating something else entirely.

If the ending instead is a **final heart-melting reprise** of the opening theme, then take your time—pull out all the emotional stops and let the audience enjoy the nostalgia.

If the piece has been a **furioso toccata**, then you might let the abrupt and angry final notes ring around the room, and then produce a sudden bow to match.

Hidden in the score of every piece are **clues** to possible ending types. Stay attuned, and when you settle on your solution **don't do it by halves**—the five seconds before the applause is due is no time for bland, safe or ordinary.

When inspiration won't come

Sometimes the perfect ending will elude you, but that doesn't mean that it isn't out there still **waiting to be discovered**.

Handle it in the same way that you would a flat dynamic patch—in other words, you need to Experiment➲135. Try a dozen different ways of ending the piece, **without any expectations** as to what will work and what won't. Listen to each from an audience's point of view, and you'll be amazed how often you'll stumble on a solution.

And remember, a poor solution **executed boldly** is better than no solution at all. Unless you want your performance to be greeted with the same polite applause that everybody else gets, then it's time to dial things up a little.

VIP practice session

In the final couple of weeks leading up to your performance, **set aside a practice session** where the *only* thing you work on are the openings and endings.

You won't have time to do this for every passage in your piece—but these aren't just any passage in your piece. They're special, so they get the VIP treatment.

That practice session will be a mixture between Boot Camp➲43, Experimenting➲135 and Cementing➲64. You'll loop these passages through **under performance conditions**, each time trying to extract a little more, and to discover sparks that you may have missed earlier.

Your aim? It's not just to polish these passages, but to ensure that they feel like **old and reliable friends** on concert day. When you start your performance, there's something **very reassuring** about knowing that the two most strategically important locations have been so thoroughly worked...

...and that confidence boost will then cascade through the rest of your piece.

Becoming a collector of openings and endings...

Stravinsky once said that good composers borrow, but great composers steal. The same is definitely true of **performers**. When you see a brilliant ending that triggers an instant ovation, chances are that the performer has themselves seen an ending just like that in the past. They were impressed by it, remembered it... and **used it** for themselves.

You can do this too. One of the great things about having a **well-stocked recording library** is that you'll have access to hundreds—maybe thousands—of openings and endings from the **world's best performers**. (Even if you don't have a well stocked recording library, your teacher might, and your local library definitely should)

The best recordings to listen to are **live performances**. When you hear an opening or ending that works well, make a note of the characteristics. What **exactly** was the performer doing?

Then you can go to work ensuring **you** can do it too.

Eventually, you'll end up with a collection of effective openings and endings to **call on**—the more, the better.

Painting the scene
Giving your performances a cinematic edge

Stan has a **great imagination**, but a **dull** sounding piece.

He's **double checked** all the score markings, and is obediently playing everything that's asked for, but the piece still sounds... **unconvincing** somehow.

What can he do to **connect better** with what he needs to play, and create a more **compelling experience** for himself, and whoever listens to him?

INJECTING LIFE INTO unconvincing passages can be a **frustrating** affair. One technique to turn to is EXPERIMENTING➲135, forcing you to break out of the familiar and **embrace the untried**. Often you'll stumble across some solutions that you never would have discovered otherwise.

But there's **another way,** and it works completely differently. In fact, it's modelled on a phenomenon that have been manipulating the **hearts and minds** of hundreds of millions of people over the past century.

Film music.

Raw emotional power

Film music doesn't exist just to cover up **awkward silences** in the dialogue. A well-composed **film score** can make you look at a wide-eyed newborn kitten...and feel *fear*.

It can turn a clumsily written and badly directed final scene into a compelling **ten-kleenex tragedy.** It can make you feel cavalier or claustrophobic, wistful or wary—**even before** the events that should trigger those emotions occur.

And the whole time it's **messing with your head** like this, you might not even notice that the music is *there...*

This raw emotional power is good news for film directors.

And it's good news for music students too. What if you could unleash that force in your own practice?

Create your own movie scene

The next time you're struggling with a piece that feels "flat", ask yourself **this question:**

*"If this piece were **background music** for a scene in a movie, what would be **happening** in that scene?"*

Be **specific** with your answer—it's not enough to come back with "something sad is happening". **Who** is sad? **Why** are they sad? Is it sadness caused by **loss**? Or **loneliness**? Or a **nostalgic yearning**?

The more real you can make the scene in your own mind, the greater the impact it will have on your playing.

And then, once you've settled on the details, add the special **background**

music for that scene:

Your piece.

Trying it for yourself

Instead of the music influencing the scene, you're going to use your imaginary scene to influence the music.

In other words, this movie you've created in your head is going to **change** how you play your piece.

Not convinced? **Try this experiment** right now.

Choose a piece that you can already play well. Then **perform** the piece five times—each performance will be background music for a **different scenario** from below:

• An **old lady,** being helped by her grandchildren as she lays flowers at the grave of her husband of 50 years.

• A **young gymnast** finding out that her dream has come true, and she will be representing her country at the Olympics.

• A **desert waste-scape.** Nothing but the occasional tumbleweed, mirages and a sky too bright to look at.

• **Children exploring** an abandoned doll factory in the dead of night, when suddenly their flashlight fails...and the machines start running all by themselves...

• A **circus clown,** tripping over his own oversized shoes, and landing face-first in a conveniently located wedding cake.

I **don't know** which piece you chose, and at least some of those scenes will have been completely inappropriate for the music.

But even so, you should have ended up with **five completely different performances**. Chances are that your tempo for the graveside scenario was **slower** than the circus clown. Your desert waste-scape dynamics were probably **flat,** while the doll factory adventure would have featured a **wider range,** and **more sudden** changes.

The point is that connecting with scenarios will help you to see your piece in a **different light**—which increases enormously your chances of discovering a compelling performance.

Your own custom-made scene

Chances are, none of the scenarios above would have been exactly right for your piece.

That's ok. Part of your job now is to come up with a scenario that *does* suit the piece perfectly.

If you get stuck, enlist some **expert help.** Play your piece for family members and friends, have them each **list** three things that the piece could be about. Look for the common items, and then switch your imagination into overdrive.

Remember, once you can clearly picture a scene that perfectly matches your piece, the right dynamics, rubato, color and articulation will just **suggest themselves**.

You'll end up making dozens of changes to your original concept, without ever actually **setting out** to make changes. All you really need to do is make your own mood match the scenario—*the music will then take care of itself.*

The point is that it's much easier to perform with imagination and from the heart, if your heart and imagination were **actively involved** in the practice process. Painting a scene like this is great way to guarantee that.

Sources of inspiration
Even if your family and friends prove no help, there are plenty of other options to help you come up with a scene that's meaningful. Consider these:

> **News stories.** You'll see prison breakouts, sporting triumphs,

> It's much easier to perform with imagination and from the heart, if your heart and imagination were *actively involved* in the practice process.

disasters and new-born baby seals at the zoo—all in the same half hour. Plenty of raw material here

Novels/movies. The more of emotional punch they packed for you, the better.

Events in your own life: If you have a piece that is sad, then calling on a time that you were sad will help bring it alive.

In fact, people listening to it will start to feel sad too, *without them ever realizing why.*

Raw imagination: No limits—just start daydreaming. Create yourself an epic and detailed

scenario—then go make it happen as a piece of music. You're the screenwriter, producer, director, actor *and* music for this movie, so you might as well make it huge.

Your scene can be secret
If you have a scene which is **highly personal,** or involves elements you wouldn't be comfortable discussing with anyone, then that's fine.

Nobody needs to know what your scene is, or even that one exists. What they *will* know, along with the rest of the audience, is that there is something...connected... about your performance, making it impossible **not** to listen to.

Practice Buddies

Using the power of competition and co-operation

Sophia's practice has been a little **flat** lately. Her teacher has a suggestion, but he's being a bit **mysterious** about it.

"Here" he says, handing her a scrap of paper. "Everything you need is on there". Sophia was hoping for answers, but instead it's just a **name**, with a **phone number** and **email address** underneath.

She looks puzzled, but as her teacher explains, she starts to smile. "That sounds like fun" she eventually says "and I *know* it will make me work".

What was the plan?

WHEN FITNESS instructors are coaching, they'll **push you** hard—so that you push *yourself* hard.

But if they really want to see your best, there's a **simple tactic** they can use:

Pair you up with **another person**.

Then, instead of having to yell at you "push-it, push-it, push-it!", they can let your competitive spirit take over.

Even if you don't think of yourself as a **competitive person**, you're not going to want to be the **first one** to stop. In fact, it's no fun even being the first person to *slow down*.

End result? You'll work a little harder, trying to **keep up** with... or better still, **get ahead** of...your training partner. Before you know it, you've done more situps than you ever thought you could do.

It's an easy but **powerful** trick. But it's not just for gyms. You can use it when you **practice** too. And as we'll see, having a buddy opens up a wealth of new practice options.

So what exactly is a Buddy?

Your Practice Buddy is another student from your teacher's studio who is going to support and challenge you *between* lessons—just as you'll be supporting and challenging them.

Unlike the gym scenario, they won't actually be *with* you when you're practicing, but you'll both be very **aware** of what the other is doing—which is why you'll need at least one reliable way to contact them.

The plan is that you would **work closely together** for around ten weeks or so. But long before ten weeks is up, you will have transformed each other's practice—and discovered some new ways of doing things too.

Sharing weekly goals

Each week you'll have **tasks** you need to complete for your teacher, and perhaps some **additional goals** you set for yourself.

Instead of keeping these goals to yourself though, start your practice week by **sharing** them with your Practice Buddy. If you're planning on learning the first two pages of a brand new piece, then **tell them** that.

Why? Because at the end of the week, they're going to **ask you** "So, how did you go?"

At that point, you'll tell them what you actually did. Naturally, they will be **comparing** that with the goals you had set yourself.

So if you only get halfway to your goal, it's not just that you didn't get there. You have to *admit* to someone that you didn't get there. And that's no fun at all.

As a result, you'll work hard each week to make sure that you've got the best chance of being able to tell your buddy "Mission accomplished"—just as they'll be working hard to ensure their report back to you is also good.

Share midweek checkpoints

You and your buddy can also help each other **during the week** too. One way is to schedule an early LESSON PREFLIGHT CHECK➲174— where you set yourself a **mini-goal** that is halfway to your practice target for the week. So if you had set yourself two pages to learn for the week, by the time this Preflight Check arrives, you should have learned **at least one**.

Again, **share** the results with your Practice Buddy, just as they'll tell you theirs.

Early intervention

The advantage to the midweek preflight check is that it's **early enough** in the week to be able to **do something** about it if you're falling behind.

If you are behind, then you would need to tell your Buddy **how** you plan to **catch up**.

Again, when the week is complete, you'll be **asked** how that plan went.

It's all about **being accountable**. It's not enough any more just to *make* practice plans and goals—if you don't stick to them too, you have to **own up** to somebody.

A little competition is good...

If you really want to **set things alight**, don't just be accountable to your Practice Buddy. Set up a competition.

So as well as your weekly practice goals, you might have a **race** to be the first to be able to **memorise three brand new pieces** that your teacher has given you. Or you might both have a Monster Scales Quiz to prepare for, knowing that you'll be comparing results afterwards. Or you might set yourself six weeks to see who can complete the most sightreading drills.

Sometimes you'll win. Sometimes they will. But it won't be because you *let* them win, and even if you end up losing, you will done a lot of great work in the process.

The point is, for both of you, no matter what the scoreboard *between* you says, your playing and practicing will be winners.

Find out their practice tricks

One thing this book should make clear is that there are **countless** different ways to practice, meaning that your buddy will almost certainly use **different** practice tactics from you.

When you get their weekly "How did I go?" report, don't just settle for a report on the **outcomes** of the week. Make sure you find out what **practice techniques** they used.

Which sections did they pick on? How much time did they spend on each? What tricks did they use to memorise page three so well? How were they able to speed up that passage on page two?

And then get ready for a surprise. You'll have your own favorite practice techniques, but they **won't necessarily** be your Buddy's favorite techniques. Make a **note** of what they do differently, and—particularly if it seemed to produce good results for them—give some of their ideas a try.

Write each other prescriptions

If you really want to experience how your Buddy works, then have them write a **prescription** this week for how you should practice. You choose the **goals**, but they choose the **techniques** that will get you there, and the **tests** you would use to assess your own progress. You would also write a similar prescription for them.

Even if their recommended practice tactics **seem bizarre**, give them a try. The way you have always done things is simply that—the way you have always done things. It doesn't mean it's the *best* way, or the *only* way.

At the very least, you might be able to forever strike some tactics off your list. But you'll **be surprised** how often you end up permanently adding elements from these prescriptions to your own practice toolkit.

Issue one-off challenges

Both you and your Practice Buddy **have the right** once in the ten week campaign to **issue a challenge.**

The aim is to set your Practice Buddy a goal that will feel slightly out of reach. They'll have to **push themselves** and use every practice trick they know to get there. In fact, you'll be **giving suggestions** of your own as to how they can reach the target.

Of course, at some stage in the ten weeks, they'll be doing the same for you.

Similar to the MARATHON WEEK⤵191, the aim is to **extend the boundaries** of what's possible, but with the added interest of having the goal set for you by somebody else.

Whenever these challenges are set, you and your buddy are going to work very much **as a team**. If they set you a tough target, and you get there, then they win too.

You'll also learn a thing or two about the tactics they use in **high-pressure-short-deadline** situations, so you can adopt them for yourself.

Remember, there's no shame in **stealing ideas**. In fact, it's really the whole point.

Rotating Buddies

Once the ten week campaign is up, it's time to team up with **somebody new.** By then, you will have discovered most of your previous partner's practice tricks, and you'll be ready for some fresh ideas.

Everything will be completely different with your new Buddy. They'll write different prescriptions. They'll **work** either less or more hard than your previous buddy. They will need either less or more **encouraging.** The **challenge they set** will be easier or harder. And they'll have a brand new set of **practice tactics** to learn, to try, and sometimes, to copy.

In this way, you will work with **four or five different people** each year, and your practicing will be permanently different because of it.

Teamed buddies

Another way to inject some competitive spice into your practice is for you and your buddy to be competing not **against** each other, but **as a team** against another practice buddy pair.

So if there is to be a Monster Scales Quiz, then you might end up **adding** your score to that of your buddy. That total will go head-to-head with the total of another team.

Knowing this, you and your buddy will **encourage each other** in your scales preparation, and work out creative ways of making your scales bulletproof.

You could similarly have competitions based on learning the most number of **new pieces,** having the most days **without skipping practice** at all, coming up with the best **practice hints** for 50 different works for your instrument...whatever. Tell your teacher that you and your buddy are ready for whatever another team can throw at you—your teacher will have no problem coming up with a competition.

Multiple buddies

It's usually easiest to manage just a pair of Buddies, but there's no reason that there couldn't be **three or more** in your practice group.

Again, you'd have to **send** your goals for the upcoming week, and assessment of the previous week to all the Buddies in the group. It's more work, but you also get to see more practice techniques sooner... and it makes competition within the group much **more interesting**.

Non-musician buddies

Musicians aren't the only ones who need to spend time at home preparing. You can **learn a lot** from a Buddy who is a ballet dancer, a swim squad member or someone preparing for the Math Olympiad. They'll still have **goals** and practice **techniques**. They'll still have times when they feel **motivated**, and times when they don't. They'll still have **performances** that go well, and some that bite them hard.

But they'll also have a completely **different perspective** on preparation, based on the type of activity that they are involved in.

It's the reason that the **Australian Rugby team** once spent a week with the **Australian Ballet**—swapping ideas, comparing techniques for minimizing injury, learning about different approaches to preparing for big events. They quickly discovered that they had more in **common** than they had differences.

And then cheer on your buddy

Whether they're musicians or not, on the day of your Buddy's big performance, make sure you're there as their **#1 supporter.** Take the trouble to bring some family and friends with you, and then take a moment to **congratulate** your Buddy afterwards.

Music is known as being a **lonely pursuit.** It doesn't *have* to be that way though.

Your Practice Suite

Setting up the ultimate practice space

Krystal has been learning her instrument for 10 years now. In that time, she's had over **three thousand practice sessions**...all of them in the same room, using the same resources.

She doesn't feel the need to change though. It's quiet, well lit, with a music stand and all her music on a special shelf.

But is that really *everything* she needs?

Could it be that she's limiting her **practice** by limiting the **space she works in**...?

THERE ARE SAYINGS about bad workers blaming tools, but let's be fair—**broken tools** certainly don't make the job any easier.

A **badly set up** practice room *is* a broken tool, and it can make your job *much* harder each week. Which at the very least means that you'll be doing more practice than you really need to.

Unfortunately, most students don't think much about the **space they work in**—they simply use whichever room they have always practiced in, as is.

If they knew how much **time** they could be costing themselves, they'd be a **little pickier**.

Which is why you shouldn't settle for working in a **mere practice room** any more...

...it's time to create your very own **state-of-the-art Practice Suite**.

Your Practice Suite: the ultimate practice space

To a **casual visitor**, it might look just like any other living room, bedroom or garage. But any **musician** would quickly realise that they are **surrounded** by items that make this a **practice haven**.

And why not? You'll be spending plenty of time in there over the years...it might as well contain **everything you need** to produce your best:

Pencil

To mark errors, record ideas, improve fingering, write down questions, define segments, create reminders...all of which you would otherwise have to **keep in your head**. Keep one on your music stand, and a box of spares handy.

Notebook

For the notes you take that **don't belong** on the score. See for example LESSON AGENDA➲171, SESSION AGENDA➲305, PRESSURE TESTING ➲249, BREAKTHROUGHS DIARY ➲46

THIS WEEK!
Memorise page 3
* Prepare for scales test
* Complete theory sheet

Practice instructions

Don't even think about practicing without these. To make sure you can't overlook anything, **write your own** practice instructions as part of a LESSON REVIEW➲178

Fresh Photocopies of all your scores

It's not a piracy thing—you'll still own the original score—but having multiple copies of each score opens up a **whole new world** of practice options. See FRESH PHOTOCOPIES➲151

Color Highlighters

For markings and reminders that communicate the information you need *at a glance.* Helps keep your scores clutter free, and a **powerful pairing** with Fresh Photocopies. See COLOR CODING➲84

Recordings of as many of your pieces as possible

The people at Suzuki have known it for years. Immersing youself in the recording is a **huge head start** for any piece that you're about to learn. See RECORDINGS➲277 and SCOUTING➲299

Something to play back the recordings on

MP3 player or a discman, or the room might actually have its own sound system or PC. Whatever the gadget, when you're practicing, you've got to be able to listen to things **regularly and conveniently,** so you'll need *something.* See RECORDINGS➲277 and RECORDING YOURSELF➲270

Your own space

It doesn't have to be your own space *all* the time—just while you're practicing. And by "your own space", I mean that other people are not going to be coming in and out, or even *visible* to you.

This is why trying to do your practice in a **central high-traffic area** of your home is asking for trouble. If your practice space is normally also the **shortcut** from the front door to the fridge, then you're going to get disturbed a lot by hungry family members in the afternoon.

This means either finding a space that is not a high traffic area, or **negotiating** with family to regard the space as a **no-go zone** while you're working.

How? Make yourself a couple of **big signs**, and put them up whenever you start your practice session:

> "I'm *Practicing.* I won't be here all afternoon...but please go around this room until I'm done. Thanks!"

And then do take the time to **thank** the rest of your family every so often... they're doing you a favor, and deserve some recognition. (They don't HAVE to go around)

Minimal aural pollution

Which is a **fancy** way of saying "make sure your practice environment is *not too noisy*."

Your sign may well be encouraging your family to go **around** your practice space, but that doesn't help if your sister and ten of her friends are having a **karaoke competition** in the next room with a stereo that's turned up so loud that your music keeps **falling off** the stand.

Practicing is about listening carefully, and being able to concentrate on **fleeting moments**—external noise distractions will do more than test your resolve. They'll make the job at hand **impossible**.

If you genuinely are having trouble getting the necessary co-operation, then you might want to look at **rescheduling** your practice. Pick times when the noisy family members are at basketball training, or out shopping.

Calendar or Countdown Charts

So you don't get **ambushed** by deadlines. Also helps you create **checkpoint deadlines** for major-but-distant events…just so you're always on track. See Countdown Charts➲99

Pack of playing cards and dice

Both for **pressure** testing, and introducing the power of **random** elements to your practice. See Pressure Testing➲249 and Randomizing➲262

Internet access (if possible)

If you've got an internet-ready computer handy, the official **IMT Books website** has loads of online resources and help to make your practice easier. Check out **www.insidemusicteaching.com** for more details.

Contact details of your Practice Buddy

You *can* work by yourself, but it's much easier (and more fun) with **support**. For more information on how this works, see the chapter on Practice Buddies➲226.

Some way of recording yourself

A whole world of self-assessment options open up once you're able to sit back and **listen** to what you just played. See RECORDING YOURSELF⊃270

Kitchen timer

It's **not** to measure how long you practice (that's a terrible idea, see CLOCKWATCHERS ⊃76), but instead is there to give you wake-up calls if you're susceptible to working on **autopilot**. Just set and forget. See ENGAGING AUTOPILOT ⊃120

Family members

Ok, so you won't want them **permanently stationed** in your practice room, but from time to time you'll need an **audience** to put yourself under a little pressure. See DRESS REHEARSALS⊃115 and PRESSURE TESTING⊃249

Hiding distractions

Most people (not just Oscar Wilde) can resist anything except **temptation**, so by far the smartest thing to do is to simply **remove** that temptation.

Don't practice in the same room as your **games console**. Or near that **book** that you're busting to keep reading. Or a window which looks outside at the rest of your family having fun in the **pool**. Or the **television** that's showing programs you know your friends are probably watching right now.

It's the reason that the computer I write books on **cannot play games**. I'm not nearly so tempted to try to level-up my Level 23 character, or just have one quick Formula One race if I can't even **see** the computer that I would do that on...

This book ☺

There will still be plenty of practice ideas in here you haven't tried—keep your *Practiceopedia* handy so that whenever you get **stuck**, there's **help nearby**.

Practice Traps

Bad practice habits that waste your time and wreck your playing

Bethany does plenty of practice each week, but is finding it **increasingly difficult** to be ready for lessons.

Her teacher is **not alarmed** though. "I'm just wondering" he says, reaching for a list "if you spend any of your time using some of *these* practice techniques..."

She **reads** for a moment, and then looks up, red faced. "How did you know?" she says.

Bethany, you've been **found out.** Just *what* was on that list though?...

Practice traps: An introduction

Every activity has associated **bad habits** that can get you into trouble. **Golfers** who take their eye of the ball at the moment of impact. **Security guards** who fall asleep at their post. **Writers** who don't prooffread they're work propperly.

It's **no different** for practicing musicians. There are a number of classic bad habits that might seem harmless enough, but which unleash all manner of calamities upon your practicing, your playing and your lessons.

So **what are** these classic Practice Traps? And how can you **avoid** them?

Beginners

How the trap works

The title of this practice trap has **nothing to do with** being new to music lessons —instead it's used to describe students who always **start** their practice **from the beginning** of their piece. It's such a common trap that it has it's very own chapter—see BEGINNERS⊃33 for the ugly truth.

Shiny Object Polishers

How the trap works

Shiny Object Polishers spend most of their practice time working on passages and issues that are **already in good shape**. They'll pick on old pieces, comfortable passages, reliable scales—anything that they know they can already play well.

Why it causes problems

If you're a Shiny Object Polisher, it's not what you do that's so bad. It's what you *don't do*. The tough runs. That scale with the awkward position shift. The technical work that you messed up at your last lesson. The second half of your new piece.

And so, **despite the fact** that there might be plenty of practice happening, *you're not going to be ready for your lesson.* The problems from last lesson will remain unsolved, the new passages will remain unlearned, and your teacher will remain unimpressed.

Symptoms to look out for

If there is a **huge gap** in quality between the passages you play best and those you struggle with—*and that gap is widening*—then you might be a Shiny Object Polisher. Passages that are already rated at 9 for quality will go up to 9.5 (because of the extra attention they're getting), while zeroes will stay at zero.

But the most **telling indicator** that you might be suffering from this practice disease is your answer to this question:

*Do you **sound good** most of the time when you practice?*

If your answer is "yes", then you've **tested positive** to Polishing Shiny Objects. The only way to sound good most of the time is to **dodge** the many, many practice tasks that can have you sounding bad.

So your neighbors might be enjoying all this **clean mistake-free** playing, but they might not enjoy your **next concert** quite so much.

And you're certainly not going to enjoy your next lesson.

How to escape the trap

• Don't just *practice*. Create Session Agendas➲305 and stick to them. Using this system, as soon as you've completed all your tasks for the session, you can **stop practicing**—a great incentive to concentrate only on what needs the work. Of course, the flip side is that you **can't stop** *until* it's all done...so polish shiny objects, and you'll be there all day.

• Use Blinkers➲38 so that you **cannot even see** passages you can already play well. The only things **visible** to you should be passages that need work.

• Keep a Breakthroughs Diary ➲46. To ensure that you'll actually have something to record each day, you'll *have* to focus your energies on solving problems, and building new skills. If all you do is **paddle around** in passages that are already concertworthy, then your Diary will **remain blank**.

• Work with a Practice Buddy ➲226. They'll **quickly notice** if you're always telling them the same things—reports from Shiny Object polishers tend to read identically every time.

> ...when you're working this way, you're not actually practicing anything. You're just *playing stuff*.

Running Red Lights

How the trap works

Red Light Runners **hate stopping** when they're playing... which means that even if they notice a problem, *they'll just keep going anyway*. Straight through the red light.

As they mess up, they **tell themselves** things like "I must work on that bit", but next thing they know, they're at the end of the piece (again), and they **can't remember** where "that bit" was, or just what about it needed fixing.

...and that goes for each of the other six "that bits" that they noticed en route.

But even more alarmingly, because their **focus** is on getting to the end of the piece, they might not even have **noticed** many of the problems in the first place. In other words, like the worst of drivers, they ran the red lights *without even knowing they were there*.

Why it causes problems

I hate to break it to you, but when you're working this way, you're not actually practicing anything. You're just *playing* stuff.

All these problems that you **scooted straight past** will be waiting for you at your next lesson...and at your performance...

Symptoms to look out for

Red Light Runners will **often complain** "I always mess that bit up". It's true. They *do* always mess that bit up. But it's no wonder, *because they've* *never tried to fix it*—they just trip over it every time, and keep going. As a result they then need to be **reminded** about the same issues week after week, because those issues are never actually being tackled.

How to escape the trap
• The next time a passage gives you a hard time, don't just keep going. Give *it* a hard time. See Boot camp ➲43.

• Use blinkers➲38 to **narrow** the chunk of the piece you work on at once. If the passage you're playing is only 8 measures long, even if you're just playing straight through in a loop, you'll be forced to see the **same red light** dozens of times in a single practice session—it will **yell** louder at you each time, until it's impossible to ignore.

• Practice some **positive discrimination.** Run practice sessions where the **only** thing you are doing is identifying and reacting to problems. Bugspotting➲53 and coral reef mistakes➲89 are two techniques that can help you find all the problem sections. You can then use Clearing obstacles➲72, Isolating➲164 and Exaggeration➲124 to target those problems.

• Record yourself➲270 to split your practice into **two clear phases**—playing and analysing. So you can run the red light when you play the piece through, but you'll pick up all the mistakes on the action replays.

• Sharpen your focus by tackling your piece one issue at a time—see Thematic practice➲330

Speeding

How the trap works
Most students **know** that practicing too fast is bad, but few realize just how much damage those extra beats-per-minute can cause.

Again, like *Beginners*, this trap is so common that it has it's own chapter. See Speeding➲320 for the full story.

Skimming

How the trap works
Skimmers will practice a problem passage until they **experience success for the very first time**—then they'll immediately declare the passage "cured", and move on to something else.

In other words, the very first time they **fluke** a good playthrough, *all work on that passage stops.*

Why it causes problems
Skimming might not actually *cause* any problems, but it certainly **doesn't fix any** either. Your pieces aren't going to get better, because you keep stopping your practice just as things are about to **get interesting.**

It would be like learning to ten-pin-bowl, and then deciding no further practice is needed after your **very first strike**. A strike is nice, but it's not a sign that your first 300 game is approaching.

Symptoms to look out for
Skimmers have a catchphrase:

"...but it didn't sound like this at home!"

Yes it did. It's just that you are comparing what you **just played** with the **one attempt** at home that happened to go well—conveniently overlooking the 129 other attempts where the ending wasn't so happy.

So for skimmers, lessons and concerts are **rolls of the dice**—maybe the passage will go well, maybe it won't. But because there hasn't been any thorough preparation, they'll be disappointed more often than not.

Like red-light runners, skimmers also often need to be reminded week after week about exactly the same issues—not because they are ignoring them, but because they're **undercooking** them, and serving them up pretty much raw each lesson.

How to escape the trap
• Before you declare something to be fixed, you need to **prove** that it's actually ready. Until you can win one or more of the PRESSURE TESTS➲249 you're not done just yet.

• You should also be running LESSON PREFLIGHT CHECKS➲174, so you can face the reality of what's really ready, and what's not—anything you had skimmed will probably fall apart in the preflight check.

> # Skimming might not actually *cause* any problems, but it certainly doesn't fix any either.

This acts as a **wakeup call** that you had undercooked the passage first time, so you can be more rigorous second time around.

• RECORD YOURSELF➲270, with the aim of capturing a no-mistakes recording of your passage. **Count the takes** until you get a result you're happy with.

If it took **more than one**, then there's still work to be done. After all, on **concert day**, one take is what you've got.

Overcooking

How the trap works
Overcooking is the opposite of skimming. These students just **can't**

let go of the passage they're working on, and keep on practicing it long after it's already been adequately prepared.

It's a variation on SHINY OBJECT POLISHING➲237, except that the student is not trying to sound good all the time, or actively avoiding any other passages—*they just don't trust the work they've already done* on this passage.

No matter how much work they've done, or how many tests the passage has passed, they're **never satisfied**.

Why it causes problems
Overcooking not only wastes huge amounts of time, it's another trap that can have you turning up to each lesson **unprepared**, despite having worked hard.

What you have to remember is

that while you were overcooking your already-fixed passages, other passages that genuinely needed the help were **missing out.**

This feeling of "no matter how much I do, it's not enough" can also severely **undermine your confidence** on performance day...

...because no matter how much preparation you've done, *it's not enough.* You're not ready, ever.

Symptoms to look out for
The Overcookers **catchphrase** is *"just one more time, just to be sure".* And of course, after one more time, then they figure that maybe **still once more** might make it even better...it will only **take a moment**...

Work this way, and you'll quickly find that you always seem to be **running out of time** before you can get through everything you need to.

How to escape the trap
• There's a chapter in this book dedicated especially to knowing when you're finished with something—and then being able to move on without **feeling guilty.** Check out CLOSURE➲80.

• Overcookers also need to use PRESSURE TESTING➲249, but for a different reason to skimmers. Instead of a succesful test simply being *permission* to move on, it's a sign that you *have* to move on.

• If your overcooking means that you are returning to the same passages session after session, you might also want to consider ONE WAY DOORS➲208.

• To add pressure to keep moving forwards through a series of tasks, make sure you always work from a SESSION AGENDA➲305. If you overcook, you'll quickly discover that it becomes impossible—or takes hours—to get through your entire agenda in one session.

Sheep counters

How the trap works
Sheep counters only know one way to practice—to play the passage over and **over** and **over** and **over**...

The hope is that if they just make the number of repetitions **high** enough, they can solve *any* problem. This means that if they've already played a passage 250 times, and it's still not right, then it's a sign that they should try 300. Or *3,000.*

Why it causes problems
This is a **deadly trap.** It's not just that sheep counting fails to fix problems—it will actually **embed** them in your piece. (See CEMENTING➲64).

This happens because repetition was never designed to *fix* problems. It just takes whatever you're already doing—good or bad—and **locks it in.** So if you have a calamitous fingering for a passage, sheep counting will just ensure that you *always* use that fingering. It makes no judgement about the fingering itself—in fact, sheep counting makes no judgements about anything.

But there's an even bigger problem. Sheep counting is **boring.** It's no wonder some students don't like practicing—if practicing is *"Here. Play this 190 times"*, then you'd need to be a **special sort of crazy** to enjoy it.

Symptoms to look out for

Very easy to spot this one—if your practice is **dominated** by repetition, then you're sheep counting. Game over, put your hands up, read yourself your rights.

The **sad thing** is that all that repetition actually takes plenty of dedication—but you're actually causing massive damage to your pieces in the process.

How to escape the trap

• CEMENTING➲64—which is the **legitimate** use for repetition in your practice sessions—is just a **tiny part** of a much bigger team of practice techniques. Check out the chapter on VARYING YOUR DIET➲360 for a glimpse of the wider practice world you're missing.

• Make sure you've got a proper understanding of each phase of a practice CAMPAIGN➲58—you'll quickly notice that repetition is actually **missing entirely** from many of the phases.

• If you must practice through heavy repetition, at least ensure that you're repeating what's **actually in the score**. Check out the chapters on DETAILS TRAWLING➲110 and PROTOTYPES➲257.

Gluttons

How the trap works

Gluttons try to fix **too much at once**—the sections they work on are too big, and the list of issues too long.

So in a **single practice session**, they might try to improve the fingering, rhythm, phrasing, dynamics, fast runs, projection of melodies, part separation, articulation, balance, rubato and tone production...in their week-old 18 page Sonata.

Why it causes problems

There's a saying that if you **chase two rabbits**, both will escape. The same thing is true when you're practicing, except that gluttons don't stop at just *two* rabbits. Instead, they're dividing their concentration among a dozen issues and pages simultaneously, ensuring that nothing receives the attention it needs.

As a result, despite the fact that gluttons often work incredibly hard, they will have **little improvement** to show for their efforts.

Worse still, because there are so many notes and issues to monitor, many problems will **escape undetected**.

Symptoms to look out for

Gluttons often feel **completely overwhelmed**—like a fire crew that has to battle multiple blazes at once. Because they're aware of all these problems, but are making little headway on any of them, there can be a creeping feeling of **panic**...

...and so they work even harder, compounding the madness.

Gluttons also tend to become **exhausted** after only a short amount of practice. There's just so much going on that practicing becomes nothing short of an **assault on their senses**...including their sense of guilt and helplessness.

Twenty minutes of that takes a lot out of anybody. A few weeks of that, and you're not going to want to practice at all.

How to escape the trap

• Make yourself a SESSION AGENDA➲305, and then work on one item at a time. You'll be amazed—to the point of **needing reviving**—at how much faster you get through everything.

• Use ISOLATION➲164 to ensure that you're able to target one problem at a time—**without interference** from other problems.

• You can **narrow your focus** to individual issues by switching to THEMATIC PRACTICE➲330 , while using BLINKERS➲38 to **limit** the portion of the score you're working with.

• If you're having trouble deciding which rabbit to chase, use TRIAGE➲342 to help you **prioritize**.

Autopilots

How the trap works

Simply put, it's practicing with your brain either **off** or **elsewhere**. You'll be thinking about all sorts of things when you play...you just won't be thinking about what you're actually doing.

This is another common practice trap with dire consequences and its **own chapter**—see ENGAGING AUTOPILOT➲120.

Ignoring the map

How the trap works

Playing from memory is definitely a useful skill, but *practicing* from memory is **not always a good idea**.

Map ignorers are usually **hard-core memorizers** who only use the music to learn the notes in the first place... and then do the remaining 95% of their practice *with no score at all.*

Which means that from that point on, they have **no way** of being able to determine if the version they're playing is different from what's being asked for.

Why it causes problems

Map ignorers will **protest** that they don't need the music, because they can remember what's there. They can even play you the piece from beginning to end to **prove** it.

But here's the thing. Even if the student had **triple checked** every note when they were first learning the piece, and even if their performance never breaks down halfway, it's **still not safe** for them to permanently discard the score.

Why? Because over time, *your playing can evolve.* Like a game of **Chinese Whispers**, little errors will steadily creep in. An accidental here. An ottavo marking there. A staccato dot. A repeat that seems to have gone missing.

Bit by bit, your piece will mutate — but because it's so gradual, you **won't notice it**.

But it's not a question of just trying to **remain faithful** to what was in the score. It's what you and your teacher will have **added** to the score since you started working on it. Fingering changes. Altered dynamics. Reminders or ideas about rubato, articulation or phrasing. Practice advice.

You won't be able to see any of this. Which means that your memory is going to have to be very, very good.

As you'll see in the chapter on FRESH PHOTOCOPIES➲151, a score is **more than** just a which-note-is-next **prompt**. It allows you to plan, annotate, verify, record, question, focus, experiment...

...**and** occasionally remind yourself which note comes next, which comes in handy when you've **accidentally transposed** that final note by an octave.

Symptoms to look out for
If your lessons seem to be filled with your teacher **re-circling missed score details**, then you should be looking hard at *how* you missed them.

Another indicator is if your **reading** tends to be weak, and **picking up** from halfway through pieces impossible. It's not always a sign that you are a weak reader by design—it's just that your insistence on playing without the score means that you've had a fraction of the reading practice that most other students have had.

> # My favorite exhibit for the prosecution is when students leave their book at the lesson...
>
> ## ...and don't notice...

But my **favorite exhibit** for the prosecution is when students leave their book at the lesson...

...and don't notice.

"How did you go this week?" I'll ask when I see them next "Practice was good?"

"Oh yes." They'll reply "I did lots".

And you know something? I **believe** them. Which means at that point, I fasten my seat belt and stow my tray table in an upright position. It's going to be a **bumpy** lesson.

How to escape the trap
• Actively choose practice techniques that are **impossible without**

the score. BUGSPOTTING➲53, COLOR CODING➲84 and DETAIL TRAWLING➲110 all require a score at all times. Depending on the issue you select (eg. "phrase lengths correct) THEMATIC PRACTICE➲330 will have you reaching for the score too.

• Discover the wonders of FRESH PHOTOCOPIES➲151—scores are a **lot more fun to work** with if each one tells you something slightly different about your piece.

• Because the habit can be hard to break, **invite a family member** to come and surprise you with score *Spot Checks*.

How does this work? They'll turn up **unannounced** in your practice room and just ask you **where** the music for what you're practicing is. It's **not enough** for you just to point at your music stand. You have to be able to show them exactly where you're up to. And if that's taking **more than a second or so**, then you weren't using the music in the first place.

• You don't have to use the score **every time** you work, just often enough for regular reality checks.

So one tactic is to roll a dice at the start of every practice session—if it's a 5 or a 6, use the score. If not, then practice as you normally would. In the course of a full week, you should still have plenty of opportunity to view the source. (See also RANDOMIZING➲262)

Clockwatchers

How the trap works

If you know you're supposed to do 30 minutes of practice each day, and your main focus is on **how far through that time** you are, then you're a clockwatcher.

It's a variation on the "are we there yet" that comes from the back seat of cars on long trips. The journey has become something to get through— like a **dentist appointment**, or a **bad movie.**

Practicing this way is ineffective— but is nonetheless so common— that there's a chapter dedicated to it (see CLOCK WATCHERS➲76).

Panic Practicing

How the trap works

Panic practicers **leave** all their practice until what they think is the last possible second...and then quickly discover that the last possible second was **actually some time ago**.

Most of the time, they look like regular students—except that they're *not* practicing. Practicing is something to be done *later*. But in the 48 hours before a lesson or concert, reality hits, and they suddenly go into hyperdrive.

Like the hare waking from its **mid-race slumber**, they set off in pursuit of the finish line...but it's all too late.

Why it causes problems

This book is all about being **more efficient**, but it's certainly **not** about short cuts. Anything that has been assembled in only 48 hours *will sound like it's been assembled in only 48 hours.* So while there's plenty you can do to cut your TURNAROUND TIME➲352 for all your pieces, there's a limit.

In the end, the results will speak for themselves. Panic-practiced pieces are **brittle**, and **fall apart** under the pressure of a lesson or concert. The only question is going to be where, and how bad the damage will be.

Symptoms to look out for

If you're a panic practicer, then music lessons probably **won't be the only area** of your life you handle this way. **School projects** are going to get started the night before. Birthday invitations will be sent out **after** the RSVP date that's printed on them. Videos will be returned late. (This is exactly how my life is)

The most telling symptom though is that your performances—whether in lessons or at your concert—will always be accompanied by **fear**, and won't show the **real you**. If you're consistently disappointed by how you play on such occasions, and often feel that it was because you **just weren't ready**, then it's time to have a look at how early you're preparing.

How to escape the trap

• First things first, check out the chapter on NOT WANTING TO PRACTICE➲200. Most panic practice ends up happening simply because the students had an extended period where they **didn't want to** practice... you need to understand why, so you can do something about it.

• It's harder to get **ambushed** by your deadlines when you can **see them coming**. Make sure you have a COUNTDOWN CHART➲99 in your practice room, so you can see the numbers ticking down to the big day.

Make sure that as part of that, you set yourself **checkpoint deadlines**, so that a quarter of the way through the campaign, you can tell if you're a quarter of the way there.

• You can then use those deadlines to help create daily SESSION AGENDAS➲305—ensuring that the practice you do **today** is actually **helping prepare** you for these distant events.

• Make sure you run a LESSON PREFLIGHT CHECK➲174 as part of every week—that way, you'll be **warned** about falling behind **early enough** to be able to do something about it.

• Another way to combat procrastination is to **make yourself accountable** to somebody else. Try working with a PRACTICE BUDDY➲226— you'll find doing nothing a lot harder if you have to **admit** it to someone. And if that someone is a fellow student, then it's **harder still.**

• Alternatively, you could keep a BREAKTHROUGHS DIARY➲46. Again, it doesn't let you get away with inactivity—you'll have **blank pages** nagging you.

• Set aside one day each week to RECORD➲270 what you sound like. If you **can't tell** *this* week's recording apart from *last* week's, then you know it's time to get moving.

Bad bricklayers

How the trap works

These students practice everything in segments... but they never actually practice the joins **between** segments. This means that while the **theme** from your *Theme and Variations* might sound great—and so does **Variation 1**— getting **from** the theme **to** Variation 1 is a different story. There's a bump, like a crack in the pavement.

Why it causes problems

Quite apart from being bump-ridden, the performance itself will sound like lots of sections **glued together**, rather than a **unified** whole...

...which is, after all, how you were practicing it.

If your **sections are short**, and the **piece is long**, then these bumps can be so regular that they detract from everything else—no matter how well you might be playing what happens in between.

Symptoms to look out for

If your score is clearly divided into segments, and you **only ever use those segments,** then you're a candidate for bad bricklaying.

Apart from that though, the **between-section-bumps** are usually pretty obvious, and make the first few measures of each new section awkward. If you're not sure, RECORD YOURSELF➲270 and then listen carefully for bumps in the playback.

How to escape the trap

• The chapter on BRIDGING➲50 is dedicated to correcting the Bad Bricklaying Trap. You'll find that it doesn't take long to turn this issue right around.

• It's also worth practicing with a metronome—it won't help you with dynamic or phrasing bumps, but it will at least help you ensure that each new section arrives **on time.**

• Instead of working on passages that are defined by marked sections, work on passages where the boundaries are set by the **problem you're having.** So your practice locations would only ever reflect the specific locations of trouble spots—and

therefore would be **changing** with every practice session.

There's no chance then for bad bricklaying, because the bricks (and therefore the joins) are always being placed in different locations.

Performers

How the trap works

Perhaps the worst practice trap of all. Performers **cannot tell the difference** between *preparing* their piece and *performing* their piece.

And so every practice session resembles a performance. The pieces are always played at **full speed.** The pieces are always played from **beginning to end.** The pieces are played with **no stops.** And as soon as they have finished the performance, they'll usually **start it again.**

Why it causes problems

Performers combine several of the worst practice traps into one **ghastly practice creature** that has bolts in its head, and could only have been

brought to life by a **lightning strike** in a **mad scientist's** chamber.

Their insistence on full tempo means that they are **Speeding.** Playing from beginning to end means that they are **Red Light Runners.** Endlessly looping the performance means that they are **Sheep Counters.** The fact that they're working on the whole piece at once means that they're the worst of **Gluttons.**

And so their piece suffers the symptoms of each of these separate practice diseases. Even the most hardened ER nursing staff would **gasp with shock** when they see this patient.

Can the piece be **cured**? Absolutely. Can it be cured while the student **insists** on making every practice session a performance? No way.

This is not a Practice Trap that simply means you are working somewhat below your best—such as, say, Bad Bricklaying. This is a Practice Trap that is a **Category 6 hurricane disaster** bearing down on your upcoming performance.

Symptoms to look out for

It's very easy to spot this trap. When you practice, are you:

❑ Always playing at full speed?
❑ Always playing the whole piece?
❑ Never stopping mid-play-through?
❑ Starting again from the beginning once you're done?

If you've checked **two or more** of these boxes, then you're almost certainly a performer. In which case, your practice isn't practice at all. It's **play-acting**. Pretending to produce the performance that you want...but not actually doing anything to earn it.

The reason you have to change quickly is that there is a **fifth box** you'll be checking otherwise:

❑ *Are your performances often sloppy, error-ridden, underprepared, and a mere shadow of what you're capable of?*

How to escape the trap

• You have to switch—as soon as you possibly can—from your **performance** model to practicing that is based around **troubleshooting**.

Use techniques like Bugspotting➲53 or Coral reef mistakes➲89 to locate areas in your piece that need work. And then turn these problems into a list for attention as part of Session agendas➲305.

• To stop yourself from playing complete performances, work from Fresh Photocopies➲151 rather than the original score—and then *hide all but one of the pages.* That way, if you're dependent on the score to play, you won't be able to play more than the page you have access to. (This technique is like a **blunt version** of Blinkers➲38)

Each practice session, you'd rotate to a new page.

• If you really must play from beginning to end, then at least ensure that you are **focusing your listening** on a different issue each time. Using Thematic Practice➲330 will ensure that each performance has you **noticing** different types of potential problems.

And then, once you've completed a performance playthrough, work on any problems that affected your issue-of-the-moment **before** looping back for your next playthrough.

So if your issue had been "fingering problems", and you noticed a couple of passages where fingering was a little **haphazard**, before you start your next performance, you'd ensure the fingering problem had been fixed.

In this way, you use your performances to **identify** problems, and then the rest of your practice to **fix** them—similar to the relationship between Bugspotting➲53 and Isolation➲164.

Pressure Testing

Ensuring you can produce your best playing when it counts most

Deanne's **concert** has just finished, and she's in the car in floods of **tears**.

"It's not fair!" she says "I **practiced hard** and it sounded so **good at home,** but that was TERRIBLE and I made mistakes that I **never** usually make and... *sniff...* I'm never playing in another **stupid concert** again and everything's stupid and did I mention it's NOT FAIR..."

Not much her family can say to cheer her up now. But there's lots she could have done to make sure this **didn't happen in the first place...**

Oₙₑ ᴏꜰ ᴛʜᴇ ᴛʜɪɴɢꜱ that makes performing so exciting—and nerve-wracking—is that there's **no "undo"**. You can't let loose a stream of wrong notes, **hit ctrl-z**, and expect those notes to go away.

As a result, music **isn't** just about being able to get things right. It's about being able to get things right *when it really matters*. Goals scored before the game don't count, and so if your piece **is a smoldering wreck** at the concert, that audience isn't going to care that "it sounded great last week".

Most students are aware of this, and **hope** that the pressure won't get to them on the day.

But dealing with this by "hoping" is not dealing with it at all. Remember, *anything that you need to do on stage is something you should practice first.* If there's a trill in your performance, you'll practice it. If there's a fast chromatic run, you'll practice it.

So since playing under pressure is a part of your performance...

...you should practice that too. The question though is *how*.

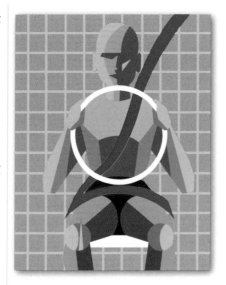

The practice room cocoon
The problem is, unlike on stage, in your practice room there *is* an "undo". When you mess things up, you *can* **simply restart** the passage, and get it right second time round. Or third time. Or whenever you like.

There's no audience, there's no teacher—and there's **no pressure**. Just re-rack the balls each time, and break again.

This might be great for staying **relaxed** when you practice, but it can be a disaster waiting to happen when you perform. *All your preparation was based on knowing you have unlimited attempts*, which is exactly what you **won't** have on concert day.

"What would happen if you only had **one shot** at this?" is the question the concert will ask of you. And when it does, you better know the answer in advance. Because if that question **hits you suddenly** for the first time when you're on stage, very, very bad things can happen.

It's not the width...
Let's imagine that you had to walk along a balance beam—but not the sort of beam you might have seen in gymnastics competitions.

Instead, this beam is **two feet wide**... and just **two inches** off the ground.

Not exactly the hardest of challenges. Two feet wide...that's practically a *path*...and with no distance to fall either, you'd have to be feeling pretty relaxed..

Because there are no consequences for messing up, walking along this beam is like playing your piece in your practice room. It's safe. It's stress free. So you'll walk along it every time without problems.

Now let's make a **minor change** to the scenario. It's exactly the same wide balance beam...

...but this time, it's **spanning a chasm** in the Himalayas that plunges almost two miles straight down. You're so high up that there are mountain goats with vertigo and cirrus clouds *below* you.

There's no handrail. No safety harness. Just a two-foot wide balance beam, and no second chances.

Now, take a look at the balance beam again and ask yourself: Is walking along this easy or not?

So what's changed?
Physically, it's exactly the same challenge as the first time. It's exactly the same length and width as the first balance beam, so it's **no harder** to balance on.

But this time, if you *do* fall off, all the kings horses and all the king's men aren't going to be able to put you together again either.

Knowing that, the bridge **looks a lot skinnier** than it actually is.

Which is where the heart of the problem really is:

The additional fear means you're more likely to fall.

Preparing for one-chance only
If you want to be able to cope with the pressure of performance day, the first thing you need to do in the practice room is **change the height** of the beam you practice on. It shouldn't always be two inches from the ground. It should sometimes be high enough that a fall will at least *hurt.*

This means having moments in your

practice where there are **consequences** for getting things wrong:

• *20 minute consequence*
Wait until the **very end** of a practice session—when you're thoroughly sick of practicing and are **looking forward** to a break. Then you choose the passage to be tested...and have **one attempt** only at playing it.

If it's all **ok**, then enjoy your time off. You've earned it. But if the **tiniest thing** goes wrong, then you need to do another 20 minutes of practice on that passage, *right there and then.*

And if that doesn't make you nervous enough, consider a 40 minute consequence...or a 60 minute. Whatever number it takes to get your **heart racing** just a little before you make that single attempt.

That way, you're not just playing the passage. You're playing it when there are **consequences for messing up**...just like concert day.

Another way to run this is the day *before* any **scheduled days off** in your practice timetable. This time, you're playing for the **right** to actually have your day off... anything goes wrong with the passage, and you're practicing tomorrow after all.

If you value your days off, this will make you **nervous**. Which is the whole idea.

• X times in a row

This balance-beam-raiser is about being able to produce **consecutive** correct playthroughs—and it's the "in a row" part that's critical here. If 5 is the magic number, then there's plenty of pressure on you once you've got 4 in a row...any mistakes now, *and you go all the way back to the first play through.*

So the higher you climb, the **more you risk losing** with a mistake. Make this game 10 in a row, and feel your **pulse quickening** after your 9th...it's a long way back to 1 if you crash at that point.

And remember—*you're not allowed to stop practicing until you win.* So there are real consequences, and they all involve messing with your free time.

• Ledger System

This game has a deceptively simple rule:

*As soon as you have played the passage correctly 10 times **more** than you've played it incorrectly, you win.*

Doesn't sound too hard, but the killer detail here is that it's the **margin** that's important—the game doesn't care whether you win 10-0, or One **Million** and ten to One Million.

Which means if you're having an **off-day**, or you **don't really know** the passage properly in the first place, then you're going to be there for a long time.

Why? Because of the scoring system, every incorrect playthrough you do *effectively erases a correct attempt.* If your score is 100-100, then you're **no better off** than you were when you started, because your margin is still zero.

(In fact, you're worse off, because you've just rehearsed 100 incorrect playthroughs—see Cementing ⮌64)

Narrowing the practice beam

The examples above are just some of the ways that you can **increase the height** of the beam...to create consequences for messing up, and then put you in a position where the way you play will either **avoid** or **bring on** those consequences.

But there's **another way** that you can increase pressure in the practice room.

You can make the beam itself *narrower.*

So, irrespective of height, instead

of walking on the same 2 foot wide beam that the main event demands, you'd **practice** on a 1 foot wide beam. Or a six inch. Or *three* inches.

That way on concert day itself, even though the beam is higher, negotiating it **feels easy** by comparison.

Narrowing the beam in the practice room is about playing those games outlined above, but **changing the circumstances** under which you play. The idea is that as well as there being **consequences** for getting things wrong, it's going to be **harder to get things right** in the first place:

• Add a metronome

It's **one type of victory** to have to play a passage correctly four times in a row...it's **quite another** if you have to stay lockstep with a metronome the whole time.

It means you can't get yourself out of trouble by slowing down—you have to keep playing, ready or not.

On concert day, you don't have to put up with demands like this, and can work with a tempo that **ebbs and flows** to suit your needs.

> **"What would happen if you only had one shot at this?"** is the question the concert will ask of you. And when it does, you better know the answer in advance...

In the meantime though, insisting on a metronome is suiting up for concert day by **exceeding its demand**s. By narrowing the beam *now*, you'll make the beam seem wider *then*.

• Play from memory

Find you're winning the pressure games easily already? Try them again, but **without the music** this time.

If you're a memorizer by nature anyway, this probably won't make things any harder, but if you normally work *with* the music, then the loss of the music will mean that the beam is suddenly looking very skinny.

Again, on **concert day**, you will have the music—which will feel easy by comparison.

• Extend the section to be tested

Obviously, the **longer** the passage you're testing, the **more likely** it is that something will go wrong. So for that reason, you wouldn't normally use these pressure tests on an entire Sonata—especially those tests that don't allow for a single error.

However, you can always make tests tougher by **gradually stretching** the length of the excerpt you're testing. It doesn't have to be the whole piece, but even a few extra measures can add enormously to the difficulty of the challenge.

So if you're **already coping well** with the introduction and first subject, maybe it's time to include the second subject as well.

• Increase the tempo demands

Don't try this until you're already comfortably winning challenges **with the metronome**. But as soon as you are, you can always make things tougher by demanding **higher speeds**.

Ideally, you want to be able to successfully pressure test tempos that **go beyond** what your concert requires—allowing you to play well within yourself on concert day.

• "Cold" tests

These are special tests that you run right at the very start of your practice session—before you get a chance to warm up. It's a technique that is particularly well suited to pressure testing **openings** (see OPENINGS & ENDINGS ➾215).

Instead of cold starts then being a monster that's **unique** to concerts, it will be something you're **used to** coping with at home as well.

• Random sections

Pressure tests can quickly start to feel **comfortable** if you always test the same passages in the same order.

If you really want to challenge yourself, throw all the possible

starting locations in a hat, and then **draw** to work out which one you use next. (See RANDOMIZING ➾262)

Or, to completely randomize things, choose both the starting measure AND the length of the passage at random. That way, you'll never see exactly the same pressure test twice...and you'll also quickly become very good at being able to pick up from absolutely anywhere. (See FIRE DRILLS ➾139)

• Add an audience

Most pressure tests are more difficult if you **know someone's watching**. Instead of just running them behind the closed doors of your practice room, invite in a family member.

Better still, create a **consequence** for messing up that the family member will hold you to. Promise to make their bed for a week if anything goes wrong. Or to cook them breakfast tomorrow. Or to cover all their chores for a couple of days.

They'll be listening very closely for any errors. Your heart will be thumping.

And by the time concert day comes around, you will be an old hand at being able to perform well under stressful conditions.

Not just for concerts

Pressure testing is a great way to prepare for performances, but that's not the only thing you'll end up using it for:

• *For Closure*

CLOSURE ⤳80 is about knowing when you can safely *stop* practicing something. If you want to be **really sure** that it's time to move on, then throw one of these tests at it—the tougher the better.

If the passage **doesn't pass**, then it's a sign that there's still more to be done.

But if you *can* pass, then you can move on to something new with **confidence**, and a **clear conscience**.

• *Preparing for lessons*

Lessons are another occasion where you **won't** have **unlimited attempts**. Your teacher doesn't have time to listen to you muddle through the opening a dozen times—in fact, if it's still a mess after the first couple of attempts, they will **assume** that you **haven't** been working on it.

That might not be completely accurate. Maybe you *have* been working on it. But you obviously hadn't been pressure testing it— otherwise you could have checked that it would have been ok despite minimal attempts.

When your fail pressure tests

You won't pass every pressure test you set yourself, but a fail **doesn't mean** you need to **panic**. When a test doesn't go so well, there are three things to try:

1) Take the test again

Sometimes it's worth attempting the test a second time round. This doesn't grant you **amnesty** from whatever penalties you incurred first time around...it just means you're taking a second shot at it. Sometimes you'll find that a second attempt is all you need.

However, if things don't work out the second time...

2) Make the test easier

Use the ideas outlined in "Narrowing the Beam" (P252), but use them in reverse:

• Try **shortening** the section
• Set yourself a **slower tempo**
• If there is an **audience** present, try the test again without them
• If you were attempting it from memory, try **using the music**.
• Take the **metronome** out of the picture, so that you can have the time you need to think between notes.

Once you've changed the rules, retest, see how you go.

If you've been steadily **dumbing down** the requirements of the test, and you *still* can't pass then...

3) Stop all testing, and trouble-shoot that passage.

It's no good just throwing endless pressure tests at a passage that's broken. Remember, Pressure Testing is **not** designed to fix problems—it's designed to ensure that you can handle under pressure passages **you already know.**

So if a passage is constantly collapsing no matter which test you throw at it, then it's a sign that the passage is simply **not ready** for testing yet.

See the PRACTICEOPEDIA USHER ⮌31 entry on "Dealing with problem passages" for suggestions as to how best to do this.

Remember, **no matter how bad** the test result, you're much better off discovering that this passage is fragile **now**...rather than on stage. Go fix it up, come back test it again, and then nail it on performance day.

Recording your triumphs

Passing a pressure test is **certification** that your *preparation has worked*. It's not just a passage that you get right when you get **lucky**—you're able to get it right under pressure, which means that it should be **fine for the concert** as well.

Whenever a passage passes a pressure test, it's worth recording the victory in your BREAKTHROUGHS DIARY ⮌46. Record the **date**, any bridge-narrowing **rules** you set yourself for the test, and the **type** of test.

That way, if any little **nagging doubts** start appearing before your concert—wondering whether you're *really* ready or not—you can actually **point to evidence** that everything is fine. For every passage in the piece, you'll see a **list** of pressure tests that you know you've passed.

So you can say to yourself:

"Am I ready? Let's see...I've tested every part of this piece with the **music**, without the music, with the **metronome** at half a dozen different speeds, up to **ten times in a row** without a single error, with and without **audiences**, starting from **random locations**...all the while with various tidy-other-people's-rooms **consequences** hanging over me...

...and on concert day, all I have to do is play it **once**. No metronomes. At three-quarters of the speed I'm capable of. With the music in front of me. And I'm actually allowed to make a few mistakes.

Am I ready?...

...you bet I am."

Prototypes
Building a model of the ideal performance

Randall has finished getting on top of the notes and rhythms in his new piece, and he's ready for **what's next**.

However, **his idea of what's next** is "Get it up to tempo".

His teacher **disagrees**. "You can speed the piece up **as soon as** you're completely clear on what the **final version** of your piece should contain, feel like and sound like."

How is Randall supposed to figure *that* out? And surely that's **not going to matter** until the performance is looming?...

L ET'S TRAVEL INTO the future for a moment. Let's imagine that you've **just given a performance** of your piece—a performance that you were proud of from start to finish.

That's **good timing**, because let's also imagine that in the audience was a **music critic**, who will be **writing up** your performance in the newspaper tomorrow.

Here's the key question:

What would you want that review to say about your playing?

Now before you **reach for the thesaurus** to look up "breathtaking" and "genius", I'm not talking about *general* superlatives. I'm talking about comments that target **specific qualities** in your playing. Were these comments directed to your intonation? Your stage presence? Your delivery of rhythms? Your use of rubato?

And if those were the elements mentioned, what exactly did the comments *say?*

This "what-do-I-want-to-be-proudest-of?" is one of the most

important things you can ask yourself. If practicing is supposed to prepare you for performance, *that preparation has to start with a clear picture of what you want your performance to offer.* That way you can **suit up** to meet the demands of that vision.

The **earlier** that picture appears, and the **clearer** it is while you practice, the more compelling your final performance will be.

So if you want your critic to be writing "effortless and precise control over the fast passages", then working towards effortless and precisely controlled fast passages needs to form part of your practice

now. Otherwise it's not going to form part of your performance *then.*

Defining your prototype
In the end, this whole exercise is a question of **values**. Obviously you want every musical element to be in good shape, but what are the elements that you *really* want to showcase? What, above all else, do you want the audience buzzing about afterwards?

Once you know, write it down, just to make it an **official wish**.

You're then going to build a model of your piece that will help make that wish come true.

Preparing your model
Ok, so you've got your piece in front of you, and a concert in three months. You've just finished creating your **list of expectations** of the performance itself:

- *Excellent **tone production** in all registers*
- *Crisp and precisely delivered **staccato notes** in the center section*
- *Perfectly **even** sixteenth notes in*

all the fast runs
• Wide *dynamic range*

Now that you've named the performance values that are most important to you, it's time to create a **prototype version** of the piece that has all those values in place.

Just what is a "prototype"?
A prototype is a version of your piece that is **performance ready** in every way *except for tempo.*

The reason for the tempo limitation is so that speed **doesn't sabotage** the other things you're trying to get right. (See SPEEDING ➲320 if you really need more convincing on this)

So one of the ways that you can tell a student is working on prototype practice is that they will have dialled the tempo **way, way down.** You need to as well—you'll need the extra time between notes to really hear what's going on when you play.

Building your prototype
Armed now with **permission** to play as slowly as you need to, it's time to work your way through your values

list, and **shape** your prototype to match.

So from our list of example values above, you might start by selecting:

"perfectly even sixteenth notes in all the fast runs"

It's definitely a worthwhile aim. But perfectly even sixteenth notes aren't going to **magically appear** in your performance just because you *hope* they might.

But they **will** magically appear in

your performance *if you build them into your prototype now.*

And so your next few practice sessions now have a clear mission. They'll be **dominated** by working on the even delivery of your sixteenth note passages, because you know that you're not just shaping a prototype here...

...you're shaping the performance itself.

Once you're done with this value, move on to the others on your list.

The whole process adds a high-sheen polish to your playing—but even more than that, it adds a clear **sense of purpose** to your practice. You're not just practicing just to "improve". You've got a prototype to prepare.

In short, you're making **real** the things you **wish for** in your playing.

How to tell when it's ready

The test is a simple one:

If somebody were to **record** your prototype, and then speed up the playback so that you were hearing it at **full tempo***, *it should match exactly what you intend the performance itself to sound like.*

In other words, your prototype is like a glimpse-into-the-future **slow-motion replay** of the best performance you could give. A prophecy, if you like. You're effectively re-living the glory of your

* There's actually a range of different software that can do exactly that WITHOUT distorting the pitch at all. Very handy for hearing what your slow version will sound like fast—or for slowing down a fast version to hear what you're *really* playing.

triumphant performance...only that performance is still yet to happen.

The **only difference** between your prototype and what you'd be hoping for on performance day is the speed itself.

And as we'll see, fixing that is going to be no problem.

Getting it up to tempo

Because you've carefully created a prototype, you've got an ideal **foundation** for speeding up your piece.

So if you **combine** your prototype now with techniques like Metronome Method ↪195,

you'll end up **having it all**—a full tempo performance that's packed with the sort of quality control that only a prototype can bring.

Make no mistake though—*this process does **not** work reliably the **other way around**.* You can't take care of tempo first and **then** try to add your preferred qualities. You just end up with a **fast mess**.

But as long as you get your carts and horses in the right order—and are careful with how you tackle each of the two stages—you'll always end up with a high quality, up to tempo performance. Always.

Prototypes are that powerful.

Matching values to pieces

Because your prototype is going to be created especially to **reflect** your wishlist of values, you need to be **careful** what that wishlist contains.

This means that you can't just have the same set of values for every piece. You may well have a favorite value of "crisp and energetic staccato", but some staccato passages just aren't meant to be delivered that way.

Instead, you've got to **tailor** your choice of values to match the special **inbuilt** qualities of the piece. So if your piece has a series of cheeky question-and answer phrases, then one of your values might actually be "delivered with a sense of humor". Build that into your prototype, and you'll completely transform your final performance.

If instead, your piece is a heartfelt adagio, then you might list "genuinely legato playing" and "sustaining the melodic line" as **two values** needed for that piece.

Again, having been listed, those two values would then be carefully **built into** your prototype...and would be evident for all to hear on concert day.

Candidates for your values list

Your ability to create compelling prototypes is *limited by the number of values you're able to think of.*

So if you could only think of **one** value—"Make sure I project well enough to fill the entire hall with sound"—then that's what your piece is primarily going to be about.

Good projection is certainly a worthwhile aim...but if it's your *only* aim, then your performance is in trouble.

It's a **balancing act** though. You're going to drown in details if you give yourself a 100 point checklist for your prototype. But too few items, and you simply won't do the piece, or yourself justice.

As a result, when you're working with prototypes, the best thing to do is to construct a list of twenty or so possibilities, and then **cull** that squad back to a team of 4-6.

Go build your prototype in the image of the values in that team, and then **enjoy the results** on concert day.

Expanding your values list

Part of the reason that you have lessons in the first place is that your teacher's musical values list will be longer than yours. As a result, your teacher is going to be a great source of values that perhaps you hadn't considered yet.

If you're working with a **practice**

buddy who has played this piece before, you might also want to ask them for **their** list of values for this piece—look out for the issues that you've never considered before. (See PRACTICE BUDDIES ⮎226)

Eliminating negatives

As well as listening for the **presence** of all the items on your values list, you're also checking for the **absence** of anything noticeably *bad* in your prototype—*even if the bad thing wasn't specifically mentioned on your list as a thing to watch out for.*

So if you **notice** your prototype getting faster and faster, you don't stop to check whether "maintain steady tempo" was on your list of values. You fix the problem there and then.

End result? You have your values list **adding sparkle** and mastery to **key elements** in your playing. And you're still scanning carefully for any non-listed items that are letting your piece down.

This twin combination ensures that your worst is not so bad...and that your best dazzles.

Randomizing

The ultimate way to end the practice ho-hums

Elsie is really **struggling** with practice at the moment. Every day seems like every other, and the whole process just makes her **feel sleepy**.

"Practicing is so...**boring**..." she complains to her teacher. "It's like watching **reruns**"

"Well, it doesn't have..." he starts to say "wait...give me two seconds..." He opens a cupboard, and takes out a **deck of cards**. "Here" he says "have you ever considered introducing a little **chaos** into your work?"

Chaos? Isn't that the *last* thing you want in the practice room?...

THERE'S A STRETCH of road between Nurina in Western Australia, and Watson in South Australia that holds an unusual **world record.**

For 478 kilometers—a whopping 297 miles—*the road is dead straight.* Not even the gentles of curves. No rises or dips. Just a ruler-drawn line on a flat and treeless landscape.

In theory, it should be the world's easiest road to drive on. No corners to negotiate, and you can always see exactly what's coming up.

But in practice, it's a **nightmare** for motorists. With no corners, traffic lights, or decisions of any sort to challenge them for 5 hours, drivers get bored.

And **sleepy.**

The problem
These drivers don't get bored because they're weak-willed. If you can always predict exactly what's coming up—**and you're always right**—then your brain quickly loses interest. We are programmed

to react to, and be fascinated by *surprises*.

Unfortunately, **practice rooms** are not always very surprising places. It's easy to end up doing the **same old thing** in the same old order.

No curves. No dips. Play this 6 times. Learn that passage. Practice these scales. Turn that page.

* yawn *

It doesn't have to be this way. In fact, with a small change, you can arrange things so that you are *always* being surprised by what's coming up.

The solution
To combat practice room predictability, you're going to introduce the element of **surprise**.

There's a problem though. You're not going to be able to surprise *yourself*—that would be like trying to say "boo!" to yourself, but when you **least expect it**. (Try it, you'll see what I mean).

So the what's-coming-next surprise instruction has to come from *outside* you.

Unfortunately your **teacher** can't be with you to give these instructions.

But that's ok. You're about to find out how a humble **pack of cards** can fill exactly the same role.

What's on your practice cards?
Every time you practice, there are dozens of **different useful instructions** you could give yourself. Memorize this passage. Fix the fingering for that passage. Listen to the recording of your new piece. Normally you would settle on one of these options, and begin.

When you're using practice cards though, instead of *choosing* one instruction, you're going to write down **all those possible instructions**. One for each card.

This means you will end up with a deck of cards that is a comprehensive collection of possible "what's next" instructions. *No matter which card you choose, you'd be told to do something* **worthwhile***.*

But since you've *shuffled* that pack of cards, you won't know exactly **which** of those useful instructions is coming your way next.

It's a small change, but it's a **powerful weapon** against stale practice sessions. In fact, it guarantees that no two practice sessions will be the same.

This is just the beginning though. As we'll see, there's a **lot more** to randomizing than just practice instructions.

So what can you randomize...?
That's what's so exciting about this technique. You can randomize just about *any* practice element.

Take some time to **read through the list** below, get your cards ready, and then fasten your seatbelt...

...anything is possible each day from then on.

...Randomizing *Segments*
Your piece should **already** be divided up into segments, but there's no rule that says you have to tackle those segments **in order**. (See Shooting the movie ➲315)

So if your piece has 14 segments, labelled A-N, you don't have to start with A each day and work your way through (See Beginners ➲33).

Instead, **create cards** for each of those segments, so that you can mix things up a little.

After you've shuffled the deck, the card you **turn over first** will be the first segment you **work on**. Once you're done with that, the **next card** will determine the next segment... and so on.

Never the same twice
You could work through the entire piece like this each day, without

Stacking the deck
If you have a particular practice element or passage that's **more important** than others, allocate several cards to the same thing. If this card appears three times in the deck while everything else appears only once, *you'll end up doing three times as much practice on it as the rest.*

So randomizing is **not** about **abandoning priorities**. In fact, in combination with a little deck-stacking, it's an effective way to ensure that the most important items receive the most attention.

any fear of having the same practice day twice—with 14 cards to shuffle, there are 87,178,291,200 combinations. It's a great way to keep practice feeling fresh during lengthy campaigns.

No more dodging
If you have segments of the piece that you really *don't* enjoy working on, then choosing "what's next" yourself can mean that you unconsciously (or consciously) **avoid** segments that **won't be fun** to tackle. (See Polishing Shiny Objects in Practice Traps➲237)

This sort of dodging **isn't an option** when the cards are setting the order of your agenda. You might **groan** whenever you turn over the "J" card, but at least it's going to get practiced now.

If you can't get through all the segments in one practice session

Simply leave the cards as they are at the end of the session, and **resume** from where you were up to next time.

In this way, getting right through a deck for a long piece might take **several practice sessions**—but it was always going to.

You don't have to **remember** what you've covered so far. Those cards will simply be **missing** from the deck next time you practice. (Because you're removing them as you practice them)

If you don't need to work on the whole piece this week

Then your deck would only have those segments that are **relevant**. So instead of having A right through to N, you might only have cards for A-F, or J-N.

There's no point in having cards in the deck that represent practice instructions you **don't need.**

...Randomizing *issues*

If you're using THEMATIC PRACTICE ⟳330, then instead of focusing on **geographic areas** within the piece, you'll be focusing on a **single issue**, and then looking for it wherever it may appear.

So your issue for Thematic Practice might be "even sixteenth note runs", in which case you would work on all passages in the score that contain sixteenth note runs.

Once you've worked out your themes though, **determining the order** to tackle them in can be hard.

So leave it to the cards. One card for each theme, shuffle, and then

surprise yourself—they're all issues that need to be taken care of at some stage.

If you spot a new issue

Sometimes you'll be busy working on one issue, and notice another that is going to need attention, but is **not on your list yet**.

No need to interrupt everything and practice it straight away. Instead, quickly **create a card** for that issue, add it to the deck, and continue on with what you were working on. Because you're steadily working your way through the whole deck, you're now **guaranteed** to cover that new issue at some stage.

...Randomizing *Tasklist items*

Another approach is to create a card for each **preparation task** your teacher set this week.

So if your **jobs** this week were:

- *Be able to play page 2 of the Sonatina from memory*
- *Come up with a fingering for the final 15 measures of your etude.*
- *Complete theory sheets 15a and 15b.*

• *Be able to pass a scales test on D, A and E Major.*

Given that some of these tasks are quite large, it's worth **splitting** them over several cards. So, for example, you might turn:

• *Be able to play page 2 of the Sonatina from memory*

into three cards:

• *Be able to play lines 1-3 from memory*
• *Be able to play lines 4-5 from memory*
• *Be able to play lines 7-10 from memory.*

Between them, that's the whole task taken care of, in manageable chunks.

So for your teacher's original 5 items, you might actually end up with **a dozen or more** cards.

Independent items, not steps

Because the order is **genuinely random,** you have to be careful to ensure that one task is **not dependent** on another being completed first. The cards might not be dealt that way.

So you wouldn't divide the memorization task into...

1) *Scout page 2*
2) *Be able to play page 2 with the **music***
3) *Be able to play page 2 from **memory***

...because the process would **only** work if the cards were drawn **in that order.** (And you've only got a 1 in 6 chance of that). If you draw step 3 first, you'll have trouble completing it, because you **skipped** the steps that were designed to lead up to it.

If working in steps is important to you, then that's fine—you need to forget about randomizing, and use something **more structured** like the LEVEL SYSTEM➲182.

...Randomizing *Practice Type*

This randomization technique will produce the greatest variety in your practice, and is **highly recommended** if you want every practice day to feel completely different from every other.

You'll need to check out the chapter on VARYING YOUR DIET➲360 for more details, but the aim is to use the cards to switch between broad **types** of practice:

• Diagnosing and Prescribing
• Quality Control
• Tempo Boosting
• Reliability Testing
• Knowing the Score
• Listening to Recordings
• Head Games
• Preparing for performance
• Locating trouble spots
• Planning
• Musical fitness training
• Theory homework

There are plenty of others. But each broad area requires a completely different set of practice tools and rules. When you're **locating trouble spots** for example, you won't actually be fixing anything—just listing issues to work on later. (See

Bugspotting↩53, or Coral Reef Mistakes↩89)

However, when you're working on **quality control**, you'll normally be focused on a single issue, and strongly in "repair" mode. (See Tightening↩337)

And while you're doing **musical fitness training**, you normally won't be working on your pieces at all (See Fitness Training↩146, or Designer Scales↩106), while **head games** and **planning** don't even require you to be near your instrument. (See Visualization ↩364 or Session Agenda ↩305)

Keeping it fresh

Since practicing means a **huge range of different things**, randomizing the practice types will make every practice day unique, and a surprise. Today is not going to feel like tomorrow...and you're not going to confuse either with yesterday.

...Randomizing *Daily Quotas*

This is a variation on the Random Schedule Triggers outlined in the Triggers↩347 chapter.

The idea is that each day you will have a quota of practice tasks to get through (see Session Agenda↩305)—but the **exact value** of that quota is determined randomly at the start of each day.

So depending on the **roll of the dice**, some days you'll have 6 tasks to get through, some days only 1.

Don't count on it though

In theory, it's possible that using this method could leave you badly underprepared—there is, for example, a 1 in 46,000 chance that you could roll a 1 every day for a whole week. In any given week though, the most likely average is **3.5 tasks each day**, for a typical weekly total of around 24 tasks. If that's not enough, then use **two** dice.

Rolling a dice to determine how much you need to get done each day? **Sounds crazy**, but it adds a fresh twist to your practice, while averaging out to fully prepared.

...Randomizing *Teleport Points*

You'll need to read the chapter on Fire Drills↩139 to understand just what Teleport Points are, but cards are a perfect way to choose a place at random in the piece where the "fire" is supposed to have broken out.

Your job will be to **jump** efficiently to the teleport point nearest that simulated fire.

Because the cards are choosing the fire-points, you'll have to be **ready for anything** —which is exactly why you'll be so calm, settled and confident during any mishaps on concert day.

...Randomizing *Improv drills*

If you're working on improvising, either as part of preparing for an upcoming performance with Fire Drills↩139 or behind-the-scenes Fitness training ↩146, cards are a great way to ensure that you're surprised by each improv request.

But because there are many possible improvisation parameters, you'll need **several** piles of cards. For example:

• One pile of cards to choose the **key**.
• Another for a **time signature**.
• Another with any **special constraining requests**—some examples:
    - *must be pianissimo*
    - *must be syncopated*
    - *not allowed to use the tonic*
    - *must be ABA structure*
    - *title is "The Battle"*
    - *title is "The Snowflake"*
• And another pile with the **musical fragment** or **idea** that you're supposed to be improvising on.

Make the cards plentiful and imaginative, and you can run drills like this **for decades** without ever having to do **exactly the same** challenge twice.

...Randomizing *Closure Tests*
When you've reached the point where you **think you've finished** with the current passage, but you're not sure, (See CLOSURE➲80) a test is the best way to find out for certain.
You'll find plenty of possible tests

to choose between in the chapter on PRESSURE TESTING➲249. But the test can feel more "official"—and definitely more daunting—if you *didn't* get to choose it yourself.

Write the names of candidate tests on cards, shuffle that deck, and turn one over. That's your test.

...Simulating *external requests*
One of the things that can make lessons challenging—and examinations **downright scary**—is that you won't always know exactly what is going to be asked for, or the order it will be asked for in.

So while you might have been asked to prepare a dozen scales for your lesson, your teacher is almost certainly only going to hear a **few** of them. Your problem is, you won't know *which* scales will make up that few.

Since you can't determine what's going to happen with any certainty, you've got to be **ready for anything**. Which means ready for any of the possible requests, and in any possible order.

Cards are a convenient and effective way to **simulate** this. Simply create one card for each item that *could* be asked for. So if you had been asked to prepare B, F, Bb and A—each learned as both Major and harmonic minor—then you'd need 8 cards.

Then draw three cards each day at random to test yourself.

That way, when the **lesson** comes around, you won't *care* what your teacher asks for. You'll be **used** to not knowing exactly what's coming next...and coping anyway.

...Randomizing *experiments*
If you're on a mission of **interpretation discovery** using the EXPERIMENTING ➲135 practice technique, part of the aim is to try things you normally *wouldn't* consider.

One way to guarantee that is to create a pile of "what if" **scenario cards.** Choose your passage, then shuffle, draw a few, and then try them each in turn:

• *Try bringing out the other part*
• *Push this forward slightly*

- *Invert your current dynamics*
- *Change your tone in some way*
- *Play it as if lost and alone*

As is always the case when experimenting, you can expect **mixed results**. But it's worth the time spent...and the bring-me-some-earplugs awful interpretations too... for the **occasional pearls** that you'll discover.

...Randomizing *technical work*

Scales and arpeggios are tailor-made for randomizing. (See DESIGNER SCALES ➲106)

Rather than creating a 20 foot high deck of all the possible scale configurations, you can recreate any of these scales with six much smaller decks—decks that combine to give you your **scale of the moment:**

- One deck to determine the **base key** of the drill. (C#, Db, F, B etc.)
- Another to determine the **tonality** (major, harmonic minor, whole tone, chromatic, melodic minor, natural minor, dorian mode etc.)
- Another to determine the **scale type** (scale, arpeggio, broken chord, dominant 7 arpeggio, etc)

- Another to determine any **inversion** of the starting note (root position, 1st, 2nd, 3rd inversion)
- Another to set the **range** of the scale (1 octave, 2 octaves, 4 octaves etc.)
- And one to set the **tempo** of delivery (120 bpm-2 notes per tick, triplets at 95 bpm etc.)

You'll easily be able to **generate** hundreds of thousands of possible unique scale requests just using these **six** piles. So having drawn one card from each pile, your scale request might be:

- F
- harmonic minor
- arpeggio
- 2nd inversion
- 2 octaves
- 60 bpm-two notes per tick

So, *F harmonic minor arpeggio in the second inversion, over two octaves, eighth notes at 60 bpm.*

Draw the next six cards, and you'll end up with something completely different:

- Bb
- whole tone

- scale
- first inversion
- 4 octaves
- 150 bpm, eighth notes

In this case, "first inversion" doesn't make a whole lot of sense, so just ignore it.

Note what you struggled with

Some of these combinations will really test you when you first try them. Make a note of the exact configurations, and **revisit** them until they're mastered.

And a final tip...

You don't need to include parameters for *every* possible scale in the universe. **Stack** these decks with the scales and figurations that your teacher is going to need to hear.

Recordings

Using existing performances to supercharge your preparation

Ben has been struggling with learning his new piece—he's making **slow progress,** and can't see how the notes he's **muddling** through are ever going to **turn into** something that people would want to listen to.

His teacher is telling him to **have faith**—that the finished version will be worth it.

If only there was some way of him being able to **taste** what that **finished version** could be like...

Eighty years ago, if a student **wanted to hear** how their piece was supposed to sound, there was only **one way** to find out:

They had to ask someone—usually their teacher—*to play it for them.*

Picture their amazement if you told them that their grandchildren would be able to listen to *any piece, any time, anywhere.* As many times as they liked. Right there in the **same room** that they practice in.

What would amaze them even more though is that despite the fact such devices are available, *the majority of music students don't use them to help their practice.* Like most of the technological wonders we're surrounded by—any of which would fill our ancestors with awe and wonder—we quickly **take them for granted.** Which means that often we end up **ignoring** them completely.

So sure, you *could* play recordings of your pieces, any time you like, as much as you like.

But **do you?**

Recordings as a practice tool

As you'll discover in this chapter, recordings are not just a way to **preview** new pieces. They're a **powerful practice tool** in their own right.

Which means that if you *don't* use them when you work, you're making things much **harder** for yourself —and paying for it by having to do **additional practice.**

In fact, recordings are such an important and versatile practice tool that playback equipment is listed as a **must-have tool** in your Practice Suite ➲231.

So what's all the fuss about? Why do recordings give you such a head start?

Let me count the ways...

1) *Aiding repertoire selection*

Instead of having to **rely on your teacher** to choose pieces for you, recordings allow you to **discover repertoire** for yourself.

If you have a big listening library of pieces for your instrument, you'll keep getting **great ideas** for pieces you'd like to work on.

2) *Creating direction for the future*

Sometimes you'll **discover a great piece,** only to have your teacher tell you "yes, but not yet". When that happens (and at some stage it will), your teacher can then tell you exactly **what skills** you need to be able to develop before that piece is an option...

...which is then a **powerful incentive** to make those advances in your playing.

So for example, a violin teacher might rule out a piece because it requires **3rd position,** which hasn't been covered in lessons yet. Knowing that 3rd position is the obstacle, if your teacher then gives you a book full of exercises that are all in 3rd position, you'll understand why, and won't mind practicing them hard.

In this way, recordings allow you to **create wishlists** for the future—and shape today's practice to help you work towards those visions.

3) Scouting

Recordings are one of your most important assets when you're SCOUTING ➲299 a new piece. You'll be able to **follow the score** along while you listen, ensuring that by the time you actually **start working** on the piece, *you already know it thoroughly.*

You'll then be able to relate the sounds you hear to locations in the score, helping you plan more effective CAMPAIGNS ➲58.

4) Background absorption

In the **first week** with a new piece, one of the best things you can do is to set the recording to **loop**, and listen to it *everywhere*. In the car, while you do homework, as replacement background music for your computer games, as the music that wakes you up when your alarm goes off...wherever.

The key word is "immersion", and it's a type of practice you can actually do **while you're busy** with other tasks. (There's not too many practice types like that!)

Unlike scouting, it's not **active** listening—you won't have the score, or be taking notes. But that's fine...your subconscious will be taking notes of its own.

5) Self correction

Because the recording will mean that you know exactly what the piece is **supposed** to sound like, you'll always know straight away if you've played something that's **wrong**.

So your teacher won't have to point out wrong notes—you'll be able to hear them for yourself.

This sort of early detection will then also save you from accidentally CEMENTING ➲64 wrong notes, so that they're a permanent wart on your piece.

6) Rhythm mentoring

Sometimes the easiest way to master a difficult rhythm is to be able to **hear it and copy it**, rather than slogging your way through counting or te-te's. You recording is obviously a great "here's how it's supposed to go" resource, and can help you with even the most complex rhythm problems.

You still need to be able to read rhythms—apart from anything else, a recording won't always be available—but if being able to **listen** to the rhythm means you work it out faster, then you're simply **wasting time** by not using the help.

7) Assembling the ultimate version

If you're lucky enough to have **multiple recordings** of the same work, then you can take big steps towards shaping **your own** interpretation by **comparing** the

different ideas in each of those recordings.

In each recording, you'll hear ideas you want to **adopt**, and others you'll want to **avoid**—but in the process, you'll learn plenty about your own vision for the Ultimate Version of this piece.

You'll also often end up with a **favorite** recording, in which case you can **reverse-engineer** it to figure out what exactly it is about that recording that you like so much. You can then apply those values to your own playing.

Multiple versions are **not always easy to find,** but this technique is definitely worth considering if you're ever learning a **well known** (and usually therefore, much recorded) work.

8) Karaoke practice

Once you know your piece well enough, you can use the recording to play along with—not so that you'll end up **cloning** that performance, but simply to give you the **added pressure** of being able to keep up.

It's also a great way to **rehearse cues** for concertos and pieces with accompaniments. Just listen to the recording and come in each time when you're supposed to.

9) Defining the gap

When you listen to a recording made by a concert artist, you'll quickly realize that you don't sound like that...yet.

Instead of despairing at the gap between what **you're** producing and what you hear in the **model version,** spend some time defining exactly what the difference is.

That way you can go and work on bridging that gap.

For example, if you notice that the recording manages to maintain a **ruthlessly controlled tempo,** whereas yours tends to **fluctuate randomly,** then as soon as you've realized that, you can do something about changing it.

In that way, the recording acts as a **constant reminder** of what's possible, and an **incentive** to polish your own efforts.

10) Keeping the prize in view

When you're in the **early stages** of practicing a new piece, it will sound **nothing like** the version you'll end up performing. You'll be playing things at half speed, in small segments, and there will be

plenty of wrong notes and dodgy rhythms.

When your piece is sounding rough like that, it can be hard to **remember** just why it was that you **fell in love** with this piece in the first place.

That's where the **recording** can come to the rescue. If your practice now is the "before" shot, the recording is a mock-up of what the "after" shot promises.

So when you're **feeling despondent** that your new piece is ugly, frustrating and pointless, stop practicing, and listen again to just what it is that you're chasing.

It's much easier to then return to the hard work, *once you've reminded yourself of what the prize is*—it would be similar to an athlete in training having a **video** on standby of athletes winning gold medals.

A recording is your instant reminder of "why am I doing all this?", while also reminding you that the **ugly-duckling** stage of your piece won't last forever.

11) The time factor

Even if all the other practice applications for using recordings leave you cold, there's one that **no student can ignore**:

When you use recordings, you'll learn your pieces faster.

In other words, you get a big fat **discount** on the amount of practice required to be ready for each lesson—and for your concert—if you're immersing yourself in recordings of your piece.

So unless you're one of these **rare students** who just has loads of don't-know-what-to-do-with-it spare time every week, you'd be crazy not to make use of anything that can help you get everything done sooner. If somebody could prove to me that wearing a **peg on my nose** would help me learn pieces faster, then I'd do it.

Fortunately, recordings are not nearly so painful.

Playback options

This technique is not just for students with stereos in their practice room. Personal MP3 players are also an option, as is your PC.

In fact, if you're using your computer, then the wonderful world of MIDI files is opened up, allowing you to play back recordings of just about any piece with tiny instantly-downloading files.

MIDI files are not so good for interpretation (they tend to sound a little "computerized"), but they're fine for getting to know the notes and rhythms—and you can also easily **change the speed** of playback.

Recording library

If your teacher's studio doesn't already have one, you might want to organize a **recording sharing co-operative** with the students in the studio. All it takes is a master list of all the recordings each student has—that way, if you start working on a new piece, you can quickly check to see if another student already has that recording.

When combined with your teacher's library, a studio of 30-40 students can create quite a **comprehensive resource**. Borrow what you need, return it when you're done, and be prepared to lend your own recordings to other students.

Playing back demonstrations

Another use for all this is to have your **teacher's demonstrations** to hand. If your teacher has their own **recording facilities**, they can quickly record the passage segment as they want it, together with any explanation they want to make.

Two minutes later, and you can have a CD with the demonstration and explanation, available for you to play back whenever you need it.

If they don't have their own facilities, you can arrange the same result by bringing **your own** recording device. Even a **dictaphone** can be enough for you to be able to remind yourself of their idea whenever you need to.

Broadening your musical intelligence

Your listening shouldn't just be **limited** to your pieces and your instrument. If you're trying to make sense of a late Beethoven Piano Sonata, then you should also be listening to his **other** late works.

Similarly, if you're about to play some Bartok for the first time, then immersing yourself in Bartok

recordings is a great way to give yourself a head start for some of the stylistic and interpretation decisions that you'll have to make later.

Listening guilt-free

Students are sometimes told that they should **avoid recordings**, because it cripples their reading, and has them producing carbon copy performances of the original.

Neither of those things are true.

Listening while you follow scores can actually enhance your reading—helping you **relate** what you hear to what you see.

And if carbon copies were possible that easily, then the fact that I listened to so much Horowitz as a student should mean that I sound like him by now. I don't. But those recordings gave me plenty of **great ideas,** and **inspired** me to practice harder.

Like every other practice technique in this book though, using recordings is **not** designed to be the **only way** you work. It's part of a much larger team—it just happens to be one of your best players.

Recording yourself
Finding out—and responding to—what you *really* sound like

Brenda turns up to lessons ready, but often leaves **disappointed**— mostly because her teacher finds flaws in her playing that she never knew was there.

"Can't you **hear**?" he would say to her "this section is gradually getting **faster**. And the passage before is **nowhere near** fortissimo..."

But Brenda *can't* hear these things—otherwise she'd **fix them**. How can she change her practice so she can hear the things her teacher does?...

Good practice is only possible if you can **listen** carefully, and then **react** intelligently to what you hear.

So if you hear that you're gradually getting faster, you can react by putting the **brakes** on. If you hear that you're tending to play sharp, you can adjust your intonation.

The only problem is that sometimes you can get **so busy** actually playing the piece, that you just **don't have time** to take in *how* you played. There's only so much you can do at once, and sometimes just getting the notes right in a tricky passage can take all your concentration.

And so *listening* becomes a casualty of *doing*.

This is why your teacher is in a **unique position** at your lesson. You do, they listen. As a result, they'll hear things that you don't—things that happened while you were too busy playing to notice.

The eventual aim of course is to be able to listen *while* you play. But in the meantime, there's a trick

you can use that will sidestep the problem entirely.

Play now, listen *later*

This trick really is very simple, and there's no time travel involved. The idea is to **record yourself**, and then listen to it *afterwards*.

In other words, you're going to **separate** doing from listening.

You "do" while you record. And then afterwards, you play the recording back—and you're completely free to listen hard to it. Find a sofa, put your feet up, close your eyes.

Free from having to play at the same time, *you'll hear things that you never noticed before.*

You will now have the **same advantage** that your teacher does— being able to give listening your full attention, without being distracted by actually having to play the piece at the same time.

In fact, you'll be able to do something your teacher *can't*. You'll be able to listen to the **same** playthrough over and over again—

as though it's been frozen in time.

But I don't have a recording studio!

Me neither. Nor do a lot of musicians who record themselves. Constantly **advancing technology** now means that a $200 gadget can capture better sound than a $10,000 setup could have done a decade ago. And it will be much easier to use.

So for the cost of a **dozen music books**, you could have the ability to capture and playback your performance anytime, anywhere.

As we'll see in the rest of this chapter, that opens up some exciting new practice options—options that probably **didn't exist** for your teacher when he or she was a student.

What sort of recording device should I get?

Technology moves too fast to make specific recommendations, although Tascam, Roland and Yamaha are likely to have products to suit. The best thing to do is to talk to your local music store, but be sure to tell them you're looking at **entry level** equipment simply to record yourself when you practice.

Remember, you're not going to be releasing these recordings commercially, so you don't need to spend up big. They're just so that you can create **instant replays** of your playing when you practice–the most basic device they have will be fine (in fact, the most basic *second hand* device they have will probably be fine too).

Another option (assuming your family already has one) is to simply use a **video camera**. The sound won't be as good, but you'll have the added advantage of being able to **see yourself** too.

Worst comes to the worst, dig around your parents' garage for an **old cassette recorder**—many of them have a basic mike built in that will make (very noisy and low-fi) recordings possible. But even the worst recording device is a much more powerful practice tool than having none at all.

What you'll use it for

Being able to record isn't **just a toy**—the list of practice applications is enormous:

...*Score reality checks*

You know you're **supposed** to play what's in the music...but do you? Are you *sure* you're not missing details?

Recording is a powerful—and confronting— way to find out.

Simply follow along the score, while you listen to the recording you just made. There's **no hiding** from the truth here—the record-

ing will either match the score or it won't. If you're **listening** to *mezzo-forte*, and **looking at** *pianissimo*, then there's a problem.

Mark in the details you overlooked, go away and practice in these changes, and then **re-record,** and compare that updated recording to the score.

The aim is to keep doing this until you **can't find** any discrepancy between your recording and the music itself. This will ensure that you'll pick up all these score details long before lesson day, *so your teacher doesn't have to.* See also DETAILS TRAWL➲110 and COLOR CODING➲84.

...*"Before and After" snapshots*

Practice isn't always about **guaranteed progress**—sometimes improvements can be so gradual that they're **hard to notice** from day to day—which can be easily confused for a piece that really isn't improving at all. (See STALLING ➲325)

The next time you're worried that a piece is **not responding** to practice, you can use recordings to **find out** whether your progress has really stalled or not.

The idea is to record the piece as it is now—**warts and all**—and then keep that recording safe. This is your "Before" shot.

Then **record it again**, but after you've done three weeks of practice on it. This will be the "After".

Once you've done that, listen to both of the recordings **side by side**.

At that point, it will often be clear that your playing *has* improved, in which case you know it's been slow progress, rather than no progress.

Of course, sometimes the news **isn't so good.** Sometimes the Before and After recordings really *will* sound the same, in which case you have evidence that this piece is **genuinely stalling**. Take your findings to your teacher, create a new plan of attack, and record it again in another three weeks.

Practicing is not about deluding yourself, and if things are stuck, you need to know. (See also "Dealing with Problem Passages" in the Practiceopedia Usher ➲31)

...Competing interpretations

Not sure whether to finish your piece with a bang or a whimper? Confused about just how steep to make that diminuendo on page 3? Record the alternative versions, then sit back and **compare** them.

Sometimes you might record **half a dozen** completely different versions of a passage—each with their own dynamics, tempo choices, rubato, articulation and phrasing—and then listen to them all to **choose the winner**. Just like you're a one-person jury at a music competition.

Having selected the winner, your practice will then be about Cementing ➲64 that version. See also Experiments ➲135 and Painting the scene ➲222 for more on choosing between interpretations.

...Practice buddy updates

If you're working with a Practice buddy ➲226, there will be times when you need to bring your buddy up to date with your progress—usually via a quick phone call or an email.

If you've got recording equipment though, instead of simply *describing* your progress, you could actually record the piece as it is, convert to an MP3 and **email** it to them.

Your practice buddy can then listen to it, and **send feedback.** And of course, you can do the same for them whenever one of their recordings turns up in your inbox.

...Midweek "is this right?" request

Being able to send recordings like this is not just useful for Practice Buddies. If you've got a rhythm that you're worried **might not be right,** or a chord that just sounds wrong no matter how many times you check it, before you start to cement it, you can email a recording of the passage **to your teacher** for either a thumbs up, or a "not quite—don't forget the tie".

If they have their own recording gear, they might even be able to quickly send you back a recording of the passage as it *should* be.

It's not something you'll need to do every week, but it's great to have the option.

...Steady beat check

If your teacher **sometimes complains** that your beat can be a little hard to follow, there's an experiment you can run for yourself—using your recording device.

Simply record the passage as you would normally play it. And then instead of just passively listening to the playback, **try to tap along** with it.

If you find that tapping hard to do, then you can listen to the same recording several times in a row to pinpoint:

- **where** you might be changing speed
- **how** you might be changing speed
- whether there are perhaps some measures with **too few** or **too many** beats.
- Whether there are any rhythms which are just downright wrong, or so **casually delivered** that the beat is lost (See Tightening ➲337)

Again, it's almost impossible to assess all of that while you're

busy actually playing. But with a recording, you can analyze and correct wandering beats—and their causes.

..."Third Party" Advice

If you really want to be able to listen objectively, sometimes it's worth recording today, but **delaying** listening to it for 48 hours.

That way, you'll be able to hear your playing with **fresh ears**.

Your job then? To make notes about what should be kept, what should be improved, and what should be overhauled completely —but to create that advice as though you were writing it for **somebody else.**

You can then turn all that feedback into practice instructions.

Then it's time to **switch places**. You would then open that advice-and-instruction-package as though it were coming from somebody else—and then rigorously **follow** all recommendations.

After all, they came from a source you can trust...

...Lesson Preflight Check

This is a recording you'll make **towards the end** of your practice week, just to see how you're progressing towards your goal of being ready for next lesson.

The idea is that you would actually make a recording of **everything** your teacher needed ready for that lesson. Straight down their **to-do list**, one item at a time.

If you find you **can't** record everything on that list yet, or that the recordings revealed some **badly undercooked** passages, then you'll still have a couple of days to do something about it. (See LESSON PREFLIGHT CHECK ➲174 for more details)

...Progress Snapshots

Instead of just **describing** what results your practice for the day produced, you can **record** the evidence.

That way, when your teacher asks "how did your practice go this week", you'll be able to actually play them short recordings from various stages in your preparation. "Here's what it sounded like on **Saturday**" you'll be able to say "And here's what it sounded like on **Tuesday**, after it had spent time in BOOT CAMP ➲43.

"And again on **Thursday**—this recording was from memory".

It's the closest thing to actually having your teacher with you while you work, and gives them a useful glimpse into how you work. See BREAKTHROUGHS DIARY➲46 for more.

...What do I really sound like?

Perhaps the most useful—and revealing—of all uses for your recorder.

Just as when people hear their own voice on tape for the first time, they protest that it "doesn't sound like me", your recordings won't often "sound like you" either. They'll be faster than you thought you played, or louder, or with shorter staccatos, or more or less projection...

This doesn't happen because you have dodgy equipment. It happens because whenever you're too busy playing to **hear** what you're actually playing, you'll put together a picture of what you *think* you're actually playing.

This picture might be detailed. It might even contain elements of the truth. But it will be a **work of fiction** nonetheless. A construction in your own mind. It's the reason that people can come off stage after a performance, and have no idea that they had just played at twice the speed they normally do.

So if you really want to **discover the truth**—to find our what your performance *truly* sounds like to others—you have to record it, and then step away from your instrument to listen. When you do, get ready for a **shock**.

And then, if you don't like some of the things you heard, you have brand new reasons for practicing in the first place.

...Single-issue based listening

If you're working with **issue-based practice techniques** such as THEMATIC PRACTICE ➲330, then recordings make everything much, much easier. These techniques are dependent on being able to listen very closely to the issue-of-the-moment (eg. *ends of phrases* **or** *tone quality in upper register playing*), but as ever, this listening is much easier if you're not busy trying to play at the same time.

To use your recording to help you with this, you'll play it back **dozens of times**—*each time with a different issue as your focus.*

What you'll build up is a comprehensive report of that single performance, and a clear picture of what still needs work.

...Performance simulation

Use your recording device to capture your DRESS REHEARSALS ➲115. You can then analyze those recordings afterwards to create a

"what's next" list for your practice, or take them with you to your lesson.

If you're like most students, just knowing that you're being recorded will make you a little **nervous**—which is perfect for performance simulations.

It's really not an optional item

It should be clear by now that being able to record yourself is simply too useful to ignore—in fact, I've included it in your PRACTICE SUITE ➲213 essential items list.

If you don't yet have some way of recording yourself yet, **don't panic**, but it is something you want to change as soon as you can.

Otherwise what you *think* you sound like, and what you *actually* sound like, may well remain two **completely different** things.

The long term goal though...

...is to train your own listening skills so that you can accurately hear what you're really playing—*but while you're actually playing it.*

In other words, the record-yourself technique is a tool, but shouldn't be a **crutch**. You'll still always use it, but you won't be as **dependent** on it.

To **find out** whether you're ready for this real-time listening leap, start making detailed feedback *as soon as you've finished* each playthrough. Then listen to the recording of the playthrough, and make feedback on that.

When both those lists are regularly **matching** eachother, then your listening has evolved to a point that few musicians reach. You'll have the rare blessing...and sometimes curse...of **hearing the truth**.

Reflecting

Why the best practice sometimes makes no sound at all

Campbell's parents are very proud. "It's not just that he practices a lot—he works so **hard**. He never mucks around in there. **Every time** we pop in he's **playing something**."

At that point, Campbell's teacher's eyes widen. "You know something?" she says "I think that **explains a lot**. Now I know why he's **sometimes not ready for lessons**."

What had Campbell's teacher realized?

For a lot of students, practicing means *playing*. You'll hear such students describing a practice session as *solid*—when all they really mean is that they just did a lot of non-stop playing.

Here's something that might surprise you though. If you were to listen outside the practice room of a **professional musician**, you'll often hear something a little weird.

They keep *stopping*.

In fact, for several minutes, you'll sometimes hear **nothing at all**.

So what's going on?

They're not just having a **snooze** in there. They're still working hard—in fact, it's a special type of work you can't do *unless* you stop frequently.

They're *reflecting*, and they're saving themselves a lot of extra work in the process.

The power of reflection
While you're practicing, what you **do next** should normally be in

response to what **just happened**.

So if what **just happened** is:

The passage collapsed because the fingering was a mess.

Then what you **do next** might be:

Work out a good fingering

The problem is that sometimes "What just happened" isn't as obvious as the example above. Sometimes you'll be left with the **vague sense** that the passage was ok...sort of...but you're not really too sure...

Because the "what just happened" is murky, the way forward is now not clear either.

You've got two choices at this point:

You can either charge ahead and just **play something** anyhow.

Or you can **stop playing** and relive the playthrough in your mind, while you **think some more...**

The second option is definitely harder work. But as any chess player will tell you, it's the only option that will help.

The dangers of blitz chess
Good chess players are renown for thinking carefully before moving. But there's a form of chess known as "blitz" chess which gives both players a very short amount of time to get through an entire game—sometimes only **5 minutes**.

This means that both players *have* to move without stopping to reflect.

The result then is that no matter how good at chess both players **usually** are, the transcripts from the game will reveal blunders, miscalculations and just **plain bad chess** that they *never* would have produced were they taking the time to think as they normally might.

It's not surprising then that a lot of chess grandmasters are **wary** of playing too much blitz chess, because they know they can get into some very **bad habits**.

For a lot of students, music practice can be a lot like blitz chess. As soon as one move is made, the next one appears. So every passage is followed immediately by **another** passage—maybe the next one, maybe the same one, maybe one from somewhere else in the piece entirely.

But wherever that next passage comes from, there's no stopping to consider the state of play. "What's next" just *happens*.

> # Just like blitz chess can produce some ugly chess, blitz practice can produce some ugly practice.

Which means that just like blitz chess can produce some ugly chess, **blitz practice** can produce some ugly practice.

"What just happened?":
If working out what's next should be based on what just happened, then you have to *know* what just happened. The best way to answer the "What just happened" question is to **quiz yourself** on some more specific issues:

> *Am I getting closer to the sound my teacher wanted me to make? Or further away? Was I relaxed throughout? How was my intonation? My breath control? Did those dynamics make sense? Were they obvious enough?*

Did that new fingering help? Were the staccatos short enough? Did I use too much pedal? Not enough? Was that bowing effective? Did I feel in control of the tempo throughout?

Without knowing the answers to questions like these, there's **no point** in simply leaping straight back into another playthrough. You might actually be in the process of making things *worse*.

No matter which questions you ask yourself though, two things are worth noting:

1) You can't reliably answer questions like these while you're **busy** playing something else.

2) To ask and then properly consider these questions **takes time**.

Hence the need for reflecting—it ensures you're not busy playing something else, **and** are able to take some time for consideration.

So when you're reflecting, you're not pausing for effect—you're pausing to get a job done.

In fact, the job is not going to get done any other way.

"What should I do next?"

Remember, the answer to the "What Should I Do Next?" question is going to be based directly on "What Just Happened?" You'll be **reacting** to any problems you just heard, and **trying possible solutions**:

Perhaps I should try this fingering instead? Or try lowering my right shoulder a little? Or brightening my tone? Or taking a snatch breath mid-phrase? Or tightening those triplets a little? Or starting that crescendo a bar earlier?

Or maybe it would help to play this from memory now? Or combine it with the previous passage? Or 20 bpm faster? Or just tap the rhythm only?

Most of these questions are then perfect candidates for running an EXPERIMENT➲135.

When you can't figure out what to do next...

It's certainly not game over. If you really are stuck, add this passage to your LESSON AGENDA➲171. But once you have, don't keep blundering blindly forwards through *this* passage—move on to another passage instead.

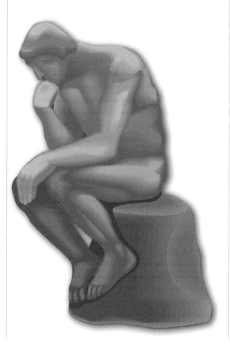

In the end, not being able to figure out what to do next is simply a sign that you **don't know enough** practice techniques yet. Keep reading this book—as you add more and more techniques to your list, you'll get better at being able to recognize problems, *and* knowing what to do about them.

So **for example**, if the "What just happened" reflecting revealed that there was a **gap** as you moved from one passage to the next, then your "what's next" might be to use the BRIDGING➲50 technique. But you can only do that if you *know* the bridging technique.

Likewise, if "What just happened" was that you have a section that is still nowhere near **up to tempo**, then "what's next" might be METRONOME METHOD ➲195, or CHAINING➲69, or CLEARING OBSTACLES➲72.

The more techniques you know, the more likely it is that a solution will pop into your head.

Making reflecting automatic

Stopping like this is **harder than it**

sounds. Most students are used to diving straight back into the passage they were just playing, or **charging ahead** to the next bit.

If you're a play-all-the-time kind of practicer, there are a few things you can do though to encourage reflection:

1) Write a reminder on your score
You're simply going to write "What just happened?" - several times on every page, so that you'll see it regularly. Whenever you see that, you should be able answer the question—if you can't, it's a sign that you should **down tools** for a moment, and **think** about what you're doing.

Alternatively, if you can **draw** at all (I really can't, so you're not going to get examples), then add some clouds or meadows or monks in lotus position...anything you like that supports the reflection message.

Or, if you want to be less gentle about all this, a big, unsubtle, yelling-at-you-to-freeze **stop sign**.

Once your reminder is in place,

you at least will have eliminated the possibility that your lack of reflection is due to forgetting that you're supposed to.

2) Set a kitchen timer
It's not there to pressure you into moving forwards faster—instead, it's similar to the technique for combatting AUTOPILOT ⟳120. Instead of reminding you that you're supposed to reflect, it will regularly ask you whether you *have been*.

Set a kitchen timer for 5 minutes, and when it goes off, ask yourself:

How many times have I stopped to actually think about what I'm doing in this past five minutes?

If the answer is **less than three**, then there's almost certainly too much doing and not enough thinking. If the answer is **zero**, then you may well have just spent the past 5 minutes making your piece *worse*. Who knows? (You obviously don't!)

3) Keep notes
It doesn't have to be a permanent part of your practice, but at least for a couple of days whenever you

stop to reflect on what you just played, jot down a **quick summary** of what you discovered. It doesn't have to be detailed:

Measures 33–44. Tempo not steady

The real reason you're doing this is not so you have an archive of your entire practice session. It's because if you **don't stop**, you'll have **no notes**.

A blank page at the end of a practice session is proof then that you're practicing without reflecting. (See also BREAKTHROUGHS DIARY ⟳46)

So this technique doesn't remind you that you're **supposed to**, or ask you if you **have been**. It just catches you red handed (or empty handed) when you **haven't**.

4) Empty your matchbox
Start with a full matchbox, and every time you pause to reflect, **take a match out**. The pile of matches (or not) next to the matchbox is your **reflection-ometer**.

Low tech, but highly accurate.

All these techniques are simply

designed to ensure reflection is part of your thinking...so that it can become part of your practicing.

Breaking out of ruts

Another use for reflection is not so much for analysis, but to simply **break a pattern of behavior** that has been hurting your performance.

So if you have a tough run with a **top note** that you've **missed** the past ten times you've attempted it, don't adopt a "one more time will fix it" mentality and **load up** number eleven. You'll just be in for more of the same.

In fact, worse than that, all this type of keep-headbutting-the-wall practice is doing is teaching you that you **can't handle** this run. Even no practice at all would be much better than that...

...and so, for a while, *do no practice at all*. Just sit quietly for a moment or two, and feel the problem note evaporate. Then picture yourself nailing the correct note. (See VISUALIZATION➲364)

And then **leave it** completely. Switch to something else, and let your subconscious do some of the heavy lifting for a while.

Try it again in a few days' time, and see how it's traveling.

Explain yourself

A standard chess coaching tactic is to have the chess student make a move, and then have them **explain** what their thinking behind the move was. Because the chess instructor then has a better understanding of the **student's thinking**, they're better able to help.

If you want to fine tune your reflecting, set aside some lesson time to **work** on it with your teacher. Practice a passage in front of your teacher, and then **reflect out loud**. Your teacher can give you feedback, and help you with any important points you may have missed.

But most importantly, they'll get a rare window into what makes your practice sessions tick.

Using recordings

By far the most accurate way to be able to answer "what just happened" is to be able to hear an **action replay**—which is why you should be recording yourself whenever you can.

The reflecting process is then almost as if you're assessing **someone else**, because you'll be able to sit back and listen without having to play at the same time.

For more information, see RECORDING YOURSELF➲270.

Restoration
Relearning old pieces without regressing

Brianna has been **re-learning** an old piece—in fact, it's been **two years** since she last played it.

"This should be **easy**" she thinks "After all, I'm two years **more advanced** than I was then..."

Unfortunately, things aren't working out that way. Before long, Brianna is making **exactly the same mistakes** in the **same places** that she used to.

It's as if she's travelled **back in time.**

What's gone wrong? Why hasn't her **piece** improved even though **she has**? And what can she do about it?...

RETURNING TO AN old piece can be a strange experience. It can set up a direct collision between how you **used to** do things, and how the **More Experienced and Wiser** version of you would do things now.

Unfortunately, when that collision takes place, the More Experienced and Wiser version often **loses**.

As a result, it's not just an old *piece*. It's old *playing*. And it's the reason that teachers are often **reluctant** to **recommend revisiting** old pieces in the first place.

So should you be careful to **avoid** old repertoire? Absolutely not. But you do need to **work** a little **differently** when confronting these ghosts from your past.

Haunted by *solid* ghosts...

One of the central aims of practicing is to **embed behavior**. To always play notes in a certain order, with specific fingers, with a particular rhythm—without needing to think.

So it makes sense then that if you've practiced a piece over a sustained

period of time, your approach to that piece will have solidified. **Hard boiled**, in fact.

Here's the thing though. When you revisit a piece—even after an extended break—you're not going to **magically forget** what you had practiced all that time ago. It's all still there, waiting to **run the show**, just like you had trained it to.

That can be a very **good thing** if you learned it **thoroughly** and **accurately** in the first place. But if you **didn't**, then you will have become very, very *good* at playing the piece *badly*.

And guess what. The break is not going to make any difference. Even **after all this time**, you'll still be very, very good at playing the piece badly.

That's how practicing works.

Removing the trigger

So what are you going to do? If you revisit the old piece, the Old You will say "Aha! I recognise this! I can take it from here..."

The trick is to ensure that the Old Your *doesn't recognise the piece in the first place*. That from the time you first open the book, your practice experience is so different that there's no trigger for the old behavior.

And that's going to start with the score itself.

Fresh copies of stale scores

Nothing will **remind** you of your previous experience of this piece faster than working with the **score** you **used to use**.

It will have all the same underlines, fingerings, corrections and notes that you used to have. That tricky bit on page two is still going to be on page two. It's **screaming** at the Old You "Hey! Remember me?".

If you're revisiting an old piece—particularly if it's a major work—get yourself a **brand new copy** of the score, preferably a completely **different edition**.

With no pencilled-in fingerings, teacher's notes, circles or suggestions, you'll be forced to **start from scratch**.

And that tricky bit on page two? Thanks to the different edition, it's now mostly on page *three*—and it looks **completely different** (and friendlier), because this editor uses a bigger typeset.

It's as if you've returned to your old hometown, and found that they've **built a shopping mall** on the space where your old school used to be—somehow it just won't *feel* like your old hometown any more.

Sometimes a brand new score doesn't feel quite like your old piece either.

That's usually a good thing.

> **When you revisit a piece, you're not going to magically *forget* what you had practiced all that time ago. It's all still there, waiting to run the show, *just like you had trained it to*...**

Fresh sections

When you were originally practicing the piece, you might have divided it into segments—bite-sized units of one or more phrases that allowed you to practice a little bit at a time.

Segmenting is almost always a good idea, but a smart way to keep things fresh is to create **different** segments this time around—even if that means creating segments that are a little odd.

Again, it's hard to do things as you used to if you're working with **different material** than you used to.

Fresh practice techniques

Your score might well **look** different, and your segments have different boundaries, but if you set about **practicing** in exactly the same way as you used to, then you'll also soon be **playing** the way you used to.

Think back to how you used to work on this. Were there segments you always used to **start** with? Start with something else. Did you have a **favorite practice technique**? Use a different one. In fact, use *lots* of different techniques. (There are **one or two** in this book if you get stuck ☺)

Were most of your energies spent speeding the piece up? Forget about tempo, concentrate on articulation instead. Or rubato. Or phrasing. Or really anything *except* tempo. Also have a think about the issues you **never** covered in the first place. Did you ever set aside time to work specifically on projection in this piece? No? Then now is a great time.

The Old You can't run the show if it's being constantly confronted with new challenges.

Fresh analysis of old problems

Two years of additional experience doesn't just mean that you can **play better**. That extra experience also means that you'll be much better at **identifying** what causes problems.

So when you're confronted with a passage that you remember as having been hard, instead of just diving straight in and practicing it, take a moment to CLEAR OBSTACLES➲72 or use ISOLATING➲164.

You'll find yourself doing simple things like reworking a fingering, or a changing your breathing, and in the process transforming an **old problem** by applying **fresh knowledge**. (Always a better option than trying to transform problems simply by spending extra time on them—see CLOCK WATCHERS➲76)

"Who's in charge here?"

Even with all these new approaches, the Old You is not going to completely forget that it used to be Captain of this ship. You have to **watch carefully**, because when you're not looking, it will try to **take over** again.

So whenever you find yourself practicing an old piece, ask yourself this:

Am I just practicing this the way I always have—or am I practicing it the best way possible? Who's really in charge here?

The Old You is *not* in charge any more, but you'll have to keep an eye on it. Make no mistake, if you let the Old You **sneak** onto the bridge, your ship is not just going to steer off course—it's going to *travel back in time*.

Futureproofing your piece

Returning to an old piece doesn't always have to be dangerous. Remember, all that's happening is that the Old You will try to play the way it used to—that's not necessarily bad or good...

...it all depends on how well you used to play it.

If you had practiced the piece well in the first place, then having the Old You take charge is a **great** way to get a piece ready in a very **short** space of time. A piece that took you a year to learn in the first place can often be relearned in less than a week.

So the lesson is this:

Practice your new pieces thoroughly, carefully, and intelligently. Partly because they'll **sound better** that way. But also because you never know when you might need them again...

Rogue Cells

When the smallest unit of practice goes bad

Mia's practice sessions are being **controlled by forces** she can't even *see*, much less understand. Forces that are **undermining** her best efforts, and **sabotaging** concerts that she **hasn't even had yet.**

Forces that **every musician** can fall victim to, but most are **unaware** of.

...Rogue Cells.

They're not science fiction. They're **real**. And here's the scary thing...

...they're in **your practice room** too...

A N ENTIRE practice CAMPAIGN➲58 for a piece might last several months, and can be made up of **dozens** or even **hundreds** of practice SESSIONS➲305

If you **zoom** right **in** on one of these practice sessions though, something interesting appears. You'll find that it's made up of even **smaller** segments.

These segments are known as "Practice Cells", and are **so tiny** that they sometimes only last a **few seconds**.

Don't be **fooled** by their **size** though. These moments of micro-practice are what *all* your practicing—and ultimately all your playing—is **built from**. Just like the cells in your body combine to form *you*.

If your practice cells are healthy, then **everything else** about your playing will be healthy too. If they're not, then your playing will suffer.

So what are these cells? How do you **spot** them? And how can you **ensure they're fit** and working well?

A closer look at practice cells

If you were to **freeze** at any point at random during your practice and ask yourself "what exactly am I doing *right now*?", the answer will **describe** the practice cell in effect at the time.

If that cell is **healthy**, then your answer will be clear on the following **three key points**:

• The exact location of the **section** you were working on (*The coda? Measures 48-51? A particular run?*)

• The specific **issue** being addressed in that section (*Speeding it up? Making the notes secure? Working out a better fingering?*)

• The **practice technique** being using to target that issue (METRONOME METHOD➲195? BRIDGING➲50? BUGSPOTTING➲53?)

As soon as there is a **change** to *any* of those settings, the cell **dies**, and is replaced by a new one.

This is a crucial idea, and the reason that so many cells **fail** to do their job properly. It's not that

they weren't capable of completing their task—it's that they get **killed prematurely** *by moving on to something else too soon*. (See "Skimming" in PRACTICE TRAPS ➲239)

But that's not what this chapter is about. As we'll see in a second, it's not the cells that fail to fulfil their purpose that you need to be afraid of.

It's the cells that **never had** a purpose in the first place.

A healthy cell example
Let's imagine you're working out a **better fingering** for measures 24-32 in your new piece, and you're accomplishing that by EXPERIMENTING ➲135 with

different fingering combinations. This then is a description of that current practice cell:

- *Measures 24–32*
- *Working out fingering*
- *Using "Experimenting"*

As long as you're working on *precisely* that, then you'll still continue to be using **the same** cell.

But if you then start focusing on **speeding up** that same passage, then the cell you were just working with dies. You've switched issues, from *correcting fingering* to *speeding up the passage*. The old cell can't do the new job, and so it **makes way** for one that can—at which point, you want to hope that the old cell had **finished** doing *its* job.

So every time you change focus like this, you change cells, which is why a **single practice session** can be made up of many **dozens** of them.

But here's the thing. These changes don't always happen consciously. For many students, they just *happen*.

These students don't **notice** the transition from one cell to the next.

> # It's not the cells that fail to fulfil their purpose that you need to be afraid of.
>
> # It's the cells that *never had* a purpose in the first place.

They don't actively **decide** when such transitions will happen, or under what circumstances. Everything is just a series of seemed-like-a-good-idea-at-the-time.

The student might not realize it yet, but when they work like that, they're in the process of creating a monster.

Becoming cell-aware

The first step to regaining control over all your practice cells is to become aware of them. So the next time you practice, take the time to **notice** the **first half dozen** cells of the practice session.

Remember, **every time** the answer to one of the three key questions **changes** (see previous page), you've **moved on** to a new cell. Because of this, you'll find that you **change cells frequently** when you work—sometimes almost kaleidoscopically.

But you'll also quickly realize that despite the fact you've been working with practice cells for years, *you've probably never really noticed them before*. They're a bit like blinking, or swallowing—they **happen automatically**, and without you being aware of them.

It's time to stop just letting cells just happen like that (see ENGAGING

AUTOPILOT ➲120), and to take an active role in making them the best they can be. There's an **old saying** about pennies and pounds, but if you take care of the cells, your practice and your pieces really will take care of themselves.

Identifying Rogue cells

It should be clear by now that healthy cells should always have a **purpose**, and that you shouldn't be working by just "doing some practice". But how do you **check** how focused and healthy your practice cells really are?

A **useful test** is to arrange to have a family member come and interrupt your practice at **random** with a single question:

"What exactly are you working on right now?"

You should be able to give the classic **Three Part Healthy Cell** answer to that:

*1) Here's the **section** I'm working on*

*2) This is the **issue** I'm targeting*

*3) This is the **practice technique** I'm using right now to target that issue.*

If you can't easily and instantly do that, then you've got something very nasty.

You have a **Rogue Cell**—a cell that is just **doing it's own thing**.

This rogue cell may or may not be helping your piece. But it also may or may not be actively *harming* your piece. Either way, you can't trust it, and it has no place in your practice room.

And what's really scary about these cells is that they don't die when practice settings change. They *mutate*.

When rogue cells mutate

Free from being defined or supervised by you, rogue cells can work through an **astonishing** range of sections, issues and techniques in a **short** space of time. In the process, they'll create all sorts of problems for your pieces, because they **make their own changes** to your piece... without checking with you first.

They'll apply haphazard fingerings. They'll ignore accidentals. They'll trample on good phrasing and distort dynamics.

They'll make easy passages tricky, and tricky passages impossible. And they'll undermine your confidence by giving your whole piece an air of **wrongness**...that there's somehow trouble in your sonatina, but you

can't quite tell what or where...

The trouble isn't really in your piece. The trouble is that the rogue practice cells that are running the show, and are **infecting** your piece with their own strand of mindless, unsupervised and arbitrary "fixes".

And the students they **hit hardest?** *Students who practice a lot.* It doesn't seem fair, but it happens because the more you practice with rogue cells, the more they can mess things up. After all, they're running the practice session, not you.

So they can take the hard work of dedicated students and **trash it**—so badly that the teacher will wonder if the student had been practicing at all.

Immunizing yourself

If you want to protect yourself from Rogue Cells, there's only one sure defense:

Every one of your practice cells should only come into being because you actively created it.

You decide **what** each cell is for. You decide how it's defined. You decide

when it's time to **move on** the next one. And then you decide what that **next cell** will be:

> *My practice now is going to be focusing on measures 24–30 of my Nocturne.*

> *The issue I'm targeting is projection of the melody*

> *The practice technique I'm using to achieve that is* ISOLATION ➲164.

That way, your cells are always **working for you**—instead of just using up your time while they turn your piece into a horror film.

Signing off on the old cell

To make this process of supervision easier, instead of *automatically* flowing on to a new segment, new issue or new practice technique, take a moment to **officially sign-off** on the cell you were just working with (for more help with this, see the chapter on CLOSURE ➲80)

In other words, *you don't ever change segments, issues or practice techniques without first stamping your current cell as being "Complete!"*

This puts the cells **on notice**—they're not allowed to just do their thing in the background any more. You're watching them...in fact, from now on, you'll be *telling* them what to do.

It also stops legitimate cells from mutating into Rogue Cells—mutating by gradually **departing** from what they were originally set up to do.

Choosing the next cell

Now that you're controlling *when* to move on to the next cell, it's time to take a more active interest in *what* that next cell should actually be. One method is to make use of

PRESSURE TESTING➲249 to create a new cell that is based on your experience with the previous one. You'll end up with a cell that is **similar** to the one you've just finished with, but either slightly **more or less demanding**, depending on how tough you found the previous cell to work with.

So if the existing cell was **no problem** for you, then you might make the next cell a little **tougher**—bumping **the** metronome up from 120 bpm, to 135 bpm, or **extending** the boundaries of the section.

Another method to use when you're choosing the next cell is the THEMATIC PRACTICE➲330 technique to **cycle** through a list of different issues for the same passage—or to cycle through different passages for this same issue.

Alternatively, you could keep your practice **fresh** and challenging by VARYING YOUR DIET➲360, and choosing a cell that is as **different as possible** from the one you were just working on.

Whichever method you use though, there's one thing you have to ensure:

Your cell has to actively help you work towards your SESSION AGENDA➲305 —which means it should be actively getting you ready for next lesson.

If your proposed cell is instead working on something that is not on your to-do list for today, then you need to choose again.

Cell *sequences*
Another way to exercise control over your cells is to place them in a **sequence**. So the first cell you work on would be designed to prepare you for the second cell, which in turn would give you the skills needed for the third...and so on. The sequence itself is designed to deliver a goal that would have been **impossible in one step**.

So for example, if you have a passage with a **tricky rhythm**, you might create the following **cell sequence**.

1) **Write in the counting** for the passage
2) **Tap** the rhythm while **counting out loud**
3) Tap the rhythm with a variety of **different metronome speeds**

4) Tap the rhythm along with the **recording**
5) **Play** the passage while you **count out loud**
6) **Play** the passage at a variety of **different metronome speeds.**

By the time you've completed the 6th cell, you will have met your goal of being able to handle the rhythm in this passage. (See also LEVEL SYSTEM ➲182 for more information on creating sequences like this).

The reward for taming cells?
Actively determining what each cell is for, and how it will end not only eliminates rogue cells, it adds a **whole new element** to your practice.

Synergy.

Your cells are no longer just **isolated pockets** of useful practice. Their actively and logically *working together* to get you to your goal.

Like a **colony of ants**, they each have small roles that seem insignificant by themselves...but **combine** them, and you're creating plenty of reasons to look forward to your next lesson...and your next concert.

Scouting

Getting to know your new piece...*before* you start practicing it

Tyler's teacher has just given him a **brand new piece**.

"Great!" he says "I'll get started on that **straight away...**"

But instead of looking happy, Tyler's teacher is now **shaking her head**.

"Tyler, if you want to do a great job with this piece, then starting straight away is definitely **not** a good idea...there's something you should **do first**."

What did Tyler's teacher mean? How can the **first** thing you do *not* be to start?

W HEN YOU GET a new piece, it's tempting to **dive straight in** and start practicing it.

I'm the same way if I've bought something that **needs assembling.** I just want the thing to be working straight away—and so I rip open the packaging, and start fitting Part A into Part C. If they **don't** seem to **go together**, I'll toss part A over my shoulder, and try part C with something else.

But like most **short cuts,** this always takes **much longer.** Before long, I can't figure out what the heck part F is for, and why I have four screws, three spokes and a spring left over when I've "finished". And my six year old is wondering why her bike always steers to the left, and how come the front wheel keeps getting stuck. (It's catching on the bell, silly)

I could have **saved** myself a **lot of time** by reading the manual, and then taking a moment or two to look at each part, figuring out **how it fits** into the whole.

That way, when the assembling

actually starts, instead of thinking *"what on earth is this for?"*, I'm thinking *"I've seen this before. I know where it goes. And I was expecting to have to fit this together at some stage"*

Yes, you *could* just start practicing your new piece straight away. But everything is going to take **much, much longer** that way.

Instead, you should spend a little time getting to know as much about this piece as you can—*before* you do any work on it. That way, when you actually start to practice it, instead of it feeling like a Strange New Piece, it will feel like an old friend.

The technique is known as scouting, and it's a **massive head start** that's going to save you many hours of work.

Listen and follow
If you can possibly track down a recording of your new piece, then your scouting should start by **listening** while you follow the score. Before long, something very important will have happened:

You will be able to point to any passage in the score, and know what it sounds like.

So that section on page two is not just a confusing mass of triplets drowning in accidentals—you can just about *hum* it. In other words, to see it is to hear it, and you will have robbed passages of their ability to seem completely foreign.

Using recordings when you practice is so important that it has a chapter all to itself (see RECORDINGS➲277).

Create and label segments
Most of the practice you're about to do will involve working with segments, and you can **save plenty of time** by having these segments worked out before you start.

Go right through the score, defining and clearly marking the segment boundaries. It's similar to a builder pegging out on the ground where the foundations for a new house should go.

Create segment *descriptors*

When you first create your segments, they'll all just be letters of the alphabet—Section A, Section B etc. That tells you *where* they are, but doesn't tell you much about *what* they are.

Your next job is to give these segments **personalities** of their own, so that you can tell them apart, and know what to expect from each.

Take a moment to actually **describe** each segment in terms of what it contains:

> *This is the first time we hear the main theme.*

> *This is mostly arpeggios, sticks largely to flat keys.*

> *This is a direct repeat of segment B, but transposed up.*

> *This is heavily syncopated, and mostly in 3rd position.*

> # Yes, you *could* just start practicing your new piece straight away.
>
> # But everything is going to take much, much longer that way...

The very process of creating this list forces you to understand each segment better. They're not just notes any more.

This far into the scouting campaign, and you already have quite a **head start**. You know exactly what every part of the piece is supposed to sound like, have created practice segments for the whole thing, and know what to expect from each segment.

But we're not done yet. The best scouting is yet to come.

Reasons for easy

The next step is to go right through the score, **collecting evidence** that this piece is really **not** all that hard. When you then tell yourself that the piece is definitely something you can handle, you won't just be playing psychological tricks. You'll be **telling the truth**—and can back it up with proof.

So what sort of evidence are you chasing?

Repeating section discounts

Are there any passages in the piece which are simply **copies** of other passages? By being aware of these, you might slash what seemed to be a four page job to a two-and-a-half page exercise.

You're **not** just looking for **exact duplicates** though. You can also include in this category sections that are *almost* repeats—recapitulations, repeating rhythms, sequences, motifs—anything that you can learn once now, and reapply later.

Go through the piece, find all examples of this, and highlight them. One way to do this is to use Color Coding➲84 to **highlight** all related passages with the **same color**.

Friendly key signatures

This is sometimes a **big tick** that you can give the whole piece. Sounds obvious, but sometimes when you're staring at masses of sixteenth notes you can overlook the fact that they're in a key you find easy to play.

Remember, the **more keys** you're comfortable with, the greater the chance that you can give this a tick. (See Fitness Training ➲146)

Passages based directly on technical work

Scales, arpeggios, chromatics – passages like these **won't require** "learning" once they have been spotted (assuming you are on top of those elements...another reason to check out the chapter on Fitness training➲146) Every one of these features that you uncover is one passage less that you have to worry about.

"I've seen this before"

Can you see passages in this piece that **remind you** of passages in pieces you've already played?

Not only does this give you the **confidence** of knowing that you've defeated this enemy once before, it also means that you've probably **already done** much of the practice that you'll need for this passage.

Playing to your strengths

I'm not saying you're good at *everything*, but you will definitely have specific technical challenges that you cope with **particularly well**. It might be playing staccato, holding long notes without running out of breath, extended passages of *piano*, jumps or trills.

Point out such sections, and then **look forward** to being able to show off your best in a passage that was obviously designed just for you.

Nothing much happening

Some sections of the piece will look easy...because they *are* actually easy. If there are eight consecutive measures with **nothing but whole notes**, then you can add that to your growing list of Reasons This Piece is Not So Tough After All.

Quarter notes in disguise

No matter how fast the notes are actually intended to go, if the passage consists of the **same note value** being repeated over and over, it's exactly the same is if you had to learn the passage using quarter notes.

So while the passage might be difficult to play, it certainly **shouldn't be hard to learn** in the first place.

This is a great technique for **disarming** a lot of etudes (many of which tend to be endless streams of sixteenth notes!), and for helping pages not seem so "black".

Mark them all

Don't just **spot** all these Reasons for Easy—actually **mark** them on the score.

What you'll find is that most new pieces will quickly end up being **covered** with markings like these. It's very hard then to be afraid of a piece that has **so many easy things** scattered throughout.

Planning ahead for tough bits

Despite your scouting for evidence of easy, some sections will still **look like trouble**. There are three important steps you can take though to taming these monsters—again, long before your practice actually starts.

1. **Label exactly where such tough bits are.** Remember, you're

only labelling the tough bits themselves—you're not helping yourself by labelling "Page 2" as "tough" if it's really only a handful of measures towards the bottom that might cause problems.

2. **Identify exactly *what* it is that makes the passage tough.** Being able to name what's difficult about something is nine-tenths of making it easier. See the chapter on CLEARING OBSTACLES➲72.

3. **Create a plan of attack.** Decide on practice tactics that will help with the problem passage. So if the section is tough because it needs to go so fast, you might use METRO-NOME METHOD➲195, CHAINING ➲69 or VISUALIZING➲364.

So instead of just having a passage that you're dreading as being tough and leaving it at that, you know **where** it is, exactly **what** is hard about it, and **how** you're going to defeat it.

Highlight essential markings

Sometimes **very small** score markings can make a **very big** difference to what you're supposed to play. Save yourself some future "oops" moments by looking for and then clearly marking:
- Key signature changes
- Clef changes (for pianists)
- Tempo changes
- Ottava markings (those symbols that tell you to play an octave higher or lower than written)
- Any recommended simplifications or ossia passages
- Ornamentation, together with a quick **note** as to how the ornament should be played.

Commonly occurring rhythms

It won't be useful in all pieces, but if your piece has particular **hallmark rhythms** (Ravel's Bolero would be a good example of this), then you can save yourself a lot of time later by spending a few minutes now figuring out exactly how these rhythms work. (See ISOLATING ➲164)

That way, when the your practice proper starts on this, every instance of that rhythm should be **ready to go.**

Keys and figurations
This is so you can set up some DESIGNER SCALES➲106 to **complement** the piece you're about to learn. The logic is that if your piece is in Eb Major, then at the very least, you want to be thoroughly on top of Eb Major scale.

Similarly, if the passagework involves lots of broken chords, then it's time to make those a part of your technical work practice.

Again, this allows you to do **prepractice** on the piece—mastering general skills so that the specific instances of that skill in the piece require less work.

Ask your teacher for a tour
Scouting is a great way to create your own impressions about the new piece, but your teacher will be able to give you **even more** to think about.

Ask them what's going to be easy in the piece, and what might prove more challenging. Ask them how they would recommend you practice it. Ask them where they would start. (See SHOOTING THE MOVIE ➲315). The answers you get **might not agree** with your own scouting, but it definitely should be part of your thinking.

Turnaround-time predictions
Having completed all this scouting, if someone were to ask you *"So, how long will it be before you can play this from beginning to end?"*, what would you say?

You should always have an answer ready for that question—it stops pieces from just floating and being ready "whenever". Similarly, you should also get in the habit of making similar predictions for:

> *"How long will it be before you can play it from memory?"*

> *"How long will it be before you can play it up to tempo?"*

> *"How long will it be before it will be performance ready"*

Record your answers, and then **compare** them with what actually happens. Like everything else you do, your ability to predict turnaround times will get better with practice.

If you want to cut how long it takes you to get things ready, see TURNAROUND TIME ➲352.

The ultimate reward...
The better you become at scouting, the less practice you'll need to do once the scouting is over. Expert scouters can sometimes form such an accurate impression of their new piece that a sprinkling of additional practice is **all that's required** before it's ready for its first playthrough.

It's the same as **good actors** being able to quickly scan a script, and then do a good job on their **first reading.**

So the next time you're given a brand new piece, work hard on it straight away...but wait a while before you actually *practice* it.

Session Agenda
Creating and working with daily practice to-do lists

Danielle is all set to practice—her instrument is tuned, her music is open, and she has forty minutes free...

...there's **only one problem**. She has absolutely no idea where to start.

Her teacher's instructions for the **week** are clear enough. But how does that help her figure out what to do *today?*...

THE NOTES J.K. Rowling made for the Harry Potter series are said to be **longer than the books themselves**—every last detail was planned in advance, with all character descriptions, settings, plot turns and backstory details having been **worked out** long before the first sentence was written.

Not all authors work this way. Some novelists just *write*. They don't figure out what's going to happen in advance—the logic is that if they don't know what's coming next, then their readers won't either.

This make-it-up-as-you-go approach might work for some novelists, but it's **a terrible way to practice.**

Unfortunately it's exactly how most students *do* practice. They open their case, tune up and *just start playing...*

This chapter is going to recommend —no, this chapter is going to *beg*— for you to **have made a plan first.** To start each session knowing the answers to three vital questions:

• What exactly do I need to **get done** when I'm practicing today?

• How will I know when I've **finished?**

• How will today's practice **help me be ready** for my next lesson, and my upcoming performances?

It's designed to save you from just "doing some practice"—the sort of mindless drifting play-whatever-until-30-minutes-is-up catatonic note-thwack that tries to pass for practice when you're working without clear direction.

Instead, you'll have a list of *exactly* what needs to be done...

...and best of all, you'll understand *why* you're doing it.

The fifteen minutes you take to do this at the start of each week can

save you hours of wasted practice in the week itself.

A closer look at sessions

A session lasts from the time you **start practicing** until the time you **go do something else.** Your teacher would be encouraging you to have at least one practice session every day, while some days it might be possible to schedule a couple— perhaps one before school, and one in the early evening.

Throughout each practice session, you're completely free to work **however** you like, on **whatever** you like. *But that doesn't mean that your choices don't matter.*

In fact, it's because your choices matter **so much** that they're worth planning for—which is why you should be setting up an agenda.

The session agenda guarantee

Your session agenda is simply a **list of tasks** you need to have completed by the end of the session. You will have carefully worked out these tasks so that they help you cover everything in the week that you're supposed to.

Then, instead of practicing until a certain number of minutes have passed, you practice until you've **completed** all the agenda items for the session.

The guarantee? As long as you **create** your agendas carefully, and then **complete** all the agenda items each session, *you are guaranteed to be ready for every lesson and every deadline, every time.*

It's that powerful.

Creating your agenda

Your master tasklist
There's no point in trying to plan individual session agendas until you understand the bigger picture of what those agendas are supposed to be **working towards.**

Which is why everything needs to start with a *Master Tasklist.*

Ok, so that's a title that takes itself way too seriously, but your master tasklist is really just a list of **everything that has to be done by next lesson**. Your session agendas will then be designed to ensure that everything on that master list gets covered before that lesson.

Where does that master tasklist come from? Most of it will be based directly on your **teacher's practice instructions** for the week. So if they asked you to prepare particular scales for a scales quiz, then those scales will be on your master tasklist, along with everything else that was asked for.

The rest of your master tasklist will be any little **extras you set yourself** —perhaps you are planning on some extra FITNESS TRAINING➲146, or have decided that you want to surprise your teacher by getting your new etude up to full speed. You're not trying to create individual session agendas just yet—all you're doing is ensuring that you have a **comprehensive and readily accessible** listing of exactly what this week's practicing is supposed to produce.

Typically that master tasklist will have **half a dozen** or so items:

Example master tasklist

• Be able to **play through** the first two pages of my new Sonatina

• **Prepare** B,F,Bb & Eb Major and Harmonic Minor for a scales quiz next lesson

• Last minute TIGHTENING ➲337 of my Nocturne, ahead of Thursday week's **concert.**

• Complete **theory sheets** 14-16

• **Memorize** the final page of my etude

And the extra item you had set yourself:

• Take etude to **full speed**

Once you're confident you've listed everything that is needed, move on to the next step.

Sort by priority
At the moment, your list is just in **whatever order** the tasks occurred to you—the next step is to rearrange that list so that the **most important** items are on top.

Why? When you start building your session agendas, you'll be **biasing** them in favor of the most important items on your list. These items will happen **earlier** in the week, and will happen **more often**.

That way, even if you should **run out of time** this week (it shouldn't happen, but...), you still will have covered all the most urgent tasks.

The chapter on TRIAGE ⟳342 goes into more detail as to how to prioritize tasks like this, but the first thing you would look for are tasks that are working towards **imminent deadlines**.

There are **two such deadlines** on the tasklist—item 2 is needed to prepare you for a scales quiz next lesson, while item 3 is for an upcoming concert.

Even though the scales quiz is happening first, the concert is by far the more important of the two occasions. So the tighten-your-concert-piece task **goes to the top** of your list, with the scales quiz preparation coming in **second**.

> # This make-it-up-as-you-go approach might work for some novelists, but it's a terrible way to practice...

Sorting the **remaining three** items is not quite so obvious—a useful guideline though is trying to assess *each task's likelihood of being asked for next lesson* (sometimes your teacher might not get around to covering everything). So if your teacher almost **always starts lessons** by hearing how new pieces are progressing, then the work for the new Sonatina should be **listed next**.

Theory sheets and memorization tasks would come after that, while your own "take etude to full speed" is listed **last**—simply because it *won't* be asked for unless you volunteer it.

So your revised list looks like this:

> 1) Last minute TIGHTENING ⟳337 of my Nocturne, ahead of Thursday week's **concert**.

> 2) **Prepare** B,F,Bb & Eb Major and Harmonic Minor for a scales quiz next lesson
>
> 3) Be able to **play through** the first two pages of my new Sonatina
>
> 4) Complete **theory sheets** 14-16
>
> 5) **Memorize** the final page of my etude
>
> 6) Take etude to **full speed**

Having created a **comprehensive list**, and **ranked** the items in order of importance, the fun starts.

It's time to **smash everything** into bits.

Smashing the tasks

While it's important to be able to see all the tasks for the week, the list you currently have is **completely**

useless for creating session agendas.

Why? *Because these tasks are **too big** to fit into individual practice sessions.*

So instead of trying to work with 6 oversized items, you're going to smash them into **dozens of smaller tasks.** Each of these smaller tasks are now small enough that you could actually **fit several** into a single practice session—which is exactly what's going to happen. These broken up tasks will become your session agenda items.

You would do the same thing for **assignments at school.** Because the job is too big to complete in one homework session you might split it up into several tasks:

- ❑ Collect research material
- ❑ Write outline
- ❑ Create first draft
- ❑ Design title page
- ❑ Polish first draft
- ❑ Proofread
- ❑ Find graphics
- ❑ Finalize layout

Going back now to our example master tasklist, the single job of "tightening" your Nocturne could be converted into lots of separate tightening tasks, each focusing on a separate issue (see THEMATIC PRACTICE ➲330):

- ❑ Tighten intonation
- ❑ Tighten rhythmic precision
- ❑ Tighten control over tempo
- ❑ Tighten legato playing
- ❑ Tighten phrasing
- ❑ Tighten tone production
- ❑ Tighten posture
- ❑ Tighten dynamics

With the concert looming, you might also want to schedule a DRESS REHEARSAL ➲115, and some tasks that focus specifically on polishing the OPENING AND ENDING ➲215:

- ❑ Dress rehearsal 1
- ❑ Dress rehearsal 2
- ❑ Tighten opening
- ❑ Tighten ending

Looking now at the second item on your list, preparing for your **scales quiz** could be broken down by scale:

- ❑ B Major
- ❑ F Major
- ❑ Bb Major
- ❑ Eb Major
- ❑ b minor
- ❑ f minor
- ❑ bb minor
- ❑ eb minor

and also by scale type

- ❑ Right hand scales
- ❑ Left hand scales
- ❑ Contrary motion scales
- ❑ Similar motion scales
- ❑ Arpeggios
- ❑ All majors
- ❑ All minors

This is more than just practice. This is **alchemy.** What used to be just **two items** on your master tasklist has now been transmuted into **27 separate smaller tasks,** each waiting now to be allocated to particular practice sessions.

You can do the same thing with the remaining master tasklist items, by which time you will be able to see all your practice session agenda items for the week. You just won't know which sessions they belong to yet...but we're just about to fix that.

Counting your sessions
Ok, so you've now turned your master list into dozens of small items. The

idea now is to **distribute** these tasks through your practice sessions this week, so that everything gets covered.

This is basically an exercise in **division**—if you have 80 small tasks to cover, and 10 practice sessions to distribute them through, then you're looking at 8 items each day.

So before you can do any distributing, you need to work out **how many** practice sessions you'll be having this week. Write them all down, than add them up—the example below assumes that your lesson is on a Tuesday:

Wednesday
(1) Before school
(2) Straight after dinner

Thursday
Not possible to schedule practice on a Thursday- just too much on.

Friday
(3) When I get home from school
(4) 6:30pm (when Kylie goes out to dance class)

Saturday
(5) Straight after breakfast
(6) When I get home from soccer

Sunday
(7) Straight after breakfast
(8) Once we get back from weekly grocery shopping

Monday
(9) Before school
(10) Straight after basketball training

Tuesday
(11) Before school

Looks like we'd be dividing by 11 for this week. This is why it's such a **good idea** to have as many sessions in your week as you can—the bigger the number you can divide by, the easier the workload in each session.

Distributing the tasks

In our example above, you have 80 individual practice tasks to distribute among 11 sessions...so you're looking at allocating between 7 and 8 practice tasks each day.

To ensure the **most important item**s get priority, sprinkle those tasks through the **first** few days of the week.

So that very first Wednesday session—the before school one—might have the following tasks:

Wednesday Before School

Nocturne:
❏ Tighten intonation
❏ Tighten rhythmic precision
❏ Tighten control over tempo
❏ Tighten legato playing

Scales:
❏ B Major
❏ F Major
❏ Bb Major

Much later in the week, you're more likely to be focusing on items that were **further down** the list—but you'll also be including some **revision** of your most important tasks too. Remember, this whole system is biased in favor of what's

Most Important, so expect your Nocturne and scales to get more attention than anything else:

Sunday, straight after breakfast

Sonatina
❑ Pressure testing page 2
❑ Page one with metronome

Scales:
❑ Mock scales test: All Majors

Etude
❑ First half of final page from memory
❑ Second half of final page, with music but pressure tested
❑ First two pages, metronome method up to 140 bpm

Nocturne
❑ Tighten balance
❑ Dress Rehearsal 1

By the time you have completed the final practice session for the week (on the Tuesday morning just before your lesson), you will have completed all 80 tasks...

...which means you're going to be in great shape for the lesson itself.

Tuesday, before school:
1. Pressure test page 2
2. Memorize the adagio
3. A & E Major scales
4. Take coda up to 140 bpm
5. Theory sheet 14
6. Refinger the introduction

Practicing to your agenda
Ok, so let's assume that you've created your agenda, and your first session is **about to begin**. Now what?

Order of attack
While you do need to get through all the items in the session, the order you tackle them in is completely **up to you**. You can warm up with a couple of the easier tasks, dive straight into the tough stuff... or you can simply work your way down the list.

As long as they're all **complete** by the end of the session, it really doesn't matter how you got there.

Marking items as "complete"
It's not enough to say "I think I've got this now", and then tick the task off your list. You need to **demonstrate to yourself** that the task has actually been completed.

For some tasks, you can actually **prove** that the item is ready, using a Pressure test ➲249.

So if the **agenda item** is "Page one of the Sonatina with metronome", then you might set yourself the test of being able to play the page through at 100bpm, **three times in a row** without error. Once you can do that, tick the task, and move on. But *until* you can, the box remains **unchecked**.

Not all agenda tasks are suited to such testing—for example:

❑ Tighten intonation

In which case, you can't use a black and white test like 3-in-a-row to declare the task "finished", because intonation can never be perfect. Instead, once you've ensured that you've **comprehensively and methodically checked** the piece for intonation problems, and have improved intonation to a point where *further improvement in this session is unlikely*, tick it and move on. (See also CLOSURE➲80 for more help with knowing when it's safe to move on like this)

Ending a session
Unless you actually have a time constraint (for example, if you need to leave by 8am to get to school), your session continues **until you've**

tested and ticked everything. *The only way to end the session is to complete the list.*

This isn't all bad news though, because it **works both ways**. Once you have genuinely completed everything, *you can stop*—even if you haven't been practicing that long.

This acts as a powerful incentive to be smart about how you practice, and to concentrate hard. Being able to focus is now **a ticket to less practice**.

You'll quickly discover that if you're **daydreaming** (see ENGAGING AUTOPILOT➲120), practicing **too fast** (see SPEEDING➲320), always starting from the **beginning** (see BEGINNERS➲33) or allowing yourself to fall victim to any of the other various PRACTICE TRAPS➲236 listed in this book, then it's going to take forever for you to complete your agenda tasks. In fact, you could practice for several hours and not complete *any*.

On the other hand, if you work intelligently, narrowing your focus to the task that's in front of you, and choose the right practice techniques

for the job, then you'll be surprised at how long it **doesn't** take.

If you run out of time
The tasks left undone still have to be completed at some stage before your next lesson, so they need to be **allocated to other sessions**. This means that if you had three tasks left undone, three of your future practice sessions will now each have an additional item.

In this way, your practice sessions are really working as a **team**, and will be prepared to pick up any items that other sessions are forced to drop.

If a task is proving too difficult
Assuming that you've been concentrating and smart about how

you practice, a too-difficult task is usually a sign that the task had **not been broken up enough**—any task that is not readily completable in a single practice session should not be listed as a task in the first place.

Instead, it should have been **several tasks.**

So the fault here lies not with your practice, but with the instructions themselves. See the chapter on Level System ➲182 for help with splitting monster tasks.

Creating better agendas

Because you'll be following these agendas when you practice, *your practice will only be as good as the agendas themselves.*

Like everything else you do, you won't be an expert at creating agendas straight away—you can expect some **teething problems**, together with some occasional flat-out **unworkable** agenda items.

You'll improve with experience, but if you **don't want to wait around** for experience to kick in, then you should use the following guidelines:

When division is a bad idea

Dividing your tasks equally throughout your practice sessions assumes that your practice sessions will be equal—however, reality is **not always as tidy** as that. For example, if you work better in the morning than the evening, then it makes sense to schedule more work for those fresh morning sessions.

Similarly, sessions that are **seriously time-limited** (eg. you might have a session scheduled for "when you get home from school"...but have a basketball game to get to at 4:30pm) should have shorter lists. Using the same idea, weekend sessions with **a blank check for time** are worth stacking heavily.

More and smaller is better
Like all checklists, the motivation comes largely from being able to **tick things off.**

For that reason, if you're going to create tasks that are the wrong size, make sure you err on the side of **too small**, *not* too big.

That way, you're guaranteeing that each practice session will be filled

with plenty of ticks, and that every agenda item feels achievable.

Build in a buffer
Consider having a couple of sessions in the week that have no agenda allocated to them—instead they're reserved for **catchup work** for any items left incomplete from other sessions.

Review weekly
Before you start creating your agendas for the week ahead, take a moment to **reflect** on the success of the agendas from the previous week. **How much** practice did your previous agenda require? Were there any items **left undone** at week's end? Were there any agenda items that were **unworkably large?** Or **individual days** where the load was just too much?

Use what you discover to create better agenda items for the next week.

Keeping it varied
Varying your task types won't necessarily improve your practice—in fact some students will work best if each practice session has a "flavor", where most

practice tasks seem to be centered around the same issue. But if instead you **need variety** to stay focused, *then your agenda needs to be varied too.* So rather than scheduling seven separate "speed this passage up" tasks for the same session, **scatter** them through your week.

This means that if you're finding your current agenda item frustrating, you can take comfort from the fact that you won't have to **put up with** anything similar again today. (See Varying your diet ➲360)

Midweek corrections

If it's clear after a couple of days that this week's plan is just not going to work, it's not a virtue to stay loyal to it—a bad plan is not going to suddenly become good just by sticking to it harder.

Rework the agendas of the remaining sessions to fix whatever is wrong, and stick to that plan instead.

Enlisting help

There's no rule that says you have to struggle with all this by yourself—it's definitely worth running your first few plans past your teacher, and

then again in the future whenever you have a week where the plan failed you.

For that reason, when the question "how did this week go" comes up, make sure you have a copy of your session agendas handy.

Other ideas to try

Buddy plans

If you have a Practice buddy ➲226, consider writing agendas for each other. You can then either use some of their recommendations, or you can simply **adopt** their entire agenda as is.

You can also use your buddy to help **keep you on track** each day. As you tick off your final agenda item for the day, your very last practice job would be to send a quick "all done!"

message to your buddy. They would do the same for you.

Why bother? Because now leaving tasks incomplete is not just something that *you'll* know about—you're actually **accountable** to someone else too. You won't want to have to admit to your buddy that you fell short, which can help you keep going when you otherwise really **don't feel like it.**

If you do fall behind, or miss a day, the job of a good buddy is to help get you back on track, so that **lapses** don't turn into **collapses.**

Randomized agendas

If you have 80 items to distribute among 10 practice sessions, instead of allocating 8 items to each session in advance, write each item on a separate card and then **draw the 8 items at random** at the start of each session.

You'll still get through all 80, but each day you won't know what you're in for until the session starts.

Not the best way to prioritize items, but great for keeping your practice fresh and unpredictable...

(See Randomizing ➲262)

Shooting the movie

A smarter way to work out "what's next?"

Damon has just finished learning the **first two pages** of his new piece. But when he tells his teacher, she **pulls a face**.

"**Why** would you do that?" she asks

"You asked me to learn two pages, and so I did..." says Damon, looking very **confused**.

"Yes, but why would you learn *those* two pages? I mean, of all the places to start, why would you choose the **beginning**?"

Good question. There's a **better way.** Let's take a look...

IF YOU WERE TO watch a movie a **hundred times**, the events will always unfold in the **same order**. Scene three will always follow scene two, which will always appear straight after the opening sequence.

It's orderly, it's predictable...

...and it bears **no resemblance** at all to the way in which the movie was **originally shot**.

The very **first scene** to be filmed might actually be one of the **last scenes** in the movie. Actors in Peter Jackson's massive *Lord of the Rings* rendition actually started work by filming one of the *final* scenes in the trilogy. It was the portrayal of an emotional farewell, with plenty of embracing and tears...yet most of the actors **barely knew** each other.

So if there were a very **short movie** consisting of **6 scenes**, the shooting order is much more likely to be

3 - 5 - 2 - 1 - 6 - 4

than

1 - 2 - 3 - 4 - 5 - 6

Why the random mix?
It's not really random. Shooting out of order happens for lots of reasons—not least of which is that it makes sense to film at the same time **all the scenes** that use the **same location**. Otherwise you might have to fly the entire cast and crew to Hawaii for Scene 1, then to Paris for Scene 2, then back to Hawaii again for Scene 3...you can see the problem.

So if scenes 1,3,12,13,22 and 45 are all set in Hawaii, then you'd be crazy not to shoot them all at the same time.

Similarly, if there is a scene that takes place in **pouring rain**, then a weather **forecast** for rain on

Wednesday means that everyone will work hard to shoot that scene on Wednesday too—**even if** it wasn't otherwise "what's next".

As a result, if you were to **ask a director** at the start of the project exactly what order scenes will be shot in, he or she would have to say that they **don't know**. They have to be able to change their mind to take advantage of locations, conditions, actor availability, and much more.

So while it **sounds tidy** to start with Scene 1 and work your way through, it's usually a terrible idea. The combined **inflexibility** and **inefficiency** of that approach would make the film hugely more expensive, put it years behind schedule and possibly result in it **never being completed**.

Using this in the practice room
When you're working with a brand new piece, it's **tempting** to start with the first measure, and work forwards from there. By the time you're halfway through the job, you'd be halfway through the piece. And the very last passage you learned would be...well, the very last passage.

Like shooting the movie in order, this approach *sounds* tidy, but it's actually hugely inefficient.

You can save yourself a lot of practice time by being prepared to learn your pieces *out*-of-order. What's really interesting though is why...

Anti-bog technology

One of the problems with working sequentially is that until you're finished with what you're **currently** working on, you can't move on to **what's next.** So it's not just that the 4th passage comes after the 3rd passage in the score—it's also after the 3rd passage on your "to-do" list as well.

Which means that until you can cope with the 3rd passage, the 4th passage is **not going to get done**.

You can't go through it...

Let's imagine that you had a piece though where the 3rd passage is proving particularly difficult to work out. Difficult enough that you are making slow-to-no progress on it.

Like a car stuck in mud, you're now **bogged**. Not only is the 3rd passage not getting done, *nothing after that passage is getting done either*. Even if the rest of the piece is going to be relatively trouble-free, it doesn't matter...because 4 comes after 3, 5 comes after 4 and so on.

So if 3 stops, *everything* stops.

...but you can go around it

One of the great **advantages** to Shooting The Movie is that if you get stuck, you can **teleport instantly** to any other location in the piece. Which opens up section 4...or section 54, for that matter.

So instead of using all your practice time fighting with that 3rd passage, you could use the **same practice time** to learn passages 4, 17, 11, 51 and 42—leaving passage 3 until your lesson so you can get some help with it.

Same amount of practice time. Vastly different results (5 passages learned vs 0 passages learned!)

For more help with this issue, see also BEGINNERS ➲33.

Grouping similar passages

Just as our director was trying to shoot all the Hawaii-based scenes at once, it can be efficient to learn passages that are built from similar elements.

So if you're learning the **main theme** in the exposition of a Sonata, it makes sense to then work on the **return** of the same theme in the recapitulation.

And while that theme is strong in your mind, you would look through the score for **other appearances** of the same theme. So if the **development section** is heavily based around the opening motif of that theme, then the development section might be next—even though it's not "next" in the score.

Because that passage is making use of something you've **just covered**, you'll pick it up with less practice than you would have needed if you'd tackled it in isolation. And as an added bonus, making that similar passage next in your shoot order will also serve to **reinforce** what you've just done.

A couple of **other possibilities** for grouping similar passages are:

• If you've just figured out a **tricky rhythm**, you might choose to work next on all other instances of that rhythm.

• If a passage is in a particular **key**, then while that particular combination of sharps or flats is fresh in your head, you might look for other passages that use the same noteset. It will speed up your

reading—so if you're already **on a roll** with E Major, stay with it.

• If your recent behind-the-scenes technical work has been focusing on a particular **technique** (see FITNESS TRAINING ➲146), then you've got a great head start for any passages in your new piece that make use of this technique.

So if you've been doing plenty of broken chords recently, and you've found passages in your piece built from exactly that, then it makes sense to shoot them together.

...or shooting for variety
Determining your shoot order by grouping similar passages has one negative **side effect** though—it can mean that your practice session lacks variety.

If you're the sort of student who needs a little more **diversity** when you work, then another use for mixing up the shoot order is to guarantee that each new passage is *as different as possible* from whatever you were just working on—helping keep your practice fresh.

Ramping up...or down
With difficult passages sometimes being a **demotivating factor** for practicing in the first place, another way to determine the shoot order for your movie is to **rank** the passages from easiest to hardest to learn.

There are a number of possible ways to use that information:

1) Start with the **easiest passages** —wherever they are—and gradually **ramp up** to the tough stuff.

The advantage of this is that you can **quickly** get lots of the piece learned. And by the time you're looking at the really tough sections, you're actually almost at the **finish line**.

2) Start with the passages you're most **worried about**, and then gradually **ramp down** to the easiest sections.

The advantage of this method is that it gets the hardest passages **out of the way** when the piece is still freshest. It's also encouraging to know that *the more passages you cover, the easier the going will get*—you should pretty much be able to **coast downhill** for the final few passages **without having to pedal** at all.

3) The third option is to **alternate** —work on something really tough, and then, when you're weary from that effort, give yourself a couple of easy passages as a reward.

Three different methods for determining the shoot order. Three completely different outcomes.

And none of them likely to produce 1 - 2 - 3 - 4 - 5 - 6...

Seeded snippets

An **extreme** approach to Shooting the Movie is not only to mix up the order, but to work on very **small segments** as you do—snippets, if you like. Each of these snippets might only be a few measures long.

You start by choosing a snippet **at random** from the piece. Once you've learned that—and because it's so short, that **shouldn't** take **much time**—you would then jump to somewhere else at random, and learn that snippet. And so on. After not a lot of practice, what you'll end up with is a **couple of dozen snippets** scattered throughout the piece—fragments that you now know very well.

By then, even though you might not be able to play the whole piece, **no matter where you are** in the piece, you'll never be more than a few measures away from a passage that **feels familiar.**

In other words, you've "seeded" your piece with moments where you can say "Ah! This bit!" —**friends** scattered through what would

otherwise be a room of strangers at a **cocktail party.** It's a **variation** on shooting the movie that gives you a great head start when you start to learn the piece in a more methodical fashion. (In fact, it's a technique that probably should belong to SCOUTING ➲299)

Guided shoot orders

While it's important that you're able to **work out** shoot orders on your own, it also makes sense to **ask for advice** from people who have already tackled this piece.

Let your teacher know that you're planning on working out-of-order like this, and then ask for their **recommendation** as to where you should start.

Similarly, if you have a PRACTICE BUDDY ➲226 who has played this piece before, **find out** they order that they used, and the reasons they tackled it that way.

If the beginning is not always a very good place to start, it doesn't hurt to survey battle veterans about where the best place to start **really is.**

Speeding

The hidden damage caused by practicing too fast

Tatiana has just been asked to play her piece **slowly,** and she's doing her best to look horrified.

"But this is a *fast* piece" she protests "Why would you ever play it *slow?*"

Now Tatiana **knows better than this.** She's heard the lectures about practicing slowly before—but what she's really wondering is **why** it's supposed to make so much difference...

I T'S ONE OF THE leading contributors to car accidents, and produces silly mistakes in spelling tests. It causes golfers to miss putts and skiers not to miss trees. It makes you spill drinks, misdial phone numbers, stumble on stairs and misassemble furniture.

Speeding. Doing things just **as fast as you can...**

...and then discovering in the process that it's actually as fast as you *can't*.

Unfortunately, going fast is enormously **tempting**. It holds the promise of getting there **sooner**. It allows you to minimise the travel time on **unpleasant journeys** (which is why firewalkers don't dawdle).

And for musicians, it allows you to **play-act** at performing the piece the way you heard it on the recording.

But there's **another lure** that encourages musicians to speed... something that's not talked about, because it's nothing short of **sinister**.

Playing fast acts as an *anaesthetic*.

Comfortably Numb

Practicing is about reacting to what you're *really* playing—which means being able to *hear* what you're really playing.

Unfortunately, the picture of "what you're really playing" is **not** always **good news.** You'll have passages that are slightly out of time, or with badly placed accents. You'll have dynamics that are questionable paired with notes that are pure fiction. (*Science* fiction sometimes.)

Nobody enjoys finding out that they're not playing well. And so it's only natural **not to want to hear** news like that in the first place.

There are two fixes to this problem. One is **long term**—to fix up the issues that are hurting your piece, so that they don't bother you any more. You can then confront the reality of what you're playing, and be **happy** with what you see. But that can take a while, and usually involves, well, *work*.

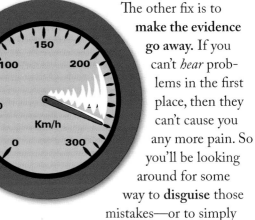

The other fix is to **make the evidence go away.** If you can't *hear* problems in the first place, then they can't cause you any more pain. So you'll be looking around for some way to **disguise** those mistakes—or to simply make it **impossible** to hear them.

Which is where practicing **too fast** comes into it's own.

Speed—the great masker
Speed is a great choice as a mistake-masker. When the notes are hurtling past at Mach 5, it can be very hard to pick up anything that's wrong—by the time you've heard the error, you're already two measures further on.

As a result, if someone were to ask you afterwards "did you notice any mistakes", you can honestly say no. *But that's very different from whether there were actually any mistakes there.*

And so the speed keeps you in blissful ignorance of what's really happening when you play. Maybe it's right. Maybe it's not. But you're nicely anesthetized—the problems are still there, you just **can't feel them** any more.

So why does speed make mistake-spotting so hard?

The pressured proofreader

Let's imagine that you've just got a job as a **proofreader.** Your employer is generous but tough—they'll give you $50 per page if you pick up every error. But if you **miss** any errors, on *any* of the pages, you get **nothing at all**.

For your **first task**, you've got a two page document to proofread, and you've been given **30 minutes.** No problems—that's enough time to read slowly and carefully, even to re-read most lines. When time's up, you can be **confident** of your $50.

But your **second task** is different.

You've been given two pages again, but this time you've only got **30 seconds.** Which means you're going to have to read as fast as you can... maybe even *faster* than you can. And the $50? I wouldn't count on it.

Exactly the same thing happens when you practice. Except that there's no mean employer *making* you play too fast. That's a completely self-inflicted injury.

Sounds bad. But it gets worse.

Collateral damage

Ok, so practicing too fast **cripples** your ability to **notice** what you're actually playing.

It's just as well. Because playing too fast also **hugely increases** the amount of **nonsense** you're playing in the first place.

So why can adding a few beats-per-minute cause such problems?

Squeezing events together

Let's imagine that you have a passage of **quarter notes.** Let's also imagine that from last lesson you have a **list** of things to get right in that passage:

- Correct notes (watch out for the F Naturals!)
- Appropriate dynamics
- Legato throughout
- Phrasing (Two short, then one long)
- Articulation (Watch the staccatos)
- Intonation (Make sure you're not tending sharp)

There's nothing unreasonable or out of the ordinary on that list. It's exactly the sort of checklist **you might have** for any passage you're working on.

If you were to play that passage at 60 bpm, then you would have **exactly one second** between each note. That's plenty of time to control your playing, and supervise each of those checklist items.

If you practice it at 120 bpm instead, then it's **not just** that you've switched from Andante to Allegretto.

It's that you now have only *half a second* between notes. **Half as much time** to get things right. **Twice as likely** to get things wrong.

But when students practice too fast, they don't set ceilings at 120. Oh no. By the time they're playing at 180, the notes have been **squeezed together** so that a brand new note is due *every third of a second*—ready or not.

And of course, sometimes they **won't** be ready. So without the proper time to think, they'll play their best guess.

It's the reason that even the **world's finest chess players** blunder horribly and regularly when they play speed chess. Constantly forced into moving before they've had time to properly assess everything, all they've got it is their instincts...and so they mess up. (See Reflecting ↪283)

And it's not like that's so fast...
The times outlined above might seem short, but they're actually just quarter notes. Picture a passage of **sixteenth notes** for a moment, being practiced at a brisk but not impossible *presto*.

So the tempo is again nudging 180, but this time you're playing 4 notes per tick...

...which means that the notes are **hurtling past** at the rate of **12 every second**. 720 every minute, and over 21,000 notes in a half hour practice session(!)...

...and you're is supposed to get these notes *right?* Along with **everything else** on your checklist?

The fast practice Whammy
It's actually a *double*-whammy, and delivers the following disasters:

1) **Plenty of mistakes** in your piece—because you simply don't have enough time between notes to get everything right.

2) **No way of noticing** those

mistakes—because of the anaesthetic factor.

So if you practice fast, you **play badly** AND you **won't know** that you are. Ouch. That's going to hurt next lesson.

So practicing fast is off-limits?
Not at all. You definitely want to have **rehearsed** your piece at full speed before you try to **perform** it at full speed.

It's a question of *when*.

Let's **back up** a step. When notes are forced close together by a fast tempo, you won't have time to supervise every note—they'll **just happen**.

But when they "just happen", it's not as random as it sounds. Because your conscious mind hasn't got time to supervise each note, *your subconscious runs the show*—and at that point, the notes and the manner in which they are played will have been **pre-decided** by the practice you have done on them previously.

So if all your earlier preparation

meant that you always played an F Natural here, then an F Natural is what you'll play now.
(See PROTOTYPES ➲257)

For that reason, playing fast is a **late-campaign** practice technique, and it's a great way to reveal just how solid the earlier practice was. If you play nonsense fast, then chances are there are gaps in your understanding of the piece slowly too.

Remember, playing fast will force your **best guess** when the note falls due—if your preparation has been good, then your best guess will be fine too.

How fast is too fast?

It's not a question you can answer with a number—you can't make a rule that says "125 bpm is ok, but 126 is too fast".

Instead, you need to administer a test:

"Is my current speed compromising *in any way* my ability to control any of the **other elements** in my playing that I need to get right?"

If the answer to that question is "yes", then you're practicing too fast. In other words, if the speed you've chosen is messing with your intonation, or rhythmic precision, or phrasing...or **anything else** on your checklist...then it's time to slow down.

When you apply the brakes...

You'll find that as soon as you do slow down, many things that **were too hard** a moment ago are **now manageable**. So the first benefit you'll notice is that most things are easier.

But because you're now playing slower, the speed anaesthetic will have **worn off**. You'll be able to scrutinize your checklist items a little more carefully, and hear problems that you hadn't noticed before.

This is good news though—those problems were always there, it's just that now you're going to be able to do something about them.

But it's not slow forever

If the answer to the speed test question is "no", then that's also a sign that maybe it's safe to play a little faster.

Increase the speed by a few beats a minute, and ask yourself the same question again. If it's still "no", then up it a little more. If it's "yes", then back off a little until you can cope. Like everything else you do when you practice, playing slowly is a **means to an end**—a tool, if you like. When you no longer have a need for that tool, you stop using it.

You can always tell

The ultimate test of whether or not you've been practicing too fast is performance day. You can **always tell** students who are careful to prepare at manageable speeds, because everything just looks easier for them on stage.

They seem to have more time. There's less doubt. There's more control. There are fewer errors.

Just like some meals are best when **slow-oven roasted**, there's a special quality about performances that have been practiced slowly.

To work any other way is like roasting your turkey in a *microwave...*

...it just doesn't taste...quite...right...

Stalling

What to do when a piece gets stuck

Travis is just about ready to **give up** on his new piece. It sounds **terrible,** and no matter what he does, it just **won't get better**.

"What's the point in practicing if it makes no difference?" he wonders.

This is a **dangerous time** for Travis. If he loses faith in the practice process, it could **cripple** his playing—and his lessons.

But he has a point doesn't he? What's the point in continuing when nothing is improving? Or is there **another way forward**...?

THE PRACTICE **promise** is very much that as long as you keep working, you'll **keep getting better**— that your musical development is about gradual but **constant improvement**.

Guess what. It's **not true**.

There will be times when you're **not improving**. And there will be other times when it feels as though you're actually getting **worse**.

It's not a sign that the process is broken. It's simply that the journey doesn't always involve steps *towards* your destination. Just like any path, it won't travel in a perfectly straight line to wherever you're going—it will **meander**, perhaps even appearing to double back on itself at times.

Your job is not to fuss about **which direction** you're facing day to day. It's to stay **on the path**.

Of course, that's easy to say.

So if you're having a week...or a month...where it feels as though you're not making progress what

can you do? What does "staying on the path" mean? And how can you tell a temporary meandering from a long term spiral into musical hopelessness?

You're not alone

The first step is to embrace the fact that backward steps happen to **every musician**—in fact, they happen to every person in every profession.

It's the reason that even the world's best athletes have **form slumps**. Or Academy Award winning directors also make **films that bomb**. And it's the reason that some of the finest musicians on the planet will talk about periods when they "just weren't playing well".

When this happens to you—and it will—it's not a sign that you're doing something wrong. But it is usually an indication that you should do something *different*.

Switching to the right tool

Sometimes you'll find yourself moving away from your destination not because the path is **turning**, but because you're just **not on** the path in the first place.

If the type of practice you're doing is **badly suited** to the problems you're trying to solve, then persisting is simply going to take you further away from where you need to be.

Which means, the **more** you persist the **worse** you're likely to get.

A **classic example** of this is if you are making extensive use of CEMENTING⊃64 practice—without having done the necessary SCOUTING⊃299 and careful LEVEL SYSTEM ⊃182 to learn the notes properly in the first place. You'll be busy playing the same thing over and over again, **without any sense** of whether what you're reinforcing is **actually right.**

Three months of hard work like that, and you will definitely have gone **backwards.** The piece will be broken, the errors deeply embedded, and it's going to take you another three months to **repair the damage**.

So the first thing you need to ask yourself is whether the practice tools you're using were designed to solve the problems you are facing. If they're not, then you're not only leaving the original problem intact—you're creating **brand new** catastrophes.

If you're having trouble telling which practice technique is suited to which type of problem, keep **checking back** with this book. Every time a practice technique is outlined, the **circumstances** under which the technique might be used will also be outlined.

Shuffling tools

You might find that you *have* been using an **appropriate tool**, but the piece still has not been responding. So, for example, you might be trying to get your piece up to tempo, and be using METRONOME METHOD ⊃195 to achieve that.

Remember though, Metronome Method is **not the only way** to get things up to speed. If it's not getting the job done, try switching to another tempo-boosting practice tool such as CHAINING ⊃69.

It's a bit like a doctor taking you off one medication and trying another. Both medications might be *listed* as being appropriate, but you might find that the second one works better for you.

You will also find that some of these tools will **complement** each other—each bringing part, **but not all** of the solution. So Metronome Method by itself might not be enough. Chaining by itself might not be enough. But that **together,** they get you where you need to go.

Focusing on foundations

Pieces that refuse to improve sometimes simply have **faulty foundations.**

So if, for example, you simply cannot get a piece up to speed, it's **tempting** to blame the tempo demands of the piece, and your own technical limitations. But sometimes the cause is **much simpler**. You might discover that there is a **bad fingering** in there that makes the passage literally *impossible* at full speed.

Fix the foundations—the fingering, in this case—and you take care of the bigger problem too.

So, in the **example above**, where the issue was that you can't get a piece up to speed, possible foundation problems to check for would include:

- Bad **fingering**

- Unworkable **bowing**/tonguing

- **Misreadings**—notes, rhythms, key signatures. And a big cause of "why can't I play this"...**tempo indications**. Maybe this piece isn't *supposed* to go at 314 bpm.

- A **flawed physical approach** to playing the passage (eg. being overly tense, breathing when you shouldn't, lifting your shoulder)

- An inability to deliver the piece correctly **slowly**. If you can't handle it at adagio, then presto is

going to see many, many notes die horrible deaths.

For **more help** with this, check out the chapter on CLEARING OBSTACLES ➲72.

Stop watching the pot

Sometimes it's easy to confuse slow progress with no progress. Which means that you might not actually be stalling in the first place.

Remember, big pieces are handled by CAMPAIGNS ➲58, not single sessions. You won't always **notice** improvement from day to day because it can be too gradual to detect.

You would have noticed this phenomenon as a small kid. Whenever you caught up with **relatives** that you **hadn't seen** in a year or more, they'll be quick to tell you how much **taller** you are than last time they saw you.

It always seems a bit strange, because you'll feel as though you're the same height you always were... that's thanks to the fact that your growing **happens gradually**.

But "gradually" doesn't mean it's not happening at all.

Sometimes the best thing you can do is to **stop looking** for daily improvement. If you must watch the pot while it heats up, check in **every week** or so instead...that way you give yourself a better chance of having made a difference you can see. (For a tricky way to achieve this, see the chapter on RECORDING YOURSELF ➲270)

Retreating

If you're certain that the battle is going badly, and that even changing practice tools hasn't helped, then it might be time for a **tactical withdrawal.**

In other words, you would **stop practicing** the piece for a while.

At the very least, if your practice has actually been making things worse, stopping the practice should also stop the rot.

But taking a break from the piece is actually more positive than that. It can produce an **unexpected**—and welcome—**side effect:**

When you return to a piece after a break, it often will have improved.

Seems completely crazy, but there are few musicians who haven't experienced this at some stage.

Perhaps it's that taking a break like this allows you to "forget" some of the things that might have been **holding the piece up** in the first place.

It also helps **break any assumption** cycles of "I can't" that you may have been trapped in.

Then again, perhaps it's as simple as helping the piece feel fresh, friendly and **fertile with possibility** once more—instead of glaring at you with the eyes of an old, embittered and entrenched **enemy**.

Be sure though to try the other ideas outlined here first (your automatic reaction to any problem shouldn't be to retreat!), but if it feels that all else has failed, a withdrawal may just help your piece live to fight another day.

Reframing

Sometimes the difficulties in a piece are there simply because you're **expecting** the piece to be difficult.

If this is the case, you can save yourself a lot of practice time by reframing how you see the piece. Instead of dwelling on what makes the piece **hard**, go through it looking for evidence that it's **easy**. (See SCOUTING➲299)

As the saying goes, whether you think you can, or you think you can't, you're right—so it's definitely worth shaping what you think. (See VISUALIZING➲364)

Restarting

This is an even more **extreme** withdrawal than retreating. If the piece feels like it is horribly broken, then it might be worth tossing everything away and starting again.

And I mean really starting again.

You'll equip yourself with FRESH PHOTOCOPIES➲151 of the scores. And then you'll start working on it *as though you've never seen it before.*

Which means that your first step will be SCOUTING➲299. Sounds insane for a piece that you used to play, but your job is to spot things that you didn't notice first time around.

Then, as you start to work on it, you would deliberately work as differently as possible from the last time.

The idea is that the notes, rhythms and score markings might be the same, but everything else about your **Campaign Version 2** will be completely different...which should mean a different outcome.

Thematic Practice

Targeting single issues on a piecewide basis

Kaylee knows that she's supposed to work on her pieces in **sections**, but right now she has one of those J.S. Bach works that **won't segment** neatly.

"It just **keeps running**, there's no way to figure out where one section ends and the next begins. It's stressing me because I have a **huge list** of things I need to get right, but I can't work on the whole piece at once..."

"Yes you can" says her teacher "And you don't *have* to practice in sections. In fact, for this piece, it's better that you don't"

Kaylee looks a little **disbelieving** as her teacher explains...an **alternative** to practicing in sections? What could it possibly be?...

YOU DON'T NEED to read a Practiceopedia to know that dividing your piece into segments can make practicing easier. That instead of tackling the piece as a whole, you would focus on **zones**:

• *the fast section on page 2*

• *that tricky bit near the end*

• *The slow introduction*

And then instead of trying to deal with the whole piece at once, you **rope off** one of these sections, and concentrate just on that. It's a good idea, and is one way of breaking a piece down into manageable chunks.

But it's not the *only* way.

The thematic alternative
Thematic practicing switches the focus from **where** to **what**. Instead of choosing and working on a **section**, you're going to choose and work on an **issue**.

You'll then be going right through your piece, working on **every instance** where that issue might arise.

Themes in action: the Party
Let's imagine that you were hosting a birthday party at your house, and needed to have the place looking great by the time guests arrive.

If you were doing this by segmenting, you'd handle it **one room at a time**. So you might start by cleaning the kitchen—and then the family room, and so on.

In this way—room by room—you'd get the whole house ready.

There's nothing wrong with working that way. But again, it's not the *only* way.

If you were using the principle behind **Thematic Practice** instead, you'd choose a **type of cleaning** that needs doing, and then apply that to the **whole house**.

So you might start by choosing the theme of "getting things off the floor". You'd then go right through the whole house and make sure there was nothing on the floor that didn't belong there.

Your second theme might then be "vacuuming". Again, you'd then go through the whole house and get all the vacuuming done.

Your next theme might be "putting up decorations" and so on.

Again, in this way—issue by issue this time—you'd get the whole house ready.

The vacuum principle
While both methods work, you'll probably find that the thematic approach is **a little quicker.**

Why? Because you don't have to interrupt the *type* of work you're doing so often—you can use momentum to your advantage, as well as the fact that you have all the resources you need at hand.

So, **for example**, once you're vacuuming, it's much easier to *continue* vacuuming—that way you don't have to keep putting it away, and then getting it out again.

Similarly, if you're already working on playing staccato, then you can **take advantage** of the work you've already done by finding *all* the passages in your piece that require staccato playing.

Themes for practicing

So what exactly are these themes? The **best person** to help you create your own list of possible themes is your teacher—there are a huge range of possibilities, of which the list below is just a **tiny sample**.

Rhythmic precision

Your focus with this theme would be on ensuring that every note happens **exactly when it's supposed to.** It's about making your triplets precisely evenly spaced, and ensuring that your dotted eighth notes really do use up three-quarters of a beat.

> # Instead of choosing and working on a *section*, you're going to choose and work on an *issue...*
>
> # ...wherever in your piece that issue might appear.

Fast runs

Wherever they may be in your piece, you'll find them and work on them. Your aim is for them to be **effortless** and **spectacular**, which means checking some thoroughly *un*spectacular issues like fingering, your slow motion version (see PROTOTYPES ➲257) and note security (see PRESSURE TESTING ➲249)

Lyrical legato lines

You'll be checking to ensure that the transition from note to note is actually legato, that the phrasing is well considered and carefully executed, and that the melody projects well. With the sort of careful listening you'll need to

do, this is a good theme to work through by RECORDING YOURSELF ➲270.

Fingering

Involves **creating** fingerings where none exist, **checking** existing fingerings for possible better alternatives, making sure that **bad fingering** is not the cause for any trouble spots that you know about, and CEMENTING ➲64 good fingerings so that you couldn't imagine ever playing the passage any other way.

Notice already that this far into the list, and there are four completely different themes, each requiring **completely different practice.** Let's look at a few more...again, you'll see that no two themes will produce even remotely similar practice:

Rests

They're such a **commonly overlooked** score detail—your job when rests is your theme is to **find** them all, and then ensure that you actually **observe** them when you're playing.

You would also look at the tricky problem of how best to introduce sound again *after* each rest.

Dynamics

Starts by find out exactly what the score asks for (see DETAIL TRAWL ⮑110). Then you would be putting your own stamp on things through EXPERIMENTS⮑135 and PAINTING THE SCENE ⮑222.

This also would be an opportunity to check for and repair any dynamic **flat spots.**

Tone production

Is your **quiet playing** clear and well-projected? Or is it breathy and thin?

And what about the **fortissimo**

sections? Is the sound still rounded, or does it become hard and edgy?

And dynamics aside, what happens to your tone production in different registers? Or when you're tired? Or before you're warmed up? Or when you have to play long held notes?

You'll need to listen especially carefully when this is your theme—changes in tone aren't always going to jump out at you the way a wrong note might.

Posture

A particularly good theme to switch to at the end of a practice session, or any other time when being tired means that your posture might otherwise be **compromised.**

When this theme is active, you'll be concentrating especially hard on how you **physically relate** to your instrument, and how you **carry yourself.** You'll already have a checklist of posture do's and don'ts from your teacher—now is your chance to put that list to work.

Security

This theme is about making the transition from right **sometimes** to right **every time**—so that you know the passage is not going to let you down if you have a "bad" day.

Best used in conjunction with plenty of PRESSURE TESTING ⮑249, to ensure that even your *worst* days are still good.

Wherever it's hiding

Just like the house-tidying scenario, once you've chosen your theme, go right through your piece and work on *all* instances where that theme could be relevant.

So if you were targeting "Intonation", then you'd look for all passages in the piece where your intonation tends to be suspect. You'd then work on that until you'd covered each of those sections...

...and then you'd choose a **new theme**. There are dozens—possibly hundreds—to choose from.

Always fresh

One of the great advantages to working with themes is that you can **dramatically reduce** the feeling of "here we go again" in your practice—themes simply provide **too much variety** for boredom to set in.

So if the idea of spending twenty consecutive practice sessions on the same passage **fills you with horror**, try it with a different theme for each session. You'll be guaranteeing that *no two of those practice sessions are alike*, while also covering a huge range of vital issues in that passage.

Linking themes to your lesson

Before you create your own theme list, *ask yourself what the issues were from last lesson*. You would then base your first choice of themes on those issues.

So if your teacher spent a lot of time correcting your **phrasing**, then phrasing is a good candidate for a theme—and the work you do on that issue means that it's less likely to be an issue again *next* lesson.

Color Coded themes

Thematic practice is a perfect complement to Color Coding ➲84. The color markings will allow you to quickly find all other instances of a particular issue in the score.

So, if for example you had a theme that was "ensuring all rests are observed", and all rests were marked in your score in orange, then they'll jump right out at you.

If there is no color code yet for the theme you just selected, then now is a good time to create one. Choose your color, and go right through the score to mark all instances of that theme.

Fresh photocopy themes

Another way to help you focus on your theme—and easily find all instances of it in the score—is to dedicate one of your Fresh photocopies ➲151 to that theme.

So if you have a dozen themes that you typically work with for your piece, you would have a dozen fresh photocopies—each dedicated to a different theme.

On those photocopies, the passages relevant to that theme would be clearly marked, and all previous work and notes you had made for that theme would also be visible.

You might even want to cover up the passages in the score that *aren't* relevant to that theme.
(see BLINKERS ➲38)

Random themes

If you **don't like to know** exactly what each practice session will consist of, write down all the possible themes on cards.

You would then start each session by drawing a theme from the deck. That becomes your #1 issue for the session.

It's an easy way to keep your practice fresh and unpredictable, while still ensuring all the important issues get covered—see RANDOMIZING➲262 for more information.

Daily themes

If you have a handful of themes that are regularly needing attention, it might be worth scheduling an entire day of practice to that theme each week.

So, Mondays might be **Making Rhythms Precise.**

Tuesdays might be **Memorizing**

Fridays might be **Posture** and **Staying Relaxed.**

You'll be practicing the same piece every day, but you'll be **learning completely different things** in each practice session.

And by the time your lesson comes around, you will have already covered many of the issues that your teacher might otherwise need to have worked on.

An alternative to Bridging

Thematic Practice is also a great way to ensure that your piece doesn't end up with "bumps" between sections.
(See BRIDGING➲50)

Because your section content and length will **change** according to the issue you've chosen, your sections won't have a chance to become established—which means neither will problems in the joins between.

Retiring themes

Sometimes you will have worked so well on a particular issue that it **no longer needs attention**, in which case you can "retire" it from your list of active themes.

It's still an issue that you listen out for—you're not abandoning it as a value—but it would no longer officially appear as one of your daily themes, or on any randomizing cards you might be using.

That way you're ensuring that the **only** themes that are receiving attention are those that genuinely need the help. **If in doubt**, check with your teacher as to whether a theme is ready to be retired yet or not.

In fact, by the time your **first performance** rolls around, you'd be hoping that **all issues** in the piece could be retired.

(Remember, you're not retiring this theme for *all time*—just for the piece you're currently working on. See One way doors ⊃208 if the whole idea of retiring themes is making you nervous)

Recurring themes

If you find the **same issue** being a problem for you in every piece you play, then you should think about doing some Fitness training ⊃146 to target that specific issue.

So if you find in the course of your Rhythmic Precision theme focus that you have trouble switching accurately from **triplets** to **duplets**, then it's worth scheduling some behind-the-scenes work on **just that**. Find an etude, or create an exercise that is *filled* with switches from triplets to duplets.

That way, instead of trying to handle it on a case-by-case basis as you meet it in pieces, you'll be fixing *all* future instances of the triplet-to-duplet switch, by mastering the core skill in advance.

In fact, if you develop the skill enough, you can **permanently retire** that issue as a theme, because it will already have been pre-practiced—it would be on your list of things you can just *do*.

One of the most satisfying things about learning an instrument is watching that list **grow**.

Themes & Prototypes

You'll need to read the relevant chapter to make sense of this, but as part of creating the slow motion Prototype ⊃257 of your piece, you will have identified a set of **core values** that you wanted your performance to showcase above all others.

So you might have selected:

- Sparkling and even runs
- Engaging dynamics
- The extended pianissimo section to be almost inaudible—without losing tone quality
- To be able to handle the coda at the marked tempo
- Clear phrasing throughout

Announcing these values is an important start, but to make them a reality in your prototype—and therefore in your performance—you'll need to practice them.

So when you're choosing your themes, make sure items on this list **feature prominently**. (They are, after all, the issues you have decided are going to be the most important in your performance!)

Tightening

Making the leap from good-enough to excellent

ennis has a **concert coming up**, but he's feeling quite relaxed about it.

Maybe a little *too* **relaxed**. Because his piece has been in good shape for some time, he **doesn't really practice it** much any more. In fact, he wonders whether there is any point in practicing it ever again.

"Definitely" says his teacher "You've got an opportunity to really make this piece sparkle now—although it's going to require a completely **different type** of work."

Improving a piece when there's nothing to fix? **How?**...

THE BETTER YOUR piece sounds, the **harder** it will be to create fresh improvements.

In fact, the **most difficult** phase of all is when a piece is *almost* ready to perform...but not quite there yet.

Motivation is the first challenge. Because nothing about the delivery of your piece is **offending** you, there will be no feeling of urgency to fix anything. Instead, there'll be a warm comfortable glow —"She'll be right mate" and "No worries" are the two expressions we'd use here in Australia.

But there's more to a great performance than simply **failing to offend** the audience. It's not just about the absence of the bad. It's about the presence of excellence.

Which is why this **next phase**— getting from 9.5 to a 10—is so **important**.

But even if you are all fired up to make this final leap, it can be an enormous challenge just trying to **figure out** what needs work in the first place. The very fact that the

piece is sounding so good means that you will already have dealt with all the **easy-to-spot** issues. The wrong notes will have been righted, the piece will be up to tempo, the monster passages will have been tamed.

The remaining issues will be **much more subtle.** You won't be looking for howling errors or gaspworthy oversights. Instead, you'll be trying to find musical elements that are still just a little loose...

...and **tighten** them.

So before you set off, wrench in hand, let's take a look at which elements are candidates for tightening in the first place.

Tightening *Rhythm*

As part of my undergraduate music degree, we would have an hour of intensive rhythm training every day.

In one of the first sessions, I can remember being handed a straight-forward rhythm—just quarter notes and eighth notes—and being asked to **tap it**.

I did, feeling a little insulted that I'd been given something **so easy.**

To my horror though, the instructor was shaking his head.

"That was a good *approximation*" he said "I could tell what you *meant* to play."

"Now this time, play it again, listen hard, and make sure every note is centered. Not the *tiniest trace* of anticipation or delay—instead, notes that are played...how would you say?... *just so.*"

And he demonstrated. This simple rhythm was **completely transformed**—the delivery was so precise, so completely without "she'll be right mate", that it was oddly moving.

"You can do that in every phrase you play. " he said "And because you can, you *should*. Now try again."

I have never been able to look the **same way** at rhythms in my own pieces since. It's added a brand new stage of work on my rhythms at a point when I used to think I was all done.

Here's the thing. In your near-performance-ready piece, you'll know how the rhythms are *supposed* to sound. You should even be able to play those rhythms so that nobody would confuse them for any other rhythm.

But **can you** place each note at the *exact* instant at which it should occur? That's a whole new dimension, and it will have a huge impact on your performance.

The basketball equivalent is **Nothing But Net**—shots so accurate that they don't touch backboard or rim. But if you want your rhythms to have this extra level of precision, you'll have to listen very carefully, and dedicate practice time specifically to tightening them.

Tightening *Articulation*

By this stage in the piece's development, you'll obviously be **making the distinction** between articulation elements such as staccato and legato passages.

But it's **not enough** just to be able to tell them apart. There are infinite degrees of staccato—the precise length of each note should be something that you've thought about, and have **complete control** over. If Tightening Rhythms is about

the precise placement of the *start* of notes, Tightening Articulation is also about controlling exactly when and how notes will *end*.

Try it yourself with a simple scale. Play each note staccato, but try to **match exactly** the same extent of staccato on every note. Very hard to get right. Exhilarating to listen to when it is though.

Tightening *Dynamics*

Again, because your piece is just about ready to perform, you'll *know* that this bit is supposed to be pianissimo, or that bit is supposed to be a crescendo.

But how good is your **control** of that crescendo? Do you end up at maximum volume with two measures still left to go? Are you controlling the **shape** of the crescendo? Are you intending a steady and linear ramp-up? Or instead a curve, where the crescendo grows more suddenly towards the end of the passage? Or does your crescendo just *happen*?

What about your pianissimo passages? Do you have some notes that don't sound, and others that jump out more than they should?

Just like tightening articulation and rhythm, you'll need to **listen very carefully** to discover what you're really playing. And then you'll need the concentration and care of a **jeweller** repairing a watch to ensure the precision you seek.

Tightening *Tempo Control*

This is a combination of ensuring there's no creeping tempo changes—in either direction—and also being able to **find** exactly the tempo you need, first time, every time.

A good tactic is to **record yourself**, allowing you to then check after you've played for any fluctuations.

Unmovable tempos will make those rhythms you tightened earlier even more compelling.

Tightening *Tone Quality*

Instead of simply reacting to and eliminating poor tone production, tightening is going to involve **actively pursuing** the best possible sound...on every single note.

What sound are you really making? What happens to the quality of your sound over **long held notes**? During pianissimo passages? Or at the top of the biggest crescendo?

It's so easy to **get used to** the sound you're currently making—for that to become not just the default, but your **standard** for excellence.

Don't get me wrong. Your sound may well be very good. But are you prepared to announce right now that it's consistently the **best sound** you could possibly make?

Until you are, then there's tightening ahead. Which means there's *always* tightening ahead.

Tightening *your own Thoughts*

With so much of performance being a mental and confidence game, **keeping your thoughts focussed** and positive is something to practice in itself. If you don't work on this skill in the practice room, you shouldn't expect to be able to do it on stage.

(See Visualizing ➲364)

You can tighten this first by **being aware** of what you're thinking, and then **steering** your focus towards the thoughts you want to have on concert day.

Getting this wrong doesn't just affect the performance itself though. If your thoughts are **running loose**, *none of your other tightening tasks are going to be possible either*—simply because they won't be getting the focus they need.

In fact, unless you have control over

your own focus and thoughts, then there's almost certainly no tightening of any sort happening, on any issue. You're just playing stuff...and worse still, perhaps on AUTOPILOT ➲120.

Tightening *Posture*

Please don't confuse this with physically tightening your posture. I'm still using "tightening" as meaning the **removal of all sloppiness** and the pursuit of the best possible.

What happens to your posture at the end of a long practice session—or for that matter, the end of a long piece? What impact does that really tough passage on page five have on how tense your wrist is?

And more importantly, vice-versa?

This goes well beyond trying to look good. It's about noticing how you sit, or stand. How you hold your instrument, how you carry yourself, how much or little you move, and how free those movements are.

But like all the other Tightening issues, you'll have a default posture that you use—without needing to

think about it. Some of that will be good, some won't be.

Until you actively check for it, *that's how it will stay.* A mix of your best... and something that's less than your best.

Find your own loose nuts

This is by no means a comprehensive list. Every aspect of your playing will have a comfortable **default state**—and that state won't change unless you take action.

Tightening is **best left** though until you already know the piece well. There's no point in trying to tightening tempo if you have to keep slowing down to read accidentals.

It all comes back to a single question from you:

> *"This piece is sounding good. What can I do to make it sound even better?"*

And for that to be a question that never grows tired.

And then relax on concert day

All of this tightening is designed to ensure that your performances shine—but because the tightening has been done **in advance**, you can still focus on losing yourself in the music during the performance itself.

Like good nuts and bolts, once your piece has been tightened well, it really should **stay that way**.

So this precision you're demanding in the practice room is not just a collection of shining moments that nobody ever gets to hear. This sort of work leaves **permanent imprints** on your piece.

Work like this enough, and it will leave permanent imprints on **you**. **Not just for music** either...once you've had a taste for the difference tightening can make to something, you'll want to re-apply it elsewhere.

Triage

When there's **too much** to do, and **not enough time** to do it in

Tiffany is in a **tangle**. She has scales to learn, her study to speed up, her Sonatina to memorise, theory to complete—and two other pieces that she's actually performing next week...

...it would have been **barely possible** with **seven** days of practice, but she and her family will be interstate for two of those days...

What should she do? With an in-tray this full, and no way of getting it *all* done, does it **matter** what she works on first? And if it *does* matter, how is she supposed to decide?...

SOME WEEKS, you're going to get **swamped**. A sudden surge of homework and a play to rehearse, in the same seven days as a birthday, a sleepover and a hockey semi-final...

...and, as ever, a dozen practice tasks.

To survive weeks like these, you have to be smart not just about *how* you work, but also a little ruthless about the **order** in which you tackle things. What you start with. What comes next. And what gets bumped to the **bottom** of your list.

Because practicing itself is so **time consuming**, musicians are more likely than most to encounter weeks like this, but we're not the only ones who have to wrestle with such overload. In fact, there's plenty we can learn from **one particular profession** that deals with such things on a daily basis.

This profession has become **very good** at prioritizing impossibly big tasklists —mostly because if someone in their job messes up the order in which problems are handled, it's **not just** that someone **won't be ready for a lesson**.

It's that somebody might *die*.

ED Triage
In the early 1800s, **doctors** on the battlefields of France were being **overwhelmed** with patients, and real-ized that they needed to create a system to work out who should be treated first.

First-come-first-served was **not going to work,** because that would mean doctors could waste their time treating minor injuries, while **more seriously injured** patients further back in the queue might be quietly bleeding to death.

As a result, **no matter when** you appeared at the field hospital, if you had a life-threatening injury, you would be **helped before** the patient who had a dislocated shoulder—**even if** that patient with the dislocated shoulder had been waiting for 24 hours already.

The system became known as **Triage**, from the French "trier", which means to **sort**. It's at the core of Emergency Departments in hospitals throughout the world, and is a system that has saved countless lives.

Practice Room Triage
Triage is based around a **short evaluation** of each patient as they come in. You're not trying to fix the patient at that point—instead, you're just assessing **how urgently** they really need help.

You can use **exactly the same technique** when you're **practicing** and time is in short supply. Before you actually start playing anything, you would quickly go through each of your possible practice tasks, and **sort** them according to urgency.

You then work on them in that order—from most urgent to least urgent.

This guarantees that **even if time is scarce,** the most important tasks have had your best attention—and that if anything is left not done by lesson day, it will be tasks that hopefully didn't matter too much anyhow.

So what's "urgent"?

An urgent practice task won't always be as **dramatic** or easy to spot as an urgent ED patient. There's no gushing head wound or coronary failures happening here. But while sorting practice tasks makes for less exciting TV than casualty ward dramas, the guiding principle behind the triage is very similar:

What would the consequences be if this task were ignored?

The more serious the consequences, the higher the item will be rated. Which means the sooner you'll work on it.

Sounds self-evident...

...but it's amazing how many students forget about this when they work.

The **classic example** is the countless students who always start their practice with scales—no matter what else is on their agenda—*simply because they always start with scales.*

In a week where *not* practicing scales has **no consequences**—but omitting other practice tasks *would* have consequences—any ED surgeon would tell you that this is not practice. It's *mal*practice.

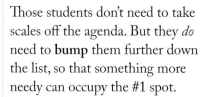

Those students don't need to take scales off the agenda. But they *do* need to **bump** them further down the list, so that something more needy can occupy the #1 spot.

That can only happen if you actually have a list in the first place though.

Triage Guidelines

What follows is a way to set up that list for yourself—items that fit into Category 1 are the **most urgent**, and would all need to be complete before you'd even **think** about practicing something in Category 2. If time constraints then mean you don't get around to Category 2, then so be it.

Similarly, Category 2 would be need to be done before Category 3...and so on...

...right down to Category 5, which could be left undone with no consequences at all.

#1: Looming performances

If you have a recital or audition approaching rapidly, then any unfinished practice tasks associated with that *have* to be the **first thing** you work on each day.

You then sort within this category according to **how soon** the performance is, and **how important** the occasion is.

So if you have a potentially life-changing audition coming up in three weeks, practice for that will **take priority** over preparing for a Neighborhood Christmas Carol singalong this weekend—**even though** the audition is further away.

Again, it sounds obvious. But if the Christmas Carol material is more fun to play, or easier, or just *there*, it can be very tempting to start with it...just for a few minutes...

You don't have time for detours like that. Once you've set your triage order, you have to be **fanatical** about sticking to it.

If you're then sorting tasks that all relate to the **same performance**, start with the passages that, if left untreated, *would have the biggest negative impact* on the performance.

In other words, feed the most dangerous animals first.

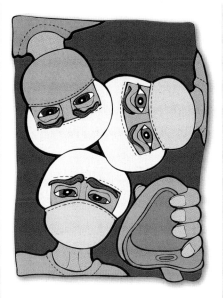

#2: Tasks due next lesson

This is your **regular to-do list** from your teacher, and it may actually contain some items that you dealt with already as part of your Category 1 concert preparation work. That's good—you can cross them off.

The problem now though is that the *to-do list itself is going to need sorting*. There might be ten different practice instructions on there, and you can't work on them all at the same time. In fact, if your week is really bad, you might

not even have time to get through them all.

Assuming that your teacher has not already **made things easy** for you by listing some tasks as being more important than others, your focus should be on setting up an order that allows you to **get through the most tasks possible.**

To do that, sort your list according to **how difficult** each task is going to be to accomplish, and then *start with the easiest of those, and work your way up.*

Why? It's all about getting runs on the board. By starting with the easiest first, if you do **happen to run out of time** before the lesson, you will have been able to "tick" more tasks than if you'd started with—*and then got bogged by*—the ugliest monsters.

That way, you can then tell your teacher next lesson that while you didn't finish everything, you did get **7 out of the 9** things. Had you started with the **toughest problems** instead, you might find that the **same amount** of practice might only have been enough for *two* tasks.

#3: Chronic Issues

Over several months of practice you'll often notice problems that keep **recurring**—you might, for example have trouble with intonation in a particular register.

Because you don't want this issue to permanently be something that undermines your playing, you'll need to be working on it in the **background**—even if that issue isn't directly relevant to the pieces you're studying right now.

Whenever you don't have category 1 or 2 practice patients to deal with, choose something from your Chronic Issues list as your "what's next". That way, you're not just tackling problems as they appear, you're also **anticipating** and **preventing** future problems.

#4: General maintenance

If you're regularly getting this far down the list, then you probably **didn't need** triage in the first place. Instead see the chapter on SESSION AGENDAS➲305.

General maintenance is non-required technical work, sightreading, listening...**behind**

> # There are countless students who always start with scales—no matter what else is on their agenda—*simply because they always start with scales...*

the scenes work that make future work easier, and **goes beyond** the technical work that your teacher may be asking for from week-to-week anyway. (See FITNESS TRAINING➲146)

It is definitely useful. It's definitely *not* urgent though. Hence the 4.

#5: Self indulgence

Playing over **old** pieces. Playing over sections in your current piece that don't *need* practice. Mindlessly looping scales. Playing movie themes by ear. Sight reading through possible new pieces.

All good fun.

And all **unaffordable luxuries** until the time crisis passes.

Unfortunately though, these are exactly the sorts of easy practice that you can lapse into if you're not paying attention—especially when you're stressed. Before you know it, you will have **lost** a sizeable slice of the **only time** you had.

Other essential skills

Triage will help you answer the vital question of **what** to work on during your most frantic weeks, but it doesn't provide any information about **how**.

For more help with getting the impossible done in insane time limits, see CLOSURE➲80, ONE WAY DOORS➲208, TURNAROUND TIMES➲352 and MARATHON WEEK➲191.

Triggers

Setting up cues that get you practicing in the first place

Cameron has just had his second week of no practice in a row, and his teacher is not smiling at him. The problem is **not** that Cameron's lazy—quite the **contrary**. He has so many things on each week that he just doesn't **get around** to practicing.

He has school, homework, art classes, swimming squad training, math tutoring and judo...and that's not even allowing for friends, TV or computer games.

How can he make practice **part** of such a full week? Is it **even possible**?...

THERE'S A LAW of **Practice Physics** that you probably don't know, but should:

*Unless practice sessions are either **scheduled** or **triggered**, then they won't happen.*

Your week is **too full** and your mind **too busy** for practicing to start all by itself. There's plenty to get on with without practicing at all.

So if you turn up to a lesson unprepared, it's not necessarily because you were **actively** avoiding the practice during the week. You might not have been hiding under your bed or feigning smallpox whenever the P-word was raised.

Instead, your non practice might have been **passive**—you simply allowed that Law of Practice Physics to run its course. As **each moment** slid past this week, there were **none** that had been specifically linked to the **start** of a practice session.

And so you used those moments for **other things**.

Creating practice triggers

Practice triggers are a way of **labelling** some of these moments in advance, so that when they arrive, they'll scream at you "it's time to practice!"

For those moments to **belong** to practicing, and to **nothing else**.

So what sorts of things can be triggers? Let's take a look at the main contenders.

Event-based triggers

Your week contains plenty of events that are guaranteed to happen. Going to school. Coming home from basketball training. Eating your breakfast.

So any practice trigger that is linked to one of these events *is also guaranteed to occur*. If you create a practice trigger that is "Straight after breakfast", then that's a sure thing. Breakfast is an every day event, which means that practice would be too.

Others to consider are:

• **As soon as you get up in the**

morning (as long as you're alive, this is the most reliable trigger of all!)

• **As soon as you get home from school/work.** Again, this is a daily thing, at least for five days in the week.

• **As soon as you get home from basketball training, cricket practice, ballet, whatever.** Usually good for a couple of triggers in each week, but you obviously can't have this as your *only* trigger. But instead of your other activities being barriers to you practicing, a trigger like this actually uses them to *encourage* practice.

• **Straight after your evening meal.** Another good daily trigger, and it also works on weekends.

• **Straight after a television show that you regularly watch.** If I had practice sessions linked to watching the first three seasons of *The West Wing*, then I would have been **guaranteeing** one practice session each week. Maybe not your favorite show, but you'll have one of your own.

Even if you decide to use the other trigger types outlined below, you should definitely have at least one Event-based trigger to kick start your practice each day.

Environmental triggers

Like Event-Based triggers, environmental triggers will link practice sessions to everyday events. However, they're a little more unpredictable, because unlike Event-based triggers, they can happen *anytime*.

That can mean that while your practice for the week is guaranteed, the **amount** can **vary wildly**. But for students who get quickly bored by

routine of any sort, this is a great way to go.

You'll come up with plenty of possible triggers of your own, but three examples are below:

• **Whenever the phone rings.** Wait until the conversation is finished, but otherwise, a phone call means a practice session. In most households, this guarantees plenty of practice, and like all environmental practice triggers, you'll never quite be sure *when*...

If your phone is **insanely busy**, this trigger can cause serious problems for you, in which case you might want to **filter** it— whenever a particular person calls, or if you have caller ID, whenever

the incoming number is even. Or it might be every *third* phone call.

• **Whenever the house is suddenly empty.** Practicing is always easiest when things are completely quiet, and particularly if you have several siblings, this can be a rare event. So if you're ever lucky enough to have all siblings and both parents out of the house at the same time, it's a perfect practice trigger.

If a *completely* empty house is simply too unlikely, then you can modify this to be "Whenever only 2 people are at home with me". In this way, dad taking a simple trip to shop for groceries, together with your little sister piping up "I want to come too" can be a trigger for you to practice.

• **As a time-out substitute.** This is not intended to link practicing to being punished, but if sibling disagreements in your home are handled with any sort of "time-out" arrangement, then instead of sitting and staring at a wall, you might as well be practicing. Check this out with parents first, but if you have a sibling that you tend to spar with a lot, then you can get a lot of practice done this way.

When you are giving your acceptance speech for your first Grammy, be sure to thank them.

"Not Now" timer trigger

This is perfect if your **parents** have just **reminded** you to practice, but you really don't feel like doing it right now. Instead of saying "later"—and thereby putting it off indefinitely—say "later", and then **set a kitchen timer**.

When the timer **goes off**, that's your trigger.

This allows you to **defer** practice sessions, but not **forget about** them, and to indirectly use reminders from parents as triggers in their own right. When they see you set the timer, they'll know that you're **acting** on their reminder—and you still get to **wait** a little longer before practicing. Everybody's happy.

You can also set this trigger when you **remember** that you need to practice, but can't really do it right now (you might be in the middle of

doing homework, for example). If you simply say to yourself "later", you could easily forget. Instead, set the timer, get on with your homework, and switch to practicing when the beeps start.

What do you set the timer to? It's up to you, but when it goes off, you **have** to practice (that's what a trigger means!), so make sure that you haven't set it to start beeping at 4:14 am.

Checkpoint trigger

This variation on practice triggers allows you to do your practice at any time, but in conjunction with a **daily checkpoint**. If you haven't practiced yet by the time that checkpoint arrives, then you will practice then.

So you might set a 6:30 pm checkpoint. If you've already completed your practice for the day by that time, then you're free to do whatever you like at 6:30. **If not**, then 6:30 *becomes* a practice session.

These triggers give you the freedom to practice "whenever", but are a safety net that guarantees practice

still happens if the rest of the day had got away from you.

Schedule-based trigger

Along with event based triggers, this is the **safest way** to guarantee that your practice gets done. Instead of linking practice to particular events though, you're linking them directly to times.

To make this work, you need a couple of **cheap alarm clocks** which are **only** used as practice triggers.

If your schedule has practice listed

on Tuesdays for 8 am and 4:30 pm, then on Monday night you would set one alarm clock for 8 am, and the other for 4:30 pm.

The next day, those **alarms** are your **practice triggers**. When the beeping starts, you stop whatever you're doing at the time, and tune up.

Random schedule triggers

This is for students who need the **security** of having scheduled practice sessions, but enjoy the **unpredictability** of the random element.

That sounds insane though. How can a schedule produce unpredictable practice times?

It's really quite simple. If you're planning on having one practice session each day, then **schedule three**.

Then get yourself three cards. Write "Not now! Enjoy the break :)" on two of them and "It's time! Go practice!" on the other. Shuffle them, put them next to the alarm clocks that were mentioned in Schedule-based triggers (above).

When an alarm goes off, turn over a card. If it says "Not now!", then you're free. Go do something else.

If it says "It's time! Go practice!", then so be it.

This adds some nice surprises into your schedule—two of those scheduled times each day are actually free time in disguise. It sounds like a silly thing, but the fact that you won't know which scheduled times are free can keep your practice feeling fresh all week.

Even more randomness...

If you want to really spice things up, get yourself 30 cards. Write "Not Now! Enjoy the break :)" on 20 of them, "It's time! Go practice" on the remaining 10.

This means that not only is the time of your practice session randomized—*the number of the practice sessions will be randomized too.*

Some days you'll draw 3 "Enjoy the break" cards, which means no practice on that day. Of course, it's possible that the **reverse** could happen too.

Normally things will be somewhere in between, but you'll always be interested to find out.

Like everything else in this book, try it, see what you think. And if the random element fires you up, there's actually a whole chapter dedicated to it—see Randomizing ➲262.

So what are *your* triggers?

Remember the warning at the start of this chapter:

Unless practice sessions are either scheduled or triggered, then they won't happen.

It doesn't really matter which of the recommended triggers you use, but you need to choose **at least one** of them.

Otherwise the week will skate past—full and busy—but empty of practice.

Turnaround Time

Mastering new pieces in weeks instead of months

Lachlan is having a mild **panic attack**. He has just been given a new piece—and the date for its first performance....

...in **four weeks.**

"Please tell me you're **kidding**" he protests "I'll need **twice** that long to do a good job..."

"Not true" says his teacher "Just because you're *used* to having twice as long doesn't mean you *need* twice as long."

Could this be true? Is it also possible that *your* pieces **could** be ready in a **fraction of the time** it currently takes?...

I F I EVER NEED to get my computer upgraded or repaired, there's only **one thing** I'm interested in when I ring around for quotes.

It's **not** *"How long have you been in business"* or *"What are your opening hours."* It's not even *"How much will this be"*.

It's *"How long will it take you to get this done?"*

Computer repairers refer to this as **turnaround time**—the time that passes from **receiving** the item to the customer being able to **pick it up** again.

And because I'm not the only customer out there who likes their jobs complete **yesterday**, businesses with good turnaround times have a huge advantage.

As we'll see in a second, **music students** have turnaround times of their own too. Just like computer repairers, music students with *fast* turnaround times also have a huge edge.

We'll take a look at **why** in a

moment. But first, let's find out exactly what "turnaround time" for a music student **actually means**.

Turnaround time for musicians

After you've been learning a musical instrument for a while, you'll come to expect that a piece of *this* size and *that* difficulty will take you *this many* weeks or months to get ready. So a short Prelude might take you 1 month. A major sonata 6 months. A huge concerto a year.

But here's the thing. These numbers are not carved in marble. You can **change** them.

Musicians are used to the idea of **improving** aspects of their playing—

improving *technique*, improving *intonation*, improving *sightreading*.

Well, guess what. Your **turnaround time** can be improved too...

...or should I say "turnaround *times*"—there are actually **two different types**.

Type 1: Time to Lesson-Ready

Lesson-Ready turnaround time is a measure of **how long** it takes you to get a piece from

never seen it before...

to

...ready to play for your teacher

This doesn't mean concert-polished, or up to tempo. It just means that you can **comfortably** and **steadily** play it from beginning to end—without having to stop to feel your way.

Any music teacher will tell you that this is a **milestone worth celebrating**. It means they can ask to hear any part of your piece, without having to listen to you **sightread** or **fake** your way through the notes.

The lesson that follows can then be about **how** you're playing rather than **what** you're playing. (Which is what lessons *should* be about).

This means that feedback from your teacher is much more likely to be **ideas** and **suggestions**, rather than "There's a sharp in front of that F".

There's plenty you can do to drastically slash your *Time to Lesson Ready*—we'll take a look at some options in a moment.

But before we do that though, there's a **second** turnaround time you need to watch...

Type 2: Time to Concert-Ready

The clock starts ticking on this turnaround time **as soon as** you've got the piece lesson-ready.

It's then a measure of how long you take to get a piece from:

ready to play for your teacher...

to

...ready to perform it anytime, anywhere.

Which is a whole different thing.

Unlike *Lesson-Ready*, *Concert-Ready* is **not just a playthrough**. You need to be able to play at full tempo, with all dynamics, phrasing and articulation worked out and polished... all stops out and ready to **show the world**.

In fact, the way you **usually prove** that something is *Concert Ready* is by actually playing it **in a concert**.

Why shorter is better

As we'll see in a moment, slashing both of these turnaround times is achievable, but it will take **careful work**. You won't necessarily have to practice any **longer** than you currently do, but you will have to practice **differently**.

Sounds like a big job. It *is* a big job. So why go to all the trouble?

• Beating the Use-By Date

Pieces might be exciting and fun when they're **brand new**, but that might not still be the case after six months. The longer you have a piece, the more likely you are to **get sick of it**—making your entire preparation campaign a race against the piece's use-by date.

Short turnaround times mean that by the time you'd normally be thinking "not *this* piece again", you would already be onto the *next* piece.

Obviously you'll meet some works that continue to delight and challenge **even after decades** of playing them—but that's not going to be true if your new piece is "Mr. Middle C does Hoppy Hops".

Granted, most of your pieces will be more interesting than that, but use-by dates is usually still an issue for all but the greatest works in the repertoire. Short turnaround times will help you finish your piece before it starts attracting flies.

• Racking up experience

If your short turnaround times

mean that you can get through **twenty pieces** in a year, then you're collecting experience *five times as fast* as somebody who only learns **four pieces** in a year.

Just picture it—after only **two years** of lessons, you will have worked with *as many pieces as that other student will have after* ***ten years***. It's a massive advantage, and it's yours to have as soon as you're ready to smash through the turnaround limits you've set yourself so far.

- ***Less hackwork practice***
  Short Lesson-Ready turnaround times don't just mean that you're ready for concerts earlier. It also means less time spent **learning the notes** in new pieces (which is the part of practice that most students *don't* like)—leaving more time to spend **making the pieces sound good** (which is the fun part).

  So if slogging through notes of a new piece is not your idea of a good time, then the best way to dodge the hackwork is to **upgrade** your Lesson-Ready turnaround time skills.

Your turnaround times are not carved in marble. You can *change* them...

- ***Say "yes" to more opportunities***
  When I was in my second year of undergraduate studies as a piano student, an **opportunity** came up to play a concerto with a major orchestra—the only catch was that it was **very short notice.** It was a work I'd never played before, and with only 3 weeks until the big day, I felt the task was **impossible**. So I passed on the chance...

  ...and it was **grabbed** by somebody who *could* get the piece ready in that time. (She'd never played it before either)

  As a music student, you'll receive **lots of invitations** to play with other people, but the time frames won't always be generous. If your turnaround times are low, you'll be able to say "yes" to opportunities that most other students will have to turn down.

- ***Cope with commitment peaks***
  Your **workload** for your music lessons and schoolwork won't always be **consistent.** Sometimes you'll have quiet weeks, with little to do. Other times, everything will be **insanely busy**. (See TRIAGE ➲342)

  If you are having one of those fortnights where everything seems to be happening at once, you're going to have to meet your teacher's **lesson targets** on a **minimum** of practice...

  ...which is exactly what students with good turnaround times are able to do. That fortnight can hit you with school exams, teetering piles of homework, sports finals and visits from family—and you'll *still* be able to make good progress in your music.

When minutes are precious, it helps to be very, very good at making every second count. Like everything else you do, it's a skill that can be learned, improved, practiced and then **unleashed**.

• *Build an imposing repertoire list*
Your rapid turnaround means that you'll be mastering **plenty of new pieces** every year—but it's not as though the works are then **discarded**. They're added to your repertoire list, and that list will be growing **very quickly**.

This gives you a huge range of **choices** for future recitals and competitions—options that **won't be open** to students with smaller and slower growing lists.

Date stamping your pieces
Ok, so life is a happier place when your turnaround times are shorter. But how do you make that happen?

Uncovering the awful truth
The first step to being able to **shorten** your turnaround times is to understand what your **current** turnaround times are.

From now on, whenever you are given a brand new piece, **write the date on the score**.

On the day that you first are ready to play the entire piece through for your teacher, **write the date again**.

Then look at the two dates, and ask yourself "how much time passed?". That number is your *Time to Lesson Ready* figure.

You can work out your *Time to Concert Ready* simply by repeating the process on the day of your **first performance**.

4 JAN 2004   1 JAN 1998
22 DEC 2009
1A NOV 1995

When you see these numbers...
You **might not like** the figures you first see—weeks turn into months *very* quickly, and can leave some **unflattering data** for your first recorded turnaround times.

That's ok though. You'll be transforming them to something much shorter soon enough.

Not just about calculation
These dates are handy for confronting the reality of your **existing** turnaround times. But there's **another benefit** too:

*As you prepare pieces in the future, simply knowing that you'll be recording dates like this **will add a sense of urgency** to your preparation.*

If you recorded the "just started the piece" date back in March—and it's June already and there's *still* no possibility of writing in the "lesson-ready" date—then that first date and its missing sibling will really start to **nag** at you. It's only natural then to start thinking about **how** you can move things forward a little.

Fortunately, it's not hard to do.

Cutting Turnaround Time

The **good news** is that there are **plenty** of measures you can take to speed up your turnaround times—mostly because there are **plenty of causes** for bloated turnaround times in the first place.

Any one of these measures can have a dramatic impact on your turnaround times. Use **all** of them though, and you **won't believe** how much faster you'll prepare your pieces.

1. Taming Parkinson's Law

Parkinson's Law states that **work expands to fill the time available**. In other words, if you allow yourself six months to learn a new piece, *then it will take you six months*.

That's not because you **needed** six months. It's simply you sticking to the plan you made for yourself.

Parkinson's law doesn't always have to work **against** you though. Remember, if the work expands to fill the time available, then it makes sense that it might contract when there's *less* time available. Guess what. It does.

What would happen if you set yourself *one* month instead of six? Or *one week*? (Before you dismiss such deadlines as impossible, check out the chapter on MARATHON WEEKS ➲191)

The point is that much of your turnaround time is based on how long you *think* you'll need. If you **expect** your pieces to take less time, then they will.

2. Improving your sightreading

If your sightreading is **strong enough**, then your *Time to Lesson Ready* can be a figure that's very hard to beat:

Zero.

Remember, all you need for lesson-ready is to be able to play right through your piece **comfortably** and **steadily**, in which case you should be asking yourself this:

What if your reading was so good that you could do this first time—no practice required?

This is not **science fiction**. There are students who can do **exactly that**, and they lead a charmed practice life—all of their work is about making their piece **sound better**, not figuring out how to play things in the first place.

So they get to **skip completely** the note-slogging part of practice that most students hate.

3. Getting things right first time

A huge amount of practice can be **wasted** *un*practicing errors—notes, rhythms or fingerings that were **mislearned** when you first looked at the piece.

If you're fanatical about accuracy in the early stages, you can **eliminate** a lot of **corrective practice** that would otherwise need to happen later. (See the chapter on ONE WAY DOORS ➲208 for an extreme but effective solution to this problem.)

4. Not cementing too early

CEMENTING ➲64 is high-repetition practice designed to **lock in** a particular way of playing something.

But if you're at all **unsure** about the passage you're trying to cement, then something terrible can happen. *You might not be truly repeating that passage when you play it over and over*...it will be close, but there will be **tiny variations.**

When this happens, no matter how much practice you do, *the cement won't set*. Students sometimes dedicate months of practice to this sort of "repetition" work, and then wonder why they've made no progress.

That's lost time. You can't get it back, but you can **stop it from going** in the first place.

5. Scouting thoroughly

Scouting allows you to get a head start on your new pieces by becoming **thoroughly familiar** with that piece *even before you've played a single note*. It's such an important practice skill that it's had a chapter dedicated to it (see SCOUTING ➲299), but a lot of students **skip the process**, trying to save time.

The **irony** is that by refusing to scout, they're actually *costing* themselves time.

It's certainly *possible* to master a new piece without scouting. It just takes longer.

6. Not overpracticing

If you want tight turnaround times, you **can't afford** the luxury of continuing to practice passages after you've mastered them. Check out the chapter on CLOSURE ➲80, and consider using ONE WAY DOORS ➲208.

7. Starting from the cells

Fast turnaround times for an entire piece are **built from** fast turnaround times for the tasks you set yourself in each individual practice session.

Every time your **extra concentration** and **smart practicing** enables you complete a task in 20 minutes instead of an hour, you're contributing to the likelihood that the **entire piece** will be ready in a third of the time.

But it works the other way too. Every time you **daydream**, or produce **sloppy practice**, *you're actively adding to your turnaround time.*

Insist on fast turnaround times for each of those **tiny jobs**, and the whole piece is guaranteed to be faster too. (For more information on the power of practice cells—for good and for evil—see ROGUE CELLS ➲293)

8. Tracking your progress

To see proof of your new speedier results, keep a BREAKTHROUGHS DIARY ➲46. Every time you can do something new—for example, when you are able to play through the first page of the piece for the first time—make a note in the diary.

Plenty of daily entries is a sign that a good turnaround time is on the way. Similarly, if a few days go by and there's nothing new...then that strange echo you hear is your turnaround time receding into the distance.

9. *Setting milestone deadlines*

You want the whole piece Lesson-Ready within two weeks? For you to have any chance, after **one week**, you should be ready with **half**.

Setting milestone deadlines like this will allow you to see whether you're on schedule, or need to work a little harder.

Remember though, it's worth being outrageous. Slashing turnaround times is about rejecting limitations you've placed on yourself in the past—and that starts by making headier demands for the future.

10. *Being Practice Trap Aware*

There are plenty of inefficient practice habits that can eat up your time AND fill your piece with errors—hugely blowing out turnaround times in the process.

But to be able to quarantine your pieces from this sort of nonsense, you need to know what the practice traps actually are. Check out the chapter on PRACTICE TRAPS ⊃236, and then keep a careful eye on how you work to make sure that none of those problems affect you.

11. *Mind Games*

A large part of being able to succeed with something demanding is to genuinely **believe** you can, to the point of accurately being able to picture the outcome itself.

If your hand is writing down a goal of "four weeks", but your mind is honestly still picturing "eight weeks", then eight weeks it is.

Whatever you believe will happen has a very nasty habit of then coming true...so be careful what you're picturing. (See VISUALIZING ⊃364)

12. *Buddy up with a speed learner*

Next time you're choosing a PRACTICE BUDDY ⊃226, deliberately work with someone who already has turnaround times that are far better than yours.

Because they're already where you're **trying to get to**, you'll be able to learn plenty as they talk you through how they work.

Start now. Astonish yourself.

Unless all 12 of those elements have been in place, up till now—whatever you've been playing, however you've been practicing—*your progress has been a shadow of what was actually possible.*

There are two options now. You can continue to work the way you always have, and get the same results you always have.

Or you can start asking yourself "How can I get this all done—and done well—*in half the time?*"

Answering that question will give you **ideas**. The ideas will transform your **practice**. Your practice will transform your **turnaround times...**

...and those new turnaround times will then transform your **entire experience** of music lessons.

Varying your diet
Freeing yourself from dull, repetitive practice

Charlene wouldn't mind practicing so much if it wasn't so **boring**.

"It's the **same thing** every day... playing my pieces over and over again...I'd go **crazy**, except that practicing makes me too **sleepy** for that."

Her teacher **doesn't understand** this at all. "Who said that practice had to be playing your pieces over and over and over again? That doesn't sound much like practice to me—**no wonder** you're bored."

If that's not practice, then what is? What else can she try?

I T SHOULD BE clear this far into the book that "practicing" actually means **hundreds** of **different things.** There's no single magic formula that will work in all situations—otherwise this book would only have needed one chapter.

Because you have all this choice though, if you're **bored** when you're practicing, *it's your fault.* It would be like standing at a buffet with hundreds of different foods...and loading up your plate with **just one.** Practicing the same way all the time means either that you simply **aren't aware** of other practice possibilities (which is easily fixed—there are over *350 pages* of ideas in this book!), or you're actively choosing to **ignore** them.

Either way, you're not just boring yourself. You're **crippling** your practice, and your music lessons.

Variety? Such as?
Below are **just some** of the tasks that qualify as "practice". So if you're sick of the way you're working, you don't have to **abandon** practice completely—you can **change** how you work, *so that practicing becomes*

a completely different experience. (See NOT WANTING TO PRACTICE ⮌200)

• *Planning*
This involves figuring out exactly what you should be practicing, and how it fits in with the bigger picture. Planning is about knowing how **today's** session will help you be ready for **next week,** and how next week can help you prepare for the **end of the year.**

You might not actually be playing your instrument while you're doing this, but planning will save you loads of unnecessary work— and **absolutely counts** as practice. See SESSION AGENDA ⮌305, COUNTDOWN CHARTS ⮌99 and CAMPAIGNS⮌58.

• *Locating trouble spots*
You **can't fix** problems if you don't know they're there. This type of practice doesn't actually fix problems, but instead helps you create a comprehensive list of what those problems are. See CORAL REEF MISTAKES⮌89 and BUG SPOTTING⮌53.

• *Diagnosing and prescribing*
It's not enough just to know that

a problem exists—you have to understand exactly what's **causing** it. In fact, being able to name *why* something is hard is often nine-tenths of the way to making it easy.

These causes are **not always obvious** though, so you'll end up needing a technique like CLEARING OBSTACLES⮌72 or ISOLATING ⮌164.

• *Quality Control*
There will be plenty of passages that don't warrant the status "Trouble Spot", but could use some polishing nonetheless.

Quality control practice is about turning **good** passages into **excellent** passages. Check out THEMATIC PRACTICE➲330 and TIGHTENING➲337.

• Tempo boosting

Getting pieces up to speed has to be handled carefully...and with it's own unique practice methods. Set yourself up with a PROTOTYPE ➲257, and then look out for techniques such as METRONOME METHOD➲195 or CHAINING ➲69.

• Pressure testing

Ok, so you've got the passage right once. But can you get it right **every** time? PRESSURE TESTING➲249 is about ensuring that you can deliver what's needed under a range of **difficult circumstances**, and under pressure.

• Interpretation workshop

Practicing is not just about getting things right. It's also a **creative process** designed to help you discover the most compelling, credible, exciting and moving ways to perform your pieces. Look for techniques such as EXPERIMENTS➲135 or PAINTING THE SCENE➲222.

• Knowing the score

Most scores are packed with details, and teachers have to waste a lot of lesson time pointing out terms, signs and notes that students missed. You can **do this for yourself** using techniques such as DETAILS TRAWL➲110 and COLOR CODING➲84.

• Preparing for performance

A special type of practice that kicks in during the **final weeks** before a recital. Look out for DRESS REHEARSALS➲115, and COSMETICS➲94 and OPENINGS AND ENDINGS➲215.

• Listening to recordings

This is practice you can do even when you're not in your practice room. While you're doing homework, in the car, while you exercise—whenever. A great way to get to know every last note of your piece. See RECORDINGS ➲277.

• Reflecting

This is quiet time taken *between* Practice Cells (see ROGUE CELLS ➲293), analyzing what just happened, and figuring out what the next cell should therefore be. Hugely important, even though it's yet another type of practice that involves no playing whatsoever. See also REFLECTING ➲283.

• Head games

With so much of performance being a confidence game, getting your head together is a vital preparation task. Check out VISUALIZING ➲364 for more on this.

• Fitness training

I'm not talking about cardiovascular here. I'm talking about behind the scenes **skillbuilding**—items you'll never show off on concert day, but will positively affect all your playing. Includes your scales and other technical work, sightreading development, theory, improvisation skills and more.

Check out FITNESS TRAINING ➲146 for this type of "preplaying" practice.

• *Scouting*

With a chapter all of it's own, SCOUTING➲299 is a type of pre-practice that ensures you get a **flying start** with any new piece.

• *Cementing*

This is a **high repetition** practice technique that is designed to lock in a particular way of playing something. See CEMENTING➲64 for advice—and warnings—for this technique.

And much more...

It's why this book was always going to be big...and that's not counting the ideas that **didn't** make it into this edition (nobody would have bought a 900 page book though!).

So if there is a reason that your practice is always the same, it's not because you're **short of alternatives.**

Setting up dedicated days

One easy way to help your practice feel fresh and ever-changing is to have **different functions** for each day of your practice week.

So **Tuesdays** might be dedicated to listening to recordings, and then some background musical fitness training.

Wednesday might focus on reliability testing, while **Thursdays** might be all about speeding pieces up.

Friday, as the midpoint of your practice week, might always contain a LESSON PREFLIGHT CHECK ➲174.

Those won't be the only things you cover on those days—you'll still have daily practice tasks to complete.

But the days will be heavily flavored by the Practice Type Of The Day, helping prevent the awful feeling that all your days are identical.

Using the random element

Another possibility is for your practice type to be determined randomly from a list of useful possibilities.

See RANDOMIZING➲262 for more on **introducing some chaos** into your ordered practice world.

When variety is missing

When your practice diet is **overlooking** one of these key techniques, it's not just that you're making things boring. These key techniques ...well, they're key techniques. If you ignore any of them, your playing is going to suffer.

It would be like a tennis player spending all their time **practicing their serve**, but ignoring their groundstrokes, volleying, strength and conditioning, flexibility, mobility, mindset and tactics.

It's not just that they're going to be bored when they practice. They're going to get **flogged** when they play...

Visualizing
The most important practice you'll ever do

Alex has a passage that just **won't co-operate.** He's thrown every practice technique he can think of at it, but there's been **no improvement.**

"I **can't see** any way that I'll **ever** be able to play this!" he says

"And that" says his teacher "is **why** you can't".

Surely Alex is just stating a fact? He's practiced it thoroughly, it's obviously **too hard,** he might as well accept it...or is there another option left he hasn't tried?...

I N MY **OTHER** life outside of music, I'm a taekwondo instructor —the classes certainly don't **look** much like music lessons, but most of the practice principles are actually uncannily similar:

• My taekwondo students practice things **slowly** before they try them **fast.** (See PROTOTYPES ➲257)

• They practice complicated combinations in **segments** before stringing them **together.** (See BRIDGING ➲50)

• Once they understand a new joint lock or takedown, and can deliver it safely in slow motion, they **gradually speed it up** (See METRONOME METHOD ➲195)

• They focus most of their attention on the **challenges** in their techniques, rather than the skills they're already **comfortable** with (See Polishing Shiny Objects in PRACTICE TRAPS➲236)

• They often work in **pairs**—not just for sparring or self-defence drills, but to give eachother **feedback** on techniques. (See PRACTICE BUDDIES➲226)

In fact, for just about **every chapter** in this book, there is a **parallel** in taekwondo training—like my music students, my taekwondo students have skills to practice each day, and *how* they work is important.

However, there's **one technique** that features more heavily in taekwondo training than in traditional music practice:

Visualization. Being able to accurately picture what it is that you're trying to do, **without** actually doing it.

Because no matter how much you practice, in the end, *your delivery is limited by that picture.*

Visualization is not a normal part of most students' music practice, but it should be—it's simply too powerful *not* to include.

Let's take a look at how it works, and what you're costing yourself by ignoring it.

Visualization in action

There's no mystical eastern philosophy involved here—in fact, visualization is a technique used by **most elite sports** too.

It's also used by many **elite musicians**...*but you don't have to wait until you're an elite musician to benefit from it.* It's something you can build into your practice right now.

There are four key areas that visualization **transforms:**

1) Your limitations

Your **picture** of what's possible will actually **determine** what *is* possible. No amount of practice will allow you to crash through the ceilings you set for yourself. If you're convinced it's impossible, then guess what...*it's impossible.* What's exciting though is the **opposite** is true too.

2) *Your technique*

If your picture of yourself delivering a technique is not clear, *you won't be able to deliver it.* Again, the amount of practice you throw at the problem won't change this.

3) *Big occasion performances*

Your visualizations are like **prophecies** here, and are *as important as all your practice put together.* If you picture a passage collapsing on the day, it will—even if you've practiced it until your eyes bleed.

4) *Your future*

The adage "be careful what you wish for, you might get it" is true—but the warning really should be against people setting their sights **too low**. Just as visualization can inhibit or unleash individual techniques, or performances, it also is central to what you'll end up doing—and *being*—in a few years' time.

There's a lot to this—let's take a closer look at each.

Visualizing *limitations*

If I have a student who **believes** that they can do 25 pushups...but **not** 30...then they will start to flag once they hit around 25. Every time. Not because they're correct in their assessment, but because that's what they have **convinced themselves** will happen.

How do I know the limitation is self-imposed rather than real? Sometimes I will get students to do pushups, but call out random numbers while they're going, making it **impossible** for them to **keep count**. But *I'm* keeping count, in my head.

When that happens, *they almost always do many more than the ceiling they had set for themselves.*

And then, once they find out how many they've just done, something magical happens.

It becomes their new limit. From now on—even when they're keeping count—they're able to get to the new ceiling. All of this means that the maximum number of pushups you can do is not limited by your upper body strength. It's limited by your upper body strength **in combination with** your own assumptions.

So the key to a better result is not necessarily stronger arms. It's more ambitious *beliefs*.

How this works with your music

Exactly the same principle holds true in your music. You will have **many, many limits** that you will have set for yourself, perhaps without even realizing:

- How fast you can manage your **scales**

- Whether you can handle sightreading in a particular **key** or not

- Whether or not a particular piece is **too hard** for you

• The amount of time it will take you to get a **new piece** ready

• Whether you are capable of a **particular technique**

• Whether there are some styles of music that you "just don't play well"

The scary thing here? *You'll be spot on with each of these limitations.* As the saying goes, whether you think you can, or think you can't, you're right.

Which means that you need to be very careful with what you put on your "I can't" list.

That's so important, I'm going to say it again. In **bold**. With a purple highlight. And **RED TYPE** so you can't miss it:

YOU NEED TO BE VERY CAREFUL WITH WHAT YOU PUT ON YOUR "I CAN'T LIST"

Because once you have put something on that list, it becomes something that you now officially —and in reality—can't do. Even if you otherwise really *could* have done it, but for your self-sabotage.

Creating a "how can I list"

Fixing faulty assumptions is more complicated than just announcing you *can* do something. A much more powerful way is to ask *how can I?*

Once your brain starts ticking over with that question, then you'll astonish yourself with what you can achieve.

For more information on unleashing the power of "how can I?", see the chapter on TURNAROUND TIMES➲352.

Visualizing *technique*

From time to time, I ask my taekwondo class to close their eyes, and simply **picture** techniques as I name them.

They need to picture themselves **actually delivering** the technique, complete with details about stances, which leg moves first, where their arms are, which way they rotate— and a dozen other technical considerations that, when combined, add up to (say) a spinning heel kick.

They need to picture it from a

first person view...from their own perspective if they actually were delivering the technique. But then, they need to picture it from an **outside point of view**—to be able to see what they would actually look like to somebody else as they complete the technique.

Here's the important thing:

If the picture in their head is fuzzy—if there are parts of the technique they can't "see"—*then they won't be able to deliver the technique.*

So students who can deliver a particular kick well with their right leg, but not their left, will have a

less clear picture of their left leg kick.

At this point, they're wasting their time just doing the kick over and over again. Instead, they need to **fix the picture.**

Once they have, the technique will follow.

How this works with your music

The next time you have a technique that you can't manage, or a passage that won't run the way it should, **don't just hurl extra practice** at it.

Stop for a moment, REFLECT➲283, and create the most detailed picture you possibly can in your head of you delivering that technique.

What you'll often find is that there are parts of this particular video that are **out of focus**...or frames that are **missing entirely.** Concentrate on being able to fill those gaps, and you'll be most of the way towards solving the problem.

That's not always easy to do. It can take plenty of thinking and experimenting to make those fuzzy gaps clear. It can also sometimes require

> # It's your brain. It's your picture. It's your concert. They're all connected, and you can choose whatever reality you like....so you might as well choose something exciting.

the intervention of your teacher.

But once you have got the picture, the practice you then do is simply to CEMENT➲64 the physical reality of the solution you can now visualize.

So if you're a violinist negotiating a tricky double-stopping passage, try to see..and feel...exactly where your fingers will be in relation to each other on the fingerboard. How far apart are they? What angle do they make relative to the fingerboard? How high is your wrist? How straight are your fingers? What sort of breathing are you doing? How relaxed is your hand? Just how much finger pressure is there?

While the answer to questions like these remains "I don't know", then there's going to be trouble in this passage...no matter how much practice you do.

Why? Because in the absence of a clear picture, *your approach will vary slightly each time.*

Which means your results will vary too.

Visualizing *Performances*

All the students in my taekwondo class have regular examinations— "gradings", as we call them—where they have an opportunity to demonstrate that they're coping well enough with their current demands to be **promoted** to the next belt.

Like any performance or test, students get very nervous beforehand. This is partly because long before the grading takes place, they will have **formed pictures** of how it's likely to go:

• How well they think they'll cope with the sparring

• How well they'll deliver their set techniques and patterns

• How easy or hard any board breaks will be

• How well they'll cope with being pushed to exhaustion

And guess what. *They'll be right about these pictures.* Students who are fearful that boards won't break will find that the boards won't break. Students who picture making mistakes in their patterns will make mistakes in their patterns.

As a result, the students who shine on grading day are not always those who punch and kick the hardest at training. They're the ones who have

passed this grading many, many times already in their head.

How this works with your music
Whenever you have a performance coming up, you'll always have expectations and fears. This book is certainly not trying to change that.

But because of the **power** these assumptions have over what actually happens up there, *it's vital that you are in charge of those assumptions.*

You have the ability to create a **positive** image of the concert. You also have the ability to picture a **disaster**.

You have the ability to picture **enthusiastic applause**, and people **buzzing** afterwards about how well you played. You also have the ability to picture people constantly **checking their watches**—or **falling asleep**—while you're playing.

You have the ability to picture the hardest passage in the piece being tossed to the audience with **flair, control and brilliance**. You also have the ability to picture yourself having to stop half way through...in which case, know this:

You **will** stop half way through.

It's all about **choices**. Choosing the image that is most likely to result in a great performance.

But here's the thing:

Controlling and shaping these pictures doesn't just happen automatically. In fact, for many students, it's the Shadows and Terrors that will dominate if their thoughts are not **managed**.

So if you want to **create a vision** of your performance that will turn the concert into a **triumph**, you have to

work on that vision. Setting aside quiet time when you can picture it as though it were a movie running in front of you—every **sparkling run**, every "**bravo**" from the audience, every moment of **not-daring-to-breathe** from the entire hall during your adagio.

It's your brain. It's your picture. It's your concert. They're all connected, and you can choose whatever reality you like.

So you might as well choose something exciting.

Visualizing *your future*
I'm not talking about holding your palm out to **strange women at village fairs**. I'm talking about creating a picture of what you would *like* your future to be. Because as anybody with experience in goal setting will tell you, visions like that have an uncanny habit of then **coming true**.

Why? Because if you can make that picture detailed and compelling, then something powerful happens:

You start to take steps towards it.

Because this picture is something you want, and imagine yourself doing, you'll **actively** be on the **lookout** for ways to get there.

So in the taekwondo class, there might be a beginner who will see a black belt perform a spectacular spinning kick. If they then take a moment to **picture themselves** doing that one day, then for the rest of that training session, *they train a little differently*. They listen harder. They push themselves more. They pay more attention to fine detail.

And they'll notice...and copy...the intensity with which the black belt trains.

However, the student who just looks at the black belt and thinks "I'll never be able to do that" won't then have that extra spark in their training. There's **no incentive** to.

And so already, *each student has taken their first steps to what they will eventually become*—in the first student's case, a black belt, and in the second student's case, a likely train-for-a-while-and-then-quit student.

All from pictures they formed early on, and **completely unrelated** to their own natural abilities.

Making it specific
Even better are those students who can picture **specific achievements** by **specific times**:

- *In two years from now, I will be able to do side-splits*

- *By the end of this year, I will be able to do 50 pushups without stopping.*

- *By my next birthday, I will be able to break a single board with a turning kick.*

Even if they don't get all the way to their goal by their stated time, they will be well on the way—and **miles past** where they would have been without the goal.

How this works with your music
These long-term pictures have exactly the same power in your own music lessons. If you can see yourself performing a particular **concerto** in five years, then that's what you'll take steps towards. If you are picturing that same concerto with a

major orchestra, then better still.

But if, as you read that last sentence, the phrase "that's never going to happen to me" popped into your head...

...and you allow it to *stay* there...

...then guess what. **It's never going to happen.** *You've created—and limited—your own fate, with a thought.*

There are said to be no guarantees in music, but I'll give you two right now:

If you **plan for mediocrity**, or almost-there, or almost-did, or could-have-been, or it's-too-hard, or that-only-happens-to-other-people, then that's what's going to happen.

If you **plan for exciting things** though, then exciting things will happen. They might not be **exactly the same** exciting things you had scripted—you might win a big competition, or a regular place in that major orchestra instead of playing a concerto—but know this:

If right now, you could meet the person you would become through thinking like that...

...and hear them play...

...you'd be stunned.

"Show me how to do that" you'd say.

If you listen carefully, you can already hear their answer.

More from the IMT Bookstore

Preview and order online at www.insidemusicteaching.com

The Practice Revolution
Getting great results from the six days between lessons

Philip Johnston, PracticeSpot Press (2002). 324 pages.
ISBN 095819050X

The acclaimed **teacher's guide** to helping students get the most out of their practice, and shattering forever the obsession with *time spent*. A more in depth examination of many of the concepts covered in *Practiceopedia*, and a look at what goes on when students practice—what works, what doesn't, what *really* happens and how to fix it.

"This book is perhaps in the top 1% of all of the things I have ever recommended. Every sentence is new and important and this goes on for 321 pages... if teachers were to absorb the content there would, indeed, be a revolution in teaching and learning. Buy the book!"
Canadian Music Educator Association **journal**

"...idea studded book on the whole practice process...when the student leaves, it should be with the practice skills to work alone. Johnston has generously outlined hundreds of ways to do that."
California Music Teacher **journal**

"...a great success...a valuable resource for studio teachers in its wealth of strategy and stimulus to creativity"
American Music Teacher **Journal**

"...first rate. After reading only half the book, I believe it had a positive impact on my teaching...Consider buying both the book and stock in the company!"

Horn Call - **Journal of the International French Horn Society**

More from the IMT Bookstore

Preview and order online at www.insidemusicteaching.com

PracticeSpot Guide to Promoting your Teaching Studio

How to make your phone ring, fill your schedule, and build a waiting list you can't jump over

Philip Johnston, PracticeSpot Press (2003). 244 pages.
ISBN 0958190518

The ultimate **self-marketing guide** for professional music teachers, and the single biggest collection of studio promotion techniques ever assembled—240 pages of action you can take to build the studio you deserve.

Not Until You've Done Your Practice
The classic survival guide for kids who are learning a musical instrument, but hate practising

Philip Johnston, David Sutton (illustrations), FuturePerfect Publishing 120 pages, fully illustrated ISBN 064640265X

The **original** easy-to-read practice guide for young students. First published in 1989, Not Until You've Done Your Practice has quietly been one of Australia's best selling books about music for two decades.

More from the IMT Bookstore

Preview and order online at www.insidemusicteaching.com

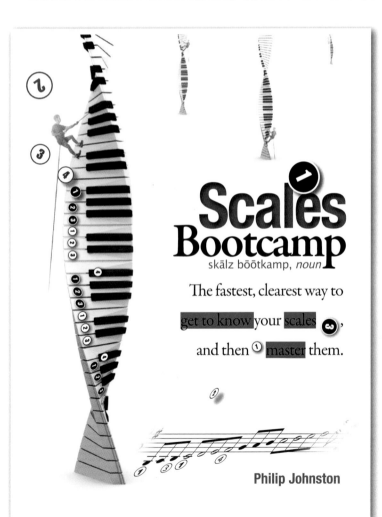

Scales Bootcamp

*The fastest, clearest way to **get to know** your scales, and then **master** them.*

Philip Johnston, PracticeSpot Press (2009). 96 pages. ISBN:978-0-9581905-4-1

Much more than just a scales manual, *Scales Bootcamp* is bursting with practice challenges, twists and variations, all leading to an extraordinary promise:

> **Complete all the listed challenges for any scale in *Scales Bootcamp*, and you'll know that scale *permanently*...**
>
> **...whether you ever practice that scale again or not.**

Take a full tour of the book at: www.insidemusicteaching.com

The first in a series of Bootcamp books.

About the author
And how to make a booking for your next conference

Philip Johnston is the founder of and chief writer for the world's largest website for music teachers and students at www.insidemusicteaching.com, while his books have stamped him as one of the world's leading experts on practicing.

Based in Australia, Philip has also recorded for Warner Music as a concert pianist in his own right, composes for Alfred Publishing, and has a Masters degree in piano performance from Indiana University. As a violin student though, he was kicked out by no fewer than six violin teachers...for not practicing.

Philip is married with three children, and juggles his time between writing, composing, performing, website development and instructing in taekwondo. His dream remains to play cricket for Australia one day, but to date, the selectors have stubbornly overlooked him in favour of players who are better than he is.

To book Philip for your next event:
A book can cover plenty of ground, but there's nothing quite like being able to actually *speak* to people. Philip is an infectiously enthusiastic and experienced presenter, and can be contacted at: **insidemusicteaching@gmail.com.**

More help at
InsideMusicteaching.com

Online Magazine

For professional music teachers: ideas, how-to guides, innovations and solutions.

Studio Stationery

Downloadable theory sheets, manuscript paper, certificates and teaching resources.

Theory drills

The web's premier collection of self-marking, randomly generated theory quizzes.

Repertoire Browser

Test-drive repertoire possibilities by listening to performances as you follow the scores online.

Eartraining drills

Streams straight from your browser. Self-marking and randomly generated.

IMT bookstore

In-depth tours of music teaching's most creative, well presented and useful texts. Ships worldwide.